Advances in Social Sc and Humanities Rese;

MW01274742

Editor-in-Chief

Wadim Strielkowski, *Centre for Energy Studies, Prague Business School, Prague, Czech Republic*

Series Editors

Jessica M. Black, *Boston College, Chestnut Hill, USA*
Stephen A. Butterfield, *University of Maine, Orono, USA*
Chi-Cheng Chang, *National Taiwan Normal University, Taipei, Taiwan*
Jiuqing Cheng, *University of Northern Iowa, Cedar Falls, USA*
Francisco Perlas Dumanig, *University of Hawai'i at Hilo, Hilo, USA*
Radhi Al-Mabuk, *University of Northern Iowa, Cedar Falls, USA*
Nancy Scheper-Hughes, *University of California Berkeley, Berkeley, USA*
Mathias Urban, *Dublin City University, Dublin, Ireland*
Stephen Webb, *Glasgow Caledonian University, Glasgow, UK*

"The proceedings series Advances in Social Science, Education and Humanities Research aims to publish proceedings from conferences on the theories and methods in fields of social sciences, education and humanities.

Topics covered by this series:
Psychology, Sociology, Education, History, Communication studies, Linguistics and language, Law and law enforcement, Political science, Religious studies, Philosophy, Globalization, Humanities, Archaeology, Anthropology, Inter-cultural studies, Development, Geography, Health, Human Factors and Ergonomics, Library and Information Sciences, Safety Research, Transportation"

Rita Martini · Sari Lestari Zainal Ridho ·
Dodik Siswantoro · Habsah Mohamad Sabli ·
Marieska Lupikawaty · Ade Silvia Handayani
Editors

Proceedings of 6th FIRST T3 2022 International Conference (FIRST-T3 2022)

ATLANTIS
PRESS

Editors

Rita Martini
Accounting
Politeknik Negeri Sriwijaya
Palembang, Indonesia

Sari Lestari Zainal Ridho
Business Administration
Politeknik Negeri Sriwijaya
Palembang, Indonesia

Dodik Siswantoro
Accounting
Universitas Indonesia
Depok, Indonesia

Habsah Mohamad Sabli
Commerce
Polytechnic Mukah
Mukah, Malaysia

Marieska Lupikawaty
Business Administration
Politeknik Negeri Sriwijaya
Palembang, Indonesia

Ade Silvia Handayani
Electrical Engineering
Politeknik Negeri Sriwijaya
Palembang, Indonesia

ISSN 2731-8060   ISSN 2352-5398 (electronic)
Advances in Social Science, Education and Humanities Research
ISBN 978-2-38476-025-1   ISBN 978-2-38476-026-8 (eBook)
https://doi.org/10.2991/978-2-38476-026-8

This Atlantis Press imprint is published by the registered company Atlantis Press S.A.R.L.,
part of Springer Nature
The registered company address is: 22 Rue de Palestro 75002 Paris France

Preface

Assalamu'alaikum wr wb,

Alhamdulillahirrobbil 'alamin, Thank to the God, almighty, due to His bless and love, we are granted good health and opportunity, so that today, on 19 October 2022, we can meet here at Beston Hotel, Palembang, South Sumatera, in the event of the 6th FIRST in conjunction with the 1st national seminar FIRST and the 4th SNAPTEKMAS 2022. This event will be held until tomorrow, on 20 October 2022.

The honourable keynote speakers, distinguished guests, all participants, ladies and gentlemen.

For the beginning of my speech, let me welcome all of you with my great warm hug. It is a great honour for us that you choose this event as your conference. I am so proud that all of us still become enthusiastic to develop the knowledge. Let us still work hard to support the development of the world through the research, science, and technology in many parts of the knowledge.

In this occasion, I would like proudly to inform you that Polsri will always be forward in supporting the education, research, and community service programs proposed by the educational ministry of Indonesia. Some of them are collaborating with the industries and implementing the research result to the real life. In order to support that development, this year, Polsri opened a new research and community service scheme, in which this program collaborated with Korem 044/GAPO which promoted an Integrated Farming System with a 4E values approach, namely Ecological, Educational, Aesthetic and Economical Values. This program becomes one of the supporters of these 6th FIRST in conjunction with the 1st national seminar FIRST and the 4th SNAPTEKMAS 2022.

The 6th FIRST, the 1st national seminar FIRST and the 4th SNAPTEKMAS 2022 as the forum to share knowledge, to search, to find, and to enlarge the link with other industries and universities have attracted so many authors from abroad, such as from Politeknik Tun Syed Nasir Syed Ismail; Politeknik Mukah Sarawak; Politeknik Melaka (PMK) Malaysia; Universiti Teknologi Malaysia (UTM); National Chin-Yi University of Technology (NCUT); Accounting Research Institute UiTM-Malaysia; Politeknik Melaka (PMK), Malaysia; Shandong University of Science Technology; Universiti Brunei Darussalam; and Ferdowsi University of Mashhad, Iran.

Welcome to all of the researchers that become the collaborators in our research and community service. It is our great honour to have you as our collaborators and participants the 6th FIRST, the 1st national seminar FIRST and the 4th SNAPTEKMAS 2022.

The honourable keynote speakers, distinguished guests, all participants, ladies and gentlemen.

In this chance, I would like to say thank you very much to Director of State Poly-technic of Sriwijaya for his full support in the development of the Research and Service Community programs. Due to his hard work and his belief to all of the committee so that this event can be held.

In this occasion, I also would like to convey my big thank you to all of the keynote speakers, invited guests, all the participants, all reviewers, and all committee of the 6th FIRST, the 1st national seminar FIRST and the 4th SNAPTEKMAS 2022. Without you all, this event will be nothing. May Allah SWT gives His reward for your sincerity. As the time goes by, it is hoped that our cooperation and coordination in the FIRST and SNAPTEKMAS can be maintained and improved. I hope that you can enjoy this conference and can get a big benefit from this event. I also wish that we can meet again in the forthcoming FISRT international conference, national seminar FIRST and SNAPTEKMAS.

Wassalamu'alaikum wr wb

Organization

General Chair

Rita Martini   Politeknik Negeri Sriwijaya, Indonesia

Program Chairs

Nyayu Latifah Husni   Politeknik Negeri Sriwijaya, Indonesia
Ade Silvia Handayani   Politeknik Negeri Sriwijaya, Indonesia

Organizing Committee

Erry Yulian Triblas Adesta   International Islamic University, Malaysia
Augustus E. Osseo-Asare   University of Sunderland, UK

Technical Committee

Siti Nurmaini   Universitas Sriwijaya, Indonesia
Ahmad Taqwa   Politeknik Negeri Sriwijaya, Indonesia
RD. Kusumanto   Politeknik Negeri Sriwijaya, Indonesia
Irsyadi Yani   Universitas Sriwijaya, Indonesia
Tresna Dewi   Politeknik Negeri Sriwijaya, Indonesia
Rusdianasari   Politeknik Negeri Sriwijaya, Indonesia

Editors

Rita Martini   Politeknik Negeri Sriwijaya, Indonesia
Sari Lestari Zainal Ridho   Politeknik Negeri Sriwijaya, Indonesia
Dodik Siswantoro   Universitas Indonesia
Habsah Mohamad Sabli   Polytechnic Mukah
Marieska Lupikawaty   Politeknik Negeri Sriwijaya, Indonesia
Ade Silvia Handayani   Politeknik Negeri Sriwijaya, Indonesia

Corresponding Author

Nyayu Latifah Husni   Politeknik Negeri Sriwijaya, Indonesia

Contents

Peer-Review Statements

Rita Martini[1], Sari Lestari Zainal Ridho[1], Dodik Siswantoro[2],
Habsah Mohamad Sabli[3], Marieska Lupikawaty[1], and Ade Silvia Handayani[1(✉)]

[1] Politeknik Negeri Sriwijaya, Palembang, Indonesia
ade_silvia@polsri.ac.id
[2] Universitas Indonesia, Depok City, Indonesia
[3] Politeknik Mukah Serawak, Mukah, Malaysia

All of the articles in this proceedings volume have been presented at the 6th FIRST 2022 during *19–20 October 2022* in *Palembang, South Sumatera, Indonesia*. These articles have been peer reviewed by the members of the *Scientific Committee* and approved by the Editor-in-Chief, who affirms that this document is a truthful description of the conference's review process.

1 Review Procedure

The reviews were *double-blind*. Each submission was examined by *at least 2* reviewer(s) independently.

The conference submission management system was https://first.polsri.ac.id/2022/ 2021/11/03/submission/.

Authors submit manuscripts via our online submission platform to the Editorial Office. The Editor-in-Chief first reviews the article; if the manuscript is suitable to the journal's purpose and scope, the Editor-in-Chief assigns a Section Editor to handle the whole review process and return a recommendation or decision to the Editor-in-Chief. The Editor-in-chief selects based on the reviewers' comments and the Section Editor's final decision to: Accept the paper as is with no revisions, Accept after revision, Request that the authors resubmit, or Reject. The reviewers should provide objective, constructive, and expert comments. Detailed comments on article recommendations. One or two sentences are insufficient; at least one paragraph is required.

The author is sent an acceptance letter, and the finished work is delivered to production. Occasionally, writers are asked to revise their article in light of the reviewers' remarks and submit the revised version to the Editor-in-chief. Depending on the discipline and type of extra evidence, information, or argument requested, the review period can range from six to eight weeks.

After review, the manuscript goes to the 'Copy Editor' who will correct the manuscript in respect of the correct referencing system in accordance with the journal style and layout. When the 'Copy Editor' finishes his/her work, the manuscript will be sent to the 'Layout editor'.

A. S. Handayani—Editors-in-Chief of the 6th FIRST 2022.

© The Author(s) 2023
R. Martini et al. (Eds.): FIRST 2022, ASSEHR 733, pp. 1–3, 2023.
https://doi.org/10.2991/978-2-38476-026-8_1

2 Quality Criteria

Reviewers were instructed to assess the quality of submissions solely based on the academic merit of their content along the following dimensions:

1. Pertinence of the article's content to the scope and themes of the conference;
2. Clear demonstration of originality, novelty, and timeliness of the research;
3. Soundness of the methods, analyses, and results;
4. Adherence to the ethical standards and codes of conduct relevant to the research field;
5. Clarity, cohesion, and accuracy in language and other modes of expression, including figures and tables.

In addition, all of the articles have been checked for textual overlap in an effort to detect possible signs of plagiarism by the publisher.

FIRST IC 2022 has a zero-tolerance policy when it comes to plagiarism. As a result, the following policy has been established, which outlines precise steps that will be taken (penalties) if plagiarism is found in an article submitted for publication in FIRST IC 2022.

Plagiarism is "the use of the language and thoughts of another author and the presenting of them as one's original work," whether the language and thoughts are used verbatim or closely imitated.

According to the policy, all submissions must be unique, never before published, and in no other stage of the publication process.

The content that has been taken verbatim from another source needs to be indicated as being different from the present original text by (1) indentation, (2) the use of quotation marks, and (3) identification of the source.

Any text of an amount exceeding fair use standards (herein defined as more than two or three sentences or the equivalent thereof) or any graphic material reproduced from another source requires permission from the copyright holder and, if feasible, the original author(s) and also requires identification of the source; e.g., previous publication. Fair use is defined as the amount of text equivalent to more than two or three sentences.

Ithenticate will be used to determine how similar each of the submitted papers is to the database.

3 Key Metrics

Total submissions	65
Number of articles sent for peer review	42
Number of accepted articles	21
Acceptance rate	32.3%
Number of reviewers	10

Any additional information about article statistics belongs to this section, but the listing should suffice in most situations. More rows can be added if necessary, but please do not delete any existing row. Numbers are for example only. "Acceptance rate" is (number of accepted articles) divided by (number of total submissions).

Competing Interests. Neither the Editor-in-Chief nor any member of the Scientific Committee declares any competing interest.

Measuring Academic Staff Job Satisfaction in TVET Institutions

Iskandar bin Reduan[1], Habsah binti Haji Mohamad Sabli[2(✉)], and Azrol bin Adenan[1]

[1] Polytechnic Mukah, Mukah, Malaysia
[2] Department of Commerce, Polytechnic Mukah, Mukah, Malaysia
habsah@pmu.edu.my

Abstract. Job satisfaction plays an important role in improving performance and quality of work. With high level of job satisfaction, employees will make a significant contribution and are committed towards their employment. Changes in the management of an organization that involve procedures and policies can affect administrative operations and in turn, cause job dissatisfaction. Moreover, issue of the transfer of personnel from Politeknik Mukah Sarawak (PMU) to their place of origin causes shortages in certain areas and skills in the workforce. Ultimately, this leads to an overburden towards other personnel (lecturers) assigned to take over the responsibilities of the transferring personnel, thus subsequently had to learn (anew) as well as to teach in the same field that is left vacant. Additionally, the replacement needs to cater their existing tasks and responsibilities. Therefore, this paper aims to identify the level of job satisfaction among academic's staffs at PMU. Several factors that contribute to job satisfaction to differ among employees. This study adopts Herzberg's Motivation Hygiene Theory Job Satisfaction includes Organizational Leadership Style and Supervision, Working Conditions, Organizational Communication, Promotion Opportunities, and Job Security, Remuneration, and Employee benefits. A total of 189 respondents were involved in the study from five main departments and two support departments. Data is collected using the questionnaire method, Google Form as a study instrument, and distributed to respondents. Data analysis is made using SPSS version 26.0 software and is expressed in the form of frequency, percentage, and mean for items related to the level of job satisfaction. The results of the study show that job satisfaction based on predetermined factors among PMU academic staffs is at a moderate level. The highest mean Organizational Leadership Style and Supervision, which (mean = 4.5026), and the lowest Remuneration and Employee Benefits (mean = 3.7778). The outcome of this research can help the decisions makers to increase the job satisfaction among PMU (Politeknik Mukah) staff.

Keywords: Job Satisfaction · Organizational Leadership Style and Supervision · Working Conditions · Organizational Communication

1 Introduction

The consistently growing field of education requires educators to always be sensitive to the latest developments. The rapid development of IR 4.0 technology and the emergence

R. Martini et al. (Eds.): FIRST 2022, ASSEHR 733, pp. 4–12, 2023.
https://doi.org/10.2991/978-2-38476-026-8_2

of Covid 19 pandemic indirectly put pressure on educators to adapt to the current needs of educations. The group of educators in Technical and Vocational Education and Training (TVET) institutions are no exception to the situation and this led to job dissatisfaction among the educators [1]. Job satisfaction is important to measure performance [2]. Satisfied employees are more productive and are more likely to stay with the company longer, while unhappy employees are less productive and more likely to leave [3]. Due to changes in organizational management such as procedures and rules, high rates of staff turnovercause work pressure among academic staffs at PMU. These are proven from the findings, [4], show job satisfaction among the university's academic staffs in Malaysia is at a moderate level. Adapted from Herzberg's Motivation Hygiene Theory, jobs at faction will be measured based on the following elements such Organizational Leadership Style and Supervision, Working Conditions, Organizational Communication, Promotion Opportunities, Job Security, Remuneration, and Employee benefits. The importance of job satisfaction among educators leads to this study. Inconsistent findings and lack of research on this matter attract authors to do this research. Hence, this paper is an attempt to identify the level of job satisfaction among academic's staffs at PMU. The findings can help the institutions, and the government implement rewards or develop facilities to help educators facing the situations. The structure of this article is as follows. It starts off by giving a summary of pertinent literature. It also discusses the research methodology and design. The research findings are then presented, discussed, and a conclusion is offered.

2   Literature Review

The motivation-hygiene hypothesis is also known as Herzberg's dual-factor theory (1959). The distinction between motivational and hygienic variables is this theory's central idea. The two factors that affect job satisfaction can be divided into two groups. Motivating variables are seen to be more significant than hygienic factors in determining job satisfaction. The urge to avoid unpleasant events is connected to hygiene components. Because of an individual's goal for self-actualization and self-development, motivational factors influence job satisfaction [5]. The factors adopt from both elements which, the Organizational Communication, Promotion Opportunities, and Job Security under motivation a elements and Organizational Leadership Style and Supervision, Working Conditions, and Remunerations and Employee Benefits under hygiene elements.

According to [6], motivators are factors that motivate people to work. These motivators result in job satisfaction. The foundation of motivating factors is a person's desire for self-improvement. Motivation variables, when present, can aid in the active creation of job happiness. If they're effective, they can inspire someone to put up an above-average effort or performance [7]. Work that is hard or stimulating, receiving recognition, opportunities for progress, responsibility, status a sense of personal accomplishment, and personal growth in the workplace are all motivating aspects. Motivational elements contribute to a higher level of job satisfaction [8]. Factors that minimized job dissatisfaction were identified as hygiene factors. The requirement for an organization to minimize unpleasantness in the workplace is the basis for hygiene factors. Employee dissatisfaction arises when these factors are deemed insufficient by the employee. Company policy and administration, sentiments of job security, financial pay, supervisory quality, and the quality of human relations and working environment are all examples of typical hygiene variables [9].

Job satisfaction is described as an individual's conduct regarding their work duties and relationships with their motivation. Positive behavior will lead to a balanced level of job satisfaction, whilst poor behavior will lead to job discontent(Scott et al. 2005).Employees who are satisfied with their jobs are more likely to stay with the company in the long run, caring more about the quality of their work and being more loyal to the company [10, 11]. The importance of job satisfaction in terms of performance cannot be overstated. People who are satisfied with their jobs are more driven, put in more effort, and are more likely to perform better than those who are dissatisfied [12, 13]. Considering the importance of job satisfaction among academic staffs in PMU, and the existence of various factors and associations between variables according to previous research, becomes a reason to carry out this research.

3 Methodology

This study used a survey method to determine how satisfied academic staffs at Politeknik Mukah were with their jobs. From October 2021 to April 2022, Mukah Polytechnic's academic departments all participated in the data collection. All academics received self-administered questionnaires, and a total of 189 lecturers responded to the questionnaire. The sampling size indicated by [14] was employed in this research to find the targeted survey respondents. The questionnaire used for this study was adapted from the Herzberg Motivation Hygiene Theory (Employee Satisfaction Survey). It was then modified to suit the current study context. The questionnaire consisted of two sections; the first was related to lecturers' demographic profile and the second section focused on the lecturers' job satisfaction. Section two comprises of six factors that includes, consist of six factors including (1) Organizational Leadership Style and Supervision; (2) Working Conditions; (3) Organizational Communication; (4) Promotion Opportunities and Job Security; (5) Remuneration and Employee Benefits; and (6) Personal Job Satisfaction. The SPSS Version 26 software was used to analyze the data collected from this questionnaire. The demographic data was described using a frequency distribution, while mean scores and standard deviations for items linked to research perceptions were calculated. Since all of the variables' Cronbach's alpha values are greater than 0.60, the reliability tests on the variables specified for this study were judged to be acceptable and reliable. (1) Organizational Leadership Style and Supervision CR (Construct Reliability) = 0.8980, (2) Working Conditions CR = 0.9290, (3) Organizational Communication CR = 0.8420 (4) Promotion Opportunities and Job Security CR = 0.9192, (5) Remuneration and Employee Benefits CR = 0.9100 and (6) Personal Job Satisfaction CR = 0.9020.

Table 1 contains details on the demographic profiles of instructors. 52.9% of the poll participants who were lecturers were female, while 47.1% were male. Eighty one percent of the respondents (81%) were already married, with the majority of them residing far from their family (56.3%). Nearly half of the respondents were over 40, the majority of them were Muslims (83.6%) and of Malay ancestry (68.8%). 19.6% of the lecturers come from the Department of Commerce, and 57.1% have been employed for less than

Table 1. Demographic respondent profiles

Categories	Items	Frequency	%
Gender	Male	100	52.9
	Female	89	47.1
Marital Status	Single	36	19.1
	Married	153	80.9
	Widowed	–	–
	Divorced	–	–
Do You Live Far from your family?	Yes	111	58.7
	No	78	41.3
Age	<20	–	–
	21–25	–	–
	26–30	24	12.7
	31–35	35	18.5
	36–40	50	26.5
	>40	80	42.3
Religion	Islam	158	83.6
	Christianity	26	13.8
	Buddhism	3	1.6
	Hinduism	–	–
	Others	2	1.0
Ethnicity	Malay	130	68.8
	Chinese	6	3.2
	Indian	–	–
	Bumiputera Sarawak	50	26.5
	Bumiputera Sabah	1	0.5
	Others	2	1.1
Department	JKA	26	13.8
	JKE	29	15.3
	JKM	32	16.9
	JP	37	19.6
	JTMK	26	13.8
	JMSK	18	9.5
	JPA	21	11.1

12 years. Last but not least, it's significant to remember that 75% of the lecturer work 15–19 h per week.

As shown in Table 2, the level of Organisational Leadership Style and Supervision among the lecturers at Politeknik Mukah is high, with mean values are ranged between 4.50–5.00. For this category, the highest (mean = is 4.5026) is related to my head of department professionally treating me and the lowest (mean of 4.0794) which is organizational leadership style promotes fairness, courtesy, and honesty.

According to Table 3, the working conditions for lecturers at Politeknik Mukah are moderate to high, with mean values ranging from 3.50 to 4.49. The item with the highest

Table 2. Mean and Standard Deviation (SD) for Organisational Leadership Style and Supervision; among lecturers in Politeknik Mukah

Item	Mean	SD
Organizational Leadership Style and Supervision		
Transparency is encouraged by the democratic leadership style of the organisation.	4.1376	.69352
The organizational leadership style promotes fairness, courtesy, and honesty.	4.0794	.75021
My head of department professionally treats me.	4.5026	.63266
During and after evaluation, my head department offers helpful, dependable, and legitimate input.	4.3598	.70535
I am consulted in any decision-making that is related to my work.	4.2593	.71569

Table 3. Mean and Standard Deviation (SD) for Working Conditions among lecturers in Politeknik Mukah

Item	Mean	SD
Working Conditions		
The actual workspace is secure, tidy, and clean (venues, ablution facilities, parking areas, grounds).	4.2275	.79632
I have access to sufficient and suitable tools and equipment to carry out my duties.	3.8519	.89280
The company is accommodating when it comes to me taking care of my personal and family obligations.	4.2804	.72250
In the workplace, diversity in terms of colour and gender is acknowledged.	4.2804	.75137
All forms of harassment and discrimination are prohibited in the workplace.	4.2540	.83733

mean score (mean = 4.2804) for this category is "I am given adequate and sufficient tools and equipment to execute my work tasks and the organisation is flexible regarding my attending to my personal and family concerns." and the least (mean 3.8519), where I am given sufficient and appropriate tools and equipment to carry out my work tasks.

According to Table 4, the lecturers at Politeknik Mukah have a moderate to high level of organisational communication, with mean values falling between 3.50 and 4.49. The maximum score in this area (mean = 4.2169) is achieved by peer communication that is professional, efficient, and mutually beneficial, while the lowest score (mean 4.1005) is achieved by employees who are informed of issues that directly impact them.

As can be seen in Table 5, there are moderate to high opportunities for promotion and job security for academics at Politeknik Mukah, with mean values falling between 3.50 and 4.49. The maximum score (mean = 4.3175) in which I feel certain that my employment is secure and the lowest score (mean = −4.3175) (mean 3.9524). The

Table 4. Mean and Standard Deviation (SD) for Organisational Communication among lecturers in Politeknik Mukah

Item	Mean	SD
Organizational Communication		
Employees are advised about issues that may affect them.	4.1005	.73329
Senior management and staff communicate effectively, professionally, and for both parties' mutual benefit.	4.1587	.79640
All staff members are informed of the organization's strategic goals.	4.1217	.76562
At staff meetings, I get enough chances to interact formally with other workers.	4.1958	.74290
Peer communication is professional, efficient, and advantageous to both parties.	4.2169	.70750

Table 5. Mean and Standard Deviation (SD) for Promotion Opportunities and Job Security among lecturers in Politeknik Mukah

Item	Mean	SD
Promotion Opportunities and Job Security		
I am certain that I will keep my job.	4.1905	.74070
I have faith that my job is safe.	4.3175	.74001
Equal possibilities for both professional and personal growth are offered by the university.	4.1799	.74335
Equal possibilities for promotion and career progress are offered by the institution.	4.2275	.72646
The organization offers workers financial aid so they can continue their education and training.	3.9524	.86471

institution offers workers financial aid so they can pursue additional education and training.

The level of renumeration and employee benefits among lecturers at Politeknik Mukah is moderate to high, as illustrated in Table 6, with mean values falling between 3.50 and 4.49. For this category, the greatest rating (mean = 3.9365) is for how happy I am with the benefits that are currently provided to employees, and the lowest rating (mean 3.7778) is for how happy I am with the present performance bonus system.

The level of personal job satisfaction among instructors at Politeknik Mukah is moderate to high, as indicated in Table 7, with mean values ranging from 3.50 to 4.49. The greatest rating (mean = 4.3757) and lowest rating (mean 3.9683) for this category are, respectively, how fully committed I am to my task.

Table 6. Mean and Standard Deviation (SD) for Remuneration and Employee Benefits among lecturers in Politeknik Mukah

Item	Mean	SD
Remuneration and Employee Benefits		
With my current pay, I'm really happy.	3.8730	1.00253
The present employment advantages offered have my full satisfaction.	3.9365	.91453
With the way performance bonuses are now given out, I'm happy.	3.7778	.93589
Workers receive the appropriate praise from management for their efficient work.	3.9365	.89097
I'm appreciated for what I bring to this organisation.	3.8995	.84138

Table 7. Mean and Standard Deviation (SD) for Personal Job Satisfaction among lecturers in Politeknik Mukah

Item	Mean	SD
Personal Job Satisfaction		
I am fully committed to my work.	4.3757	.70834
I always have a good time at work.	3.9683	.89267
With my coworkers, I get along well at work.	4.3333	.71459
My confidence and morale are strong at work.	4.1376	.78015
I would heartily suggest that a friend apply for a job at this organization.	4.2804	.88767

4 Discussion and Conclusion

The primary goal of this study is to find the level of job satisfaction factors (Organizational Leadership Style and Supervision, Working Conditions, Organizational Communication, Promotion Opportunities, and Job Security, Remuneration and Employee Benefit. Among academic staffs in PMU. Their overall job satisfaction scores, which range between 3.50 and 4.49, are moderately high. These results, which are corroborated by [15], showed that work satisfaction among university faculty members in Malaysia is at a moderate level due to the collectivist ethos of Malaysians (Hofstede, 1980; 1984).

However, the top management needs to improve to factor under Remuneration and Employee Benefit where some academic staffs are not satisfied with the current system used to award performance bonuses. Remuneration and Employee Benefits also known as reward for employee and that reward practices will enhance their Increased job engagement, discretionary behavior development, and motivation. The motivation process is a strategy that encourages workers to set goals, act, and achieve those goals in order to receive a worthwhile reward that meets their needs. Achievable performance, both financially and non-financially, such as a growth in profit and product quality, can be referred to as the organization's aim.

It is important to note that, this study is limited to the academic staffs of Politeknik Mukah, and the findings does not reflect the over all results of Politeknik Malaysia academic staffs. The respondents of this study are also bound by Malaysian government circular and policies that cannot be enacted at the institutional level itself Limitations and setbacks observed from this study found out that some of the questionnaires were not return to theresearcher due to time constrains and costs.

References

1. K. Ramamurthi , A. Vakilbashi , S. Z. A. Rashid , M. Mokhber and R. Basiruddin , "Impact of Job Stressors Factors on Employees' Intention to Leave Mediated by Job Engagement and Dispositional Factors", International Review of Management and Marketing, vol. 6, no. 3, pp. 528–531, May. 2016
2. Wahi,M.F, Sabli, M.S &Redho, Z. S.R, Job Satisfaction among Academic Staff in TVET Institutions. International Applied Business and Engineering Conference, 86–89.
3. Sarker, A.H., A. Crossman, and P. Chinmeteepituck, 2003. The relationships of age and length of service with job satisfaction: An examination of hotel employees in Thailand. J. Managerial Psychol., 18: 745-58.
4. FauziahNoordin, &KamaruzamanJusoff (2009), Levels of Job Satisfaction amongst Malaysian Academic Staff. Asian Sosial Science. www.ccsenet.org/journal.html, Vol. 5, No. 5.
5. Chu, H.-C., &Kuo, T. Y. (2015). Testing Herzberg's Two-Factor Theory in Educational Settings in Taiwan. The Journal of Human Resource and Adult Learning, 11(1), 54–65. http://www.hraljournal.com/Page/10HuichinChu&TsuiYangKuo.pdf
6. Herzberg, F. (2003). One more time: How do you motivate employees? Harvard Business Review, 81(1), 86.
7. Park, S. M. (2007). A multi-level analysis of work motivation and organizational socialization: Probing the internalized motivational effects among public managers.
8. Zimmerman, F. M. (1988). Cornerstones of management: old recipes to today's problems. St.Paul, MN: University of St. Thomas.
9. Hee, O. C., Ong, S. H., Ping, L. L., Kowang, T. O., &Fei, G. C. (2019). Factors Influencing Job Satisfaction in the Higher Learning Institutions in Malaysia. International Journal of Academic Research in Business and Social Sciences, 9(2), 9–20. https://doi.org/10.6007/ijarbss/v9-i2/5510
10. Zhang, X., Kaiser, M., Nie, P., & Sousa-Poza, A. (2019). Why are Chinese workers so unhappy? A comparative cross-national analysis of job satisfaction, job expectations, and job attributes. PLoS ONE, 14(9), 1-16.
11. Alfonso Sousa-Poza, Andrés A Sousa-Poza, Well- being at work: a cross-national analysis of the levels and determinants of job satisfaction, The Journal of Socio-Economics, Volume 29, Issue 6, 2000, Pages517–538
12. Chen, S.-H., Yang, C.-C., Shiau, J.-Y., & Wang, H.-H. (2006). The development of an employee satisfaction model for higher education. The TQM Magazine, 18(5), 484–500. https://doi.org/10.1108/09544780610685467
13. Santhappar, A. S., & Alam, S. S. (2005). Job Satisfaction Among Academic Staff in Private Universities in Malaysia. Journal of Social Sciences, 1(2), 72–76. https://doi.org/10.3844/jssp.2005.72.76

14. Chuan, C. L., & Penyelidikan, J. (2006). Sample size estimation using Krejcieand Morgan and Cohen statistical power analysis: A comparison. *JurnalPenyelidikan IPBL*, 7(1), 78-86.
15. Lam, S. M., Kuok, A. C., Sze, T. M. (2022). Self-Efficacy, Stress and Job Satisfaction among Pre- Service, Novice, and Experienced English Teachers: A Study of their Occupational Health. Health Psychology Report. https://doi.org/10.5114/hpr.2022.115768

Evaluation of Occupational Safety and Health Management System at Lab Test Lembaga Air Perak

Juhaidie Zamani Bin Jamaludin[1(✉)] and Norshahida Binti Hasan Saari[2]

[1] Civil Engineering Department, Poytechnic Mukah, Mukah, Sarawak, Malaysia
juhaidiez@pmu.edu.my
[2] Operation Unit, Lembaga Air Perak, Perak, Malaysia

Abstract. All industries including the government organizations have to follows the Occupational Safety and Health Act (OSHA) 1994 which required the employers to perform minimum duties to ensure the safety, health and welfare of their workers, and joint the responsibilities between employer and employees. With the aim to evaluate the occupational safety and health management system at lab test Lembaga Air Perak a quantitative cross-sectional descriptive survey research was conducted at the laboratory test department of Lembaga Air Perak located at Ipoh in the Kinta district from the 4th October 2021 till the 31st March 2022. The data were collected in two phases; The first phase, the consented laboratory worker was interviewed using a pretested structured questionnaire as a guide focusing on the demographic characteristic and the sources and types of hazards encountered by them throughout the working period. On the second phase researcher naturalistic observe the participant and laboratory implementation towards the occupational safety and health management system based on Lembaga Air Perak Laboratory Quality Manual. This research found most of the participants are Laboratory Assistant with the median age of 39 years old and have been working between one to three years. Majority of the participants implement to occupational safety and health management system in general and within 12 elements been observe the laboratory fail to implement two of the requirements of the Lembaga Air Perak Laboratory Quality Manual. This study hypothesized that the occupational safety and health management system been implemented well at the laboratory of Lembaga Air Perak. This study provides a conceptualization of safety culture that can be used in future study.

Keywords: Occupational Safety and Health Management System · laboratory · implementation

1 Introduction

National Occupational Accidents Statistics 2020 by the Department of Statistic Malaysia shown that the number of reporting occupational accidents in year 2020 was 32, 674 cases compared with year 2019, 40,811 cases was reported [1]. The same report also shown that the pattern of the accidents rate in Malaysia was decreasing years by years

R. Martini et al. (Eds.): FIRST 2022, ASSEHR 733, pp. 13–24, 2023.
https://doi.org/10.2991/978-2-38476-026-8_3

[1]. The employers of all industries including the government organizations cannot feel relieve to see this data because as we witness how the COVID-19 pandemic changes our daily life substantially the statistical decline of the accidents rate in Malaysia may due to the measures of closure and restrictions imposed by the government on economic activities to overcome the spread of the COVID-19 and the Department of statistics Malaysia reported the total working hours dropped till 28.2% [1]. However, employers of all industries including the government organizations have to follows the [9]. This Act states that employers and employees are responsible for safety and health practices in the workplace [9]. Thus, there is no exception for the Lembaga Air Perak organizations.

Lembaga Air Perak is a corporation that been established on January 1990 under the Lembaga Air Perak Enactment 1988 [2]. The purpose of Lembaga Air Perak been established was to provide clean water supply services in the state of Perak which included more than 2.5 million people. Lembaga Air Perak is the third largest water operator in Malaysia after Selangor and Johor [2]. Thus, it is very important for the Lembaga Air Perak to have a laboratory that safe from potential hazard such as chemical, biological, physical and also safety hazards. Safety awareness is very wide concepts that refers to the avoidance and know of any kind of accident leading to harm or injury to human beings [3].

To be the best benchmark in Malaysia, Lembaga Air Perak had a visionary mission which to provide clean water for the needs of all including the population in and outside the city as well as the commercial and industrial sectors [2]. This shown that Lembaga Air Perak being an efficient and also responsible corporation that very concern with the aspect of environmental safety and also want to ensure the human health at the highest quality. In addition, there is a responsibility for an organization to provide a safe system of work for every worker which includes the layout, the raining, supervision, the provision of warning, personal protective clothing, special instruction and methods of work adopted [4]. The laboratory department is one of the important facilities to ensure that Lembaga Air Perak can always achieve their mission and be in a good direction. However, laboratory activities may expose the laboratory employees, and also the public to potential hazardous and toxic chemicals also increase the risk of incidents [5].

Therefore, the Lembaga Air Perak have to make sure their management system that managing the risk in the laboratories. Which included the occupational health, the prevention of any disease related to the laboratory facilities and activities also the protection of the environment always been compliance by all the laboratory employees and aligned with the Standard Operation Manual provided by Lembaga Air Perak.

2   Literature Review

Generally, a hazard can be defined as any source which can be any condition or situation also any behaviour of potential damage, harm or adverse health effects on something or someone [6]. To prevent any hazardous, it must be identified because the unidentified hazards will cause unmanageable risk [7]. Thus, it is so important for an organisation to identify the source also type of hazards in their facilities. There was a way to detect the hazards, based on the literature search this recommended process are applied in the National Institute for Occupational Safety and Health United States, Western Sydney

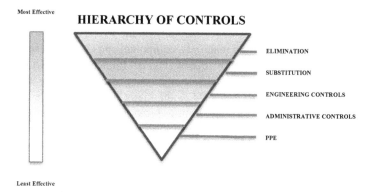

Fig. 1. Hierarchy of Control

University and also at the Department of Occupational Safety and Health, Ministry of Human Resources Malaysia stated in the Guidelines for Hazard Identification, Risk Assessment and Risk. This full process of hazards identification is called Risk Assessment where the organisation needs to evaluate each of work area, work task, situation, items and also thing proactively because anything may have potential to cause harm [8].

Based on Fig. 1 the Hierarchy of Control, the most preferred method of controlling risk is to eliminate the hazard although most of the cases found that the hazards are not possible to be eliminate [10]. Then, it must move to the substitution, where the hazard will be replaced with anything that give no risk or more lower risk [10]. Engineering control also be one of the alternative procedures because is consist of variety ways to minimizing the risk such as enclosure and isolation even though the level of effectiveness controlling the risk was moderate [10]. Policies, guidelines, training and schedule controls are among the Administrative Controls that can be implemented [10].

Focusing on the laboratory, the safety programs involving the laboratory began in the late of 1980s and it required uniformity and continuity throughout the facilities such as chemical labelling and the ways of reporting any accidents or exposure [31]. Safety is the most import element in management of laboratory science [32]. Besides that, Occupational Safety and Health also want all the laboratory staff to subcommittees to ensure shared expertise and tasks including the risk management, hazardous material, infection control, laboratory safety, life safety involving utilities equipment and radiation and many more [8]. Surprisingly, 93 cases accidents related to exposure to or contact with harmful substances or radiation reported by National Occupational Accident 2020 [1]. If the Occupational Safety and Health management system being priorities over the past decade, why the accidents still occur.

Accidents can easily happen in the laboratory if the level of implementation towards safety when working in the laboratory are low. The safety must be practicing once the worker entering the laboratory especially during conducting any experiment or any laboratory works. Safety rules in the laboratory should be observed. Workers should be responsible to avoid accidents [12]. The security and safety unit state that the laboratory is expose with high risk for accidents, injury and may cause disease as a result of the work conducted in the laboratory especially involving the use of chemical if it been handled in unsafe manner [13]. The accidents happened have significant relationship with negligence, the lack of knowledge especially on the works that been carried out as well as damage or failure either on materials, equipment and chemical used [14].

The are many factors that can influence the level of implementation of occupational and health system. From the side of government, they already provide a guiding act; Occupational Safety and Health Act 1994 as the major law that provide the provision on area including the employer's responsibilities providing a safe working environment, an appropriate training also a very good preparation to face any type of emergency [15]. Now, it clear that the top management commitment is one of the important factors that influences the level of implementation and execution of the Occupational Safety and Health Management System. Management's involvement and engagement in actions towards was the management commitment in order to achieve a goal [16].

However, there are situations that organizations face as a barrier to implement the occupation and health system. To maintain the system all the time it required high cost that must be bear by the organisation [17]. Sometime, there will be a need to changes or updating the procedures for improvement. Training is also always given however the employee still ignores the procedure [18]. Here, the leader must take an appropriate action. Leaders always concern about their leadership [19]. Thus, before an organization must overcome all the barrier before making any decision to implement any new system to ensure the organization productivity still running efficiently and safe for [20].

3 Methodology

The study mainly incorporates was a quantitative cross-sectional descriptive survey research design. With the aim to evaluate the occupational safety and health management system at lab test Lembaga Air Perak this study was conducted at the laboratory test department of Lembaga Air Perak located at Ipoh in the Kinta district from the 4th October 2021 till the 31st March 2022.

The data were collected in two phases; The first phase, the researcher used a pretested structured questionnaire as a guide to direct an interview and the second phase, the researcher used an observation checklist referring to the Laboratory Quality Manual. This study involved two sampling technique. The first sampling technique involving the participation among laboratory workers. By using formula with finite population estimating a proportion with the setting of precision level 5%, confidence level at 95% and adapting the assumption that 50% of the laboratory worker have implement to the occupational safety and health management system. However, there is no sample size calculation needed in due to the small number of populations.

where,

$$n = \frac{NZP(1-P)}{d(N-1) + ZP(1-P)}$$

n = Sample size with finite population correction

N = Population size
Z = Statistic for a level of confidence
P = Expected proportion (if the prevalence is 20%, P=0.2)
D = Precision (if the precision is 5% then d = 0.05)

The second sampling technique for this study involving the facilities sampling. With the objective to evaluate the level of implementation of occupational safety and health management system at Lab Test Department of Lembaga Air Perak, researcher also interest in linked the facilities with analytics value to see the practices of occupational safety and health management system in all the laboratories of Lembaga Air Perak. The data collection of this study was carried out in two phases thus there are two different data collection instruments. In the first phase, the researcher used a pretested structured questionnaire as a guide to direct an interview. In the second phase, the researcher used an observation checklist referring to the Lembaga Air Perak Laboratory Quality Manual. Table 1 showed the sources and types of hazards or hazardous situations provided.

The returned questionnaires and also the observational list was encoded by hand to ease data entry and to minimize errors. The collected data analysed using with Statistical Package for Social Science (SPSS version 22.0 for windows). Descriptive analysis been used to describe the demographics and baseline characteristic of the respondent. Mean and standard deviation presented the normal distributed continuous data, meanwhile categorical data presented in frequency and percentage.

Table 1. The Sources and Types of Hazards Encountered by The Participant at The Laboratory

Types of Hazards	Sources of Hazards
Chemical: *Waste spills*	Hazardous chemical waste spills at the time pouring
Chemical: *Waste spills*	The occurrence of waste leakage
Working environment: *Confined space hazard*	Inhalation of strong acid vapor in the laboratory
Chemical: *Toxic*	Skin contacts with strong acid material
Energy: *Electrical*	Leakage of current on electrical
Radiation: *Expose to radiation*	Skin or eye disorder due to the exposure to any radiation
Working environment: *Falls, trips, slip etc.*	Falling or slippery during the working in the facilities
Working environment: *Worker behaviours*	Use improper devices, equipment tools or material
Energy: *Acoustic/noise*	Expose to the noise that more than 80 dB

4   Data Analysis and Result

Table 2 summarizes the socio-demography characteristics of all the study participants. With the median age of 39 years old (IQR: 16.75) and the number of male and female participants are equal which 4 (50.0%) person respectively. Half of the respondent have been working in the laboratory between one to three years (n = 4, 50.0%) and majority of the participant's was designation in the laboratory of Lembaga Air Perak was Laboratory Assistant (n = 3, 37.5%).

Table 3 shown the frequency and percentage of the sources and type of hazards encountered by the participants throughout their working period at the laboratory of Lembaga Air Perak. Half of the participants experienced the hazardous chemical waste spills at the time pouring (n = 4, 50.0%) and also the occurrence of waste leakage (n = 4, 50.0%) respectively. However, majority of the participants do not encounter the moments of inhalation of strong acid vapor in the laboratory (n = 6, 75.0%) and leakage of current on electrical (n = 5, 62.5%) but experience their skin been contacts with strong acid material (n = 5, 62.5%).

Table 4 below shown the level of implementation of occupational safety and health management system among the participants. Research used the Lembaga Air Perak Laboratory Quality Manual as the references to categories the participants either implement toward the manual or not. First, the researcher observes the level of implementation towards the general laboratory safety rules which contain 15 rules under this section such as it is forbidden to enter the laboratory without any arrangements, no eating, drinking and smoking in the laboratory and it is forbidden to work alone in the laboratory without supervision. However, majority of the participants do not implement the general laboratory safety rules (n = 5, 62.5%).

Table 2. Study Participants' Characteristics

Characteristics	Statistic, n (%)	
Age (median in years)	39	$(16.75)^a$
Gender		
• Male	4	(50.0)
• Female	4	(50.0)
Duration working in lab test department Lembaga Air Perak		
• Less than 1 years	1	(12.5)
• Between 1 to 3 years	4	(50.0)
• More than 3 years	3	(37.5)
Respondent's designation		
• Science officer	1	(12.5)
• Assistance science officer	2	(25.0)
• Laboratory assistant	3	(37.5)
• General assistant	2	(25.0)

Table 3. Sources and Types of Hazards Encountered at Laboratory

Types of Hazards	Sources of Hazards	Encounter, n (%)		Do not Encounter, n (%)	
Chemical: *Waste spills*	Hazardous chemical waste spills at the time pouring	4	(50.0)	4	(50.0)
Chemical: *Waste spills*	The occurrence of waste leakage	4	(50.0)	4	(50.0)
Working environment: *Confined space hazard*	Inhalation of strong acid vapor in the laboratory	2	(25.0)	6	(75.0)
Chemical: *Toxic*	Skin contacts with strong acid material	5	(62.5)	3	(37.5)
Energy: *Electrical*	Leakage of current on electrical	3	(37.5)	5	(62.5)
Radiation: *Expose to radiation*	Skin or eye disorder due to the exposure to any radiation	4	(50.0)	4	(50.0)
Working environment: *Falls, trips, slip etc.*	Falling or slippery during the working in the facilities	3	(37.5)	5	(62.5)
Working environment: *Worker behaviours*	Use improper devices, equipment tools or material	2	(25.0)	6	(75.0)
Energy: *Acoustic/noise*	Expose to the noise that more than 80 dB	6	(75.0)	2	(25.0)

Table 4. The Level of Implementation of Occupational Safety and Health Management System Among Participants.

Characteristics	Implement, n (%)		Do not Implement, n (%)	
General laboratory safety rules	3	(37.5)	5	(62.5)
Personal Protective Equipment				
• Lab Coat	7	(87.5)	1	(12.5)
• Respirator	6	(75.0)	2	(25.0)
• Face Protection	5	(62.5)	3	(37.5)
• Hearing Protection	6	(75.0)	2	(25.0)
• Mask	5	(62.5)	3	(37.5)
• Gloves	5	(62.5)	3	(37.5)

Table 5 below shown the general level of implementation of occupational safety and health management system among participants. From the results of Table 4.3.1, the participants who implement to majority of the categories will categories as implement to occupational safety and health management system in general. This study showed that majority of the participants implement to occupational safety and health management system in general (n = 6, 75.0%).

Table 6 below shown the level of implementation of occupational safety and health management system at the laboratory. Research used the Lembaga Air Perak Laboratory Quality Manual as the references to categories the laboratories at the Lembaga Air Perak either implement toward the manual or not. There are only three laboratories at the Lembaga Air Perak. First, the researcher looks up into the First AID Equipment. There are four elements under this category. However, only one of the laboratories implements the First AID box safety rules (n = 1, 33.3%). The second categories were safety rules and electrical equipment maintenance and electronics. This category contained four elements. All of the laboratories implement the general safety rules (n = 3, 100%). The

Table 5. The General Level of Implementation of Occupational Safety and Health Management System Among Participants.

Characteristics	Implement, n (%)		Do not Implement, n (%)	
General level of Implementation of Occupational Safety and Health Management System among participants.	6	(75.0)	2	(25.0)

Table 6. The Level of Implementation of Occupational Safety and Health Management System at The Laboratory.

Characteristics	Implement, n (%)		Do not Implement, n (%)	
First AID Equipment				
• First AID box	1	(33.3)	2	(66.7)
• Eye wash	2	(66.7)	1	(33.3)
• Fire extinguisher	3	(100.0)	0	(0.0)
• Fire blanket	1	(33.3)	2	(66.7)
Safety Rules and Electrical Equipment Maintenance and Electronics				
• General safety rules	3	(100.0)	0	(0.0)
• Electrical and Electronics Equipment Maintenance	2	(66.7)	1	(33.3)
• Computer rules	1	(33.3)	2	(66.7)
• Short circuit	3	(100.0)	0	(0.0)

(continued)

Table 6. (*continued*)

Characteristics	Implement, n (%)		Do not Implement, n (%)	
Safety rules for high-risk equipment in the laboratory				
• High temperature equipment	3	(100.0)	0	(0.0)
• Vacuum equipment	2	(66.7)	1	(33.3)
• High pressure equipment	2	(66.7)	1	(33.3)
• Gas compressor equipment	1	(33.3)	2	(66.7)

last categories were safety rules for high-risk equipment in the laboratory. This category contained four elements. There are many safety rules under this element and one of it was ensure the laboratory have an adequate workspace to ensure safety during operation.

5 Discussion and Conclusion

This research can summarize that most of the participants are Laboratory Assistant with the median age of 39 years old and have been working between one to three years. The sources and type of hazards encountered by the most of participants throughout their working period at the laboratory of Lembaga Air Perak was the hazardous chemical waste spills at the time pouring, the occurrence of waste leakage, their skin been contacts with strong acid material, either skin or eye disorder due to the exposure to any radiation and also been expose to the noise that more than 80db. The results of the evaluation on the level of implementation of occupational safety and health management system among the participants shown that majority of the participants do not implement the general laboratory safety rules.

[21] state that demographic factors affects the studies conducted on the occupational and health system management. However, this study was focusing on the participants characteristic as the factors that influences implementation of occupational safety and health management system at Lab Test Department of Lembaga Air Perak. The results of this study as same as the results of study by [22] reported no significant differences on the studies conducted. Meanwhile, study by Hastings et al. (1995) found that work performance is closely related to demographic factors [23]. Congruent with the study by Sattler and [24] and [23] that discovered the female employees complied with warnings. Besides that, [25] also believe female employees were found more perceive that the occupational safety and health management system elements are critical to effective occupational safety and health management system practices.

The study also states employees are forced to comply with safety and health regulations [26] because the employee does not follow the given rules while working [27]. These results may be the consequence of the relationship between employee pessimism and poor safety performance [28]. In addition, if the management put the blames to the employee for injury and accident, occupational safety and health management system performance will decrease [29]. For that reason, employers always give priority prefer-ence to practice for that reason, an organizational culture/climate is vital in determining that employees and employers give a high priority to safety and health practices. [30] found from previous research that the leadership of the organization needs to play a major role in safety, as management is accountable for most "human ware" problems. However, this was a limitation for this study because this study did not capture the how important the employee's behaviour and responsibilities will affect the implementation of occupational and health management system among the employers. However, they implement the lab coat safety rules, respirator safety rules, face protection safety rules, hearing protection safety rules, mask safety rules and gloves safety rules.

In this study the level of implementation of occupational safety and health manage-ment system at the laboratory also been evaluate. Within 12 elements that been observe, the results shown that the laboratory of Lembaga Air Perak do not implement the ele-ments under the First AID equipment which the fire blanket and also the element under safety rules and electrical equipment maintenance and electronics which was related to computer rules. Although only two out of 12 elements that do not fulfil the requirement of the Lembaga Air Perak Laboratory Quality Manual, the risk was still there and it should not happen to the laboratory that has recognized the MS ISO/IEC 17025:2005 Accreditation Certified under Laboratory Accreditation Scheme Malaysia (SAMM). To overcome this situation, everyone must take responsibility to ensure their working environment was safe.

References

1. Department of Statistic Malaysia. (2021). Big Data Analytics: National Occupational Acci-dents Statistics 2020. Release July 22, 2021 from https://www.dosm.gov.my/v1/index.php?r=column/cone&menu_id=dUgyTTlBYitlSVVrbkUveXVsZVRNZz09
2. Lembaga Air Perak. (2021). Corporate profile. https://www.lap.com.my/v4/
3. Shaari, Z., & Soebarto, V. (2013). Investigating sustainable practices in the Malaysian office building developments. Construction Innovation, 14(1), 17–37.
4. Soehod, K. & Laxman, L.K.P. (2007). Report on Law on Safety and Health in Malaysia. Uni-versiti Teknologi Malaysia. Retrieved from http://eprints.utm.my/2660/1/71777.pdf Assessed on 26 March 2015.
5. Ritch, D. & Rank, J. 2001. Laboratory safety in the biology lab. Bioscene 27(3): 17–22.
6. Leggett, D.J. 2012. Lab-HIRA: Hazard identification and risk analysis for the chemical research laboratory part 2. Risk Analysis of Laboratory Operations 19(5): 25–36
7. F. K. W. Wong et al., "Article information," J. Eng. Des. Technol., vol. 7, no. 2, pp. 130–142.
8. Department of Safety and Health (DOSH) (2008). DOSH website. Retrieved January 28, 2008, from http://dosh.mohr.gov.my
9. Occupational Safety and Health Act (Act 514). (1994). Malaysia.
10. National Institute of Occupational Safety and Health. (2020). https://www.dosh.gov.my/index.php/legislation/guidelines/general/597-04-guidelines-on-occupational-safety-and-health-management-systems-oshms/file
11. National Institute of Occupational Safety and Health. (2021).
12. Azizi, Y., Nordin, Y., Jasmi, I., Zainudin, S., Muhammad Sukri, S., Azlina, M. K.
13. Heron, R. J. L., (1999). Audit and "Responsible Care" in the Chemical Industry. Occup. Med., 49: 407–410.

14. Tharaldsen, J. E., Mearns, K. J., & Knudsen, K. (2010). Perspectives on safety: The impact of group membership, work factors and trust on safety performance in UK and Norwegian drilling company employees. Safety Science, 48(8), 1062– 1072. https://doi.org/10.1016/j.ssci.2009.06.003
15. Shaluf, I. and Fakhru'l-Razi, A. (2003). Major hazard control: the Malaysian
16. Cooper, D. (2006). Exploratory Analyses of the Effects of Managerial Support and Feedback Consequences. Journal of Organizational Behaviour Management. 26: 41–82
17. Beckmerhagen, I. A., Berg, H. P., Karapetrovic, S. V., & Willborn, W. O. (2003).
18. Zutshi, A., & Sohal, A. S. (2005). Integrated management system: The experiences of three Australian organizations. Journal of Manufacturing Technology Management, 16(2), 211 – 232.
19. Machin, M. A. (2005). Predictors of coach drivers' safety behaviour and health status. Paper presented at the 2nd International Conference in Driver Behaviour and Training, 15–17 Nov 2005, Edinburgh, Scotland. Retrieved December 20, 2007, from www.usq.edu.au/users/mac hin/Machin.2005.pdf
20. Vassie, L., Tomas, J. M., & Oliver, A. (2000). Health and safety management in UK and Spanish SMEs: A comparative study. Journal of Safety Research, 31(1), 35–43.
21. Kuenzi, M., & Schminke, M. (2009). Assembling fragments into a lens: A review, critique, and proposed research agenda for the organizational work climate literature. Journal of Management, 35, 634–717.
22. Thomas, T. L. (1999). Evaluation of training technique as a means of influencing safety knowledge, risk perception and proper respirator donning ability among respiratory protection users. Master Thesis. Faculty of the Virginia Polytechnic Institute and State University. Retrieved October 20, 2008, from http://scholar.lib.vt.edu/theses/available/etd102599151953/unrestric ted/TraciThomas.pdf
23. Rose, J., & Schelewa-Davies, D. (1997). The relationship between staff climate in residential services. Journal of Intellectual Disabilities, 1, 19 – 24.
24. Sattler, B., & Lippy, B. (1997, May 23). Hazard communication: A review of the science underpinning the art of communication for health and safety. Retrieved May 20, 2009, from http://www.osha.gov/SLTC/hazardcommunications/hc2inf2.html
25. Malle, B. (1996). Issues in social and personality psychology. Retrieved May 20, 2009, from http://darkwing.uoregon.edu/~bfmalle/issues/q9.html
26. Carvalho, M. (2008, June 22). Number of workplace accidents going down. The Star. Retrieved from http://thestaronline.com/
27. Health and Safety Executive (HSE) (2005). A review of safety culture and safety climate literature for the development of the safety culture inspection toolkit. Retrieved March 20, 2007, from http://www.hse.gov.uk/RESEARCH/rrpdf/rr367.pdf
28. Oyan, T. (2000). Putting optimism into your safety program. Occupational Hazards, 62(1), 66 -69.
29. Erickson, J. A. (2000). Corporate culture: The key to safety performance. Occupational Hazards, 62(4), 45–50.
30. Lin, J. and Mills, A. (2001). Measuring the occupational health and safety performance of construction companies in Australia. Facilities. 19: 131–138.
31. Christian, M. S., Bradley, J. C., Wallace, J. C., & Burke, M. J. (2009). Workplace safety: a meta-analysis of the roles of person and situation factors. The Journal of applied psychology, 94(5), 1103–27. https://doi.org/10.1037/a0016172.
32. Hogan, J., & Foster, J. (2013). Multifaceted Personality Predictors of Workplace Safety Performance: More Than Conscientiousness. Human Performance, 26(1), 20–43. https://doi.org/10.1080/08959285.2012.736899

Flipped Classroom Versus Traditional Classroom to Improve Students' Reading Comprehension Attainment During Covid-19 at SMA Negeri 7 Prabumulih

Welly Ardiansyah[1]([✉]), Nurul Aryanti[1], Murwani Ujihanti[1], Risnawati[1], Lutfi Asyari[2], Wasitoh Meirani[1], and Ahmad Leo Faragusta[1]

[1] State Polytechnic of Sriwijaya, Palembang, Indonesia
[2] Institut Pendidikan Indonesia, Garut, Indonesia

Abstract. The writing is intended to know if a flipped classroom design improves reading comprehension scores among students in class XI of SMA Negeri 7 Prabumulih in the year 2022/2023. This study is quasi-experimental research. There are 216 students in population and 68 students in sample, they are XIA as controlled class and XIB as experimental class. The purposive sampling was applied. The collecting data used was reading comprehension test comprising 40 question items in the form of multiple choices. Before applying a parametric-test normality and Homogeneity test were applied. Then, t-test (test of sig.) was calculated with SPSS 26. A study conducted by this research found that students teaching using flipped classroom design models were more likely to have higher reading comprehension than students taught using traditional classrooms. The experimental class had a mean score (19.000) that was much higher than the average score (14.824) of the control class. It directly implies that the use of Flipped classroom design helps students achieve greater reading comprehension.

Keywords: Flipped Classroom · Traditional Classroom · Reading Comprehension

1 Introduction

The COVID-19 pandemic has caused governments to close schools and colleges in 213 countries. Many people have been compelled to transition from traditional to online schooling as a result of this predicament. Virtual-based learning or online learning was promoted in almost all nations as a way for teachers and school staff to remain in touch with pupils [1]. In Indonesia, this situation has resulted in the transformation of the conventional teaching approach into a technology-based model. It is a drastic adjustment that poses several difficulties for a teacher to adopt in the classroom.

Flipped classroom teaching is a type of teaching where students do both in-class activities and outside activities during class. In the online learning method, teachers use digital tools to give students help to learn how quickly they want to learn, and all

R. Martini et al. (Eds.): FIRST 2022, ASSEHR 733, pp. 25–37, 2023.
https://doi.org/10.2991/978-2-38476-026-8_4

students are given assignments to learn independently at home and improve their learning capabilities. Students must actively study offline before they can join online classes. As part of the learning process, they must also be active in group work [2].

Many researches have looked at how to utilize the flipped paradigm to enhance reading comprehension, but few have looked at how critical thinking is used to support critical reading. Students can improve their English skills by using English more frequently in the flipped classroom. It will affect their academic success, learning styles, and engagement of English students have been examined by previous research (Hung, 2015). Some classrooms in high school have flipped classes, which means that students learn more about specific reading skills than they do in traditional classes. This can help improve their concentration on reading tasks. According to their findings, students given flipped directions may learn at their own speed and study outside of the classroom [3]. In a flipped classroom, the way the class is taught changes so that students can learn more about the content being taught. This allows them to understand the material in a deeper way. Surely, it also improves their achievement levels, thereby changing their roles as teachers and students. Studies have shown that flipped classrooms are highly effective and beneficial in a number of different ways [4]. Flipped classrooms have been found to boost students' achievement levels, making people want to learn different types of material [5, 6] inspiring students' desire to learn [7], enhancing the ability of students to grasp the learning materials [8], and increasing students' ability to write and their classroom engagement [9]. The influence how the flipped classroom affects different levels of reading comprehension skills of EFL learners was explored [10]. Investigating whether a flipped classroom design model is effective in teaching reading comprehension to students at SMA Negeri 7 Prabumulih is the focus in the writing. This model involves having students learn material in class, but then using resources, such as textbooks, and online to help them practice and improve their skills. This is being done in order to see if it has an effect on student reading achievement.

2   Literature Review

2.1   Defining Flipped Classroom

Engagement in learning is key to success in academics, so if a student is disengaged, their chances of doing well in school are lower. Students were able to show how engaged and interactive they were by engaging and interacting with others outside of the classroom. By engaging students in their regular school activities, teachers ensure they are meeting all behavioral, emotional, and cognitive markers while still meeting their learning goals. Positively engaged students obeyed class rules and norms well and demonstrated excellent behavior. Depending on their emotional state, students react positively and negatively to lecturers, peers, and academics. They may be engaged, interested, bored, happy, sad, or anxious. Meanwhile, achieve cognitive engagement can be achieved when they learn strategies and self-regulate to become more effective students [11]. A flipped classroom allows the lecturer to perform more activities, and students are no longer required to take notes during classes. Instead of lectures, students engage in activities and problem-solving during class time [12]. If students learn the material before class, they may be less interested in using it during the class session. In a traditional class, the material is received during the session, so students are more likely to be engaged with it. Studies show, however, that interactive online videos are more effective than in-person lectures [13, 14]. Flipping classrooms will improve student performance by increasing student engagement [15].

Through flipped classrooms, online learning is a way of getting help from teachers in a way that is different from traditional classroom learning. In online learning, teachers provide video lectures that students can watch or use for individual help. This way, students can continue their learning even if they cannot come to class. In this way, it differs from traditional online learning. In traditional classrooms, teachers often give the same lecture to everyone, no matter how different their level of understanding may be. This can make the lectures go too quickly for some students, and too slowly for others. But sometimes, depending on what students say, teachers may change the speed of the lectures to make them more accessible to everyone. In flipped classrooms, video lectures provide students with the option to fast forward or pause to review topics which may require more processing time [16].

Flipped classrooms allow students to learn English grammar in a more active way, by watching instructional videos before class. This was investigated to see how well students perform, what they think of the process, and how they feel about learning English independently. There were 43 students who were grouped into two. The first group, the experimental group, learned by watching the videos by themselves before class and practicing what they had learned under the lecturer's supervision. The second group, the control group, received traditional method only in class. The final test proved that that students' grammar performance improved when learning in a flipped classroom, even though the results of the test were not significant. Students' responses to questionnaires and interviews showed that they had positive attitudes toward learning in a flipped classroom. The survey results and interviews with students reveal that they positively respond the use of flipped classrooms in their English classes [17]. In 2013, examined the effectiveness of flipped learning at California State University Northridge by using flipped classroom in two classes. In spring 2013, this study was carried out with 50 students. The course designed is especially helpful for students who want to learn more independently. Based on the statistical data, it seems that a majority of students found the course helpful.

Several students said that they learned more effectively using the flipped classroom method, and it looks as if the students benefited from it. The majority of students considered educational films to be useful, entertaining, and difficult enough [18].

2.2 Traditional Classroom

Traditionally, a classroom consists of a lectern placed under a microscope, surrounded by pale-colored walls and rows of tables and chairs. In the past, people have focused their education on attending classes every day, and school facilities were found to affect learning. Traditional classroom education is primarily based on teaching methods and focuses on learning materials rather than learning styles and differences between learners. Learning occurs naturally when learners harmonize their techniques along with their learning ability. In the traditional classroom, the senses and the mind are not stimulated. Instead, rote learning is encouraged [19].

2.3 Reading Comprehension

The understanding of a text that one acquires from reading is called comprehension in reading. Meaning is constructed as a result of reading instruction, and it is the main objective of instruction. A reader's comprehension of a text goes beyond simply understanding words, sentences, or sentences themselves, but also has need a prior knowledge integration, language proficiency, and metacognitive strategies. To understand what is written, the reader is demanded to bridge the gaps in the information by using what the reader has already known and by understanding what the author is trying to say [20].

Readers who understand what they are reading use a variety of strategies, including connecting what they know from their own lives, summarizing key points, drawing conclusions, and asking questions to help them make sense of what they are reading. Ultimately, the goal of reading instruction is to help students understand what they are reading [20].

3   Methodology

3.1   The Method of the Research

In this study, a method called statistical analysis was used to look at data. Statistical analysis is a way of looking at data that uses mathematical tools. This type of research was done using a type of experiment called quasi-experimental. This type of experiment is where participants are not randomly assigned to groups.

3.2   Research Place

The place where the research was conducted is important because it is related to the research's variable. The research was conducted at SMA N 7 Prabumulih in Jalan. Lingkar Timur, Muara Dua, Kecamatan Prabumulih Timur, Kota Prabumulih, Sumatera Selatan 31146. Time is also important in this research, and it was held from May to July 2022.

3.3   Research Variable

The study used a quasi-experimental design, which means that it used two different groups of people. The groups were different in terms of the independent variable (X) - one group was given a treatment, while the other group was not. The independent variable (X) is a change that is made to a classroom. One way to change the way a classroom is structured is to flip the design model. The outcome of this modification in the classroom is the dependent variable (Y). This result can be measured in different ways, such as reading comprehension achieved by the students.

3.4   Research Population and Sample

In this study, researchers looked at the eleven students in the class of 2022/2023 at SMA N 7 Prabumulih. They selected a sample that is representative of the entire population, so the generalization about this group of students is likely to be precise. To get a sample, the researcher chose two groups, XIA and XIB. There were 34 experimental students in group XIA and 34 control students in group XIB. This study used a non-equivalent or non-randomized control group design to see if a specific treatment would be affected. The research objective is to see if a specific treatment would be affected or not by the study.

3.5   Research Procedures

The way the teacher was using the flipped classroom was different from the way most classes are taught. Through three phases comprising before, during, and after class, the traditional classroom provides an excellent learning environment. The flipped classroom used three phases too: pre-reading activities (planning), during-reading activities (monitoring and evaluation), and post-reading activities (evaluating what was learned) (Table 1).

3.6   Technique of Data Collection

Researchers gathered data by conducting pre-tests, treatments, and post-tests. In more detail, the test was completed as follows:

1. Pre-Test
   Before starting the treatment, the researchers want to see if the students can understand what they read well. So, pre-test is done to see how well they do. Students are required to complete a pre-test as part of the testing procedure. There were 40 multiple-choice items. If the students answered the full question properly, they would receive 100 points.
2. Treatment
   The researchers tested two different classroom designs. One used a flipped classroom design model, and the other used a traditional teaching method. The study's findings revealed that the flipped classroom design model outperformed the traditional method in terms of improving student reading comprehension.
3. Post-Test
   The study's final task is a post-test that is administered after two classes that the researchers have instructed. The post-test involved 40 multiple-choice items, just like the pre-test. The effectiveness of the flipped classroom design model is then evaluated using test results. Researchers were able to evaluate how effective flipped classroom design model was compared to a non-flipped classroom design model class in this case.

Table 1. Summary of the instruction given in both classes

Experimental Classroom	Controlled Classroom
Pre-reading activity	Before Class
Lesson objectives and background knowledge are communicated by the lecturer. The lecturer introduces the topic and activates students' knowledge during the lecture. The lecturer uploads various teaching materials in various formats (such as videos and book chapters) so students can access them before class begins.	Students were not given any lesson materials before the class.
Monitoring and evaluating while reading	In Class
The lecturers review what they have taught in class, and then asks questions to help the students understand. They then assign homework, and the students discuss what they have learned in class. The lecturers then provide more information about the materials that the students need to know, and explain that these materials will be gradually added to the WA group.	Students received the lesson and the teacher gave the entire lecture.
Post reading activity	After Class
During this phase, students were guided to reflect on the teaching and learning process and draw conclusions about lessons learned. In order to assist students who experienced difficulty implementing the flipped classroom strategy, the lecturer asked them questions related to the material. Consequently, a lecturer could evaluate the learning process by using this activity. As a result, teachers would be able to reflect on their teaching. Reflective teaching is a way of learning and teaching that focuses on thinking about teaching in a critical way. This can help teachers improve their understanding of teaching, as well as the quality of their classroom practices. In case the first teaching and learning process did not improve student reading achievement, the researcher will take another look at the classroom using the flipped classroom method.	Students were given the homework and materials to be reviewed about that day's topic.

3.7 Data Analysis Technique

The quantitative data from the research was analyzed using statistics, which involved doing calculations to see how the data was related.

Two distinct tests were carried out by the researchers to identify if two groups of students had different outcomes after students had completed a course. The independent sample t-test was used as the initial test to assess if there is any statistical proof that the associated population means differ significantly between two independent groups. The second test used was the pair sample t-test, which looked at differences in average scores between the two groups of students. A useful statistical test for examining differences between groups is the between-group t-test. It is especially helpful when one group's value for a certain parameter differs from the other group's value. When the two groups are not perfectly matched, a different kind of test called the paired-sample t-test can be applied.

a. Normality Testing
   Software called SPSS 26 is used to scrutinize whether the data was normal. The value of significance (α) was 0.05 indicating that there was a slight possibility that the data were not normal.

   1) H0: Data is normal if significance is less than 0.05.
   2) H1: Data is not normal if significance is greater than 0.05.

b. Testing for Homogeneity
   The researchers want to know whether or not the data has a consistent variance. To do this, the assumption of homogeneity of variance was adopted. Its purpose is to determine if two populations have the same distribution. If the variances are different, then the data might not be homogeneous.

   1) H0: Data are homogenous if significance is greater than 0.05.
   2) H1: Data are not homogeneous if significance is less than 0.05.

4 Results and Discussion

4.1 Results

In order to determine if the data from the pretest and post-test tests is normal, a normality test is conducted. Before choosing an analysis, determining the normality of the data is important. In this case, a normality test was used since the data was scrutinized through parametric statistics. The data is considered normal if the asymptote (2-tailed value) is bigger than or equivalent to 0.05. The results of the normality test of pre- and post-test data belong to the experimental class are displayed in Tables 2 and 3.

Typical score, according to data from the pretest, was 0.2226, and after the test, the average score was around 0.105. This suggests that the distribution of data is normal. This is significant because it means that the data are to be reliable.

Asymptotes either the pre-test or post-test is 0.181 and 0.100 separately. The asymptotes indicate that the data was distributed normally.

The homogeneity test establishes the homogeneity of the obtained data. The researchers conducted a test of variance homogeneity either on the post-test experimental or control classes using SPSS 26 by the sig. Level (α) = 0.05. The post-experiment homogeneity of variance results for the experimental and control classes are shown in Tables 4 and 5.

Table 2. Normalization test before and after the class tests on experimental class

Tests of Normality

	Kolmogorov-Smirnov[a]			Shapiro-Wilk		
	Statistic	df	Sig.	Statistic	df	Sig.
pre_test	.126	34	.191	.959	34	.226
post_test	.096	34	.200[*]	.948	34	.105

[*]This is a lower bound of the true significance.
[a]Lilliefors Significance Correction

Table 3. Normalization test before and after the class tests on control class

Tests of Normality

	Kolmogorov-Smirnov[a]			Shapiro-Wilk		
	Statistic	df	Sig	Statistic	Df	Sig
.pre_test	.103	34	.200[*]	.956	34	.181
.post_test	.126	34	.191	.947	34	.100

[*]This is a lower bound of the true significance.
[a]Lilliefors Significance Correction

Table 4. The variance homogeneity test

		Levene Statistic	df1	df2	Sig.
Post Test Results	Based on Mean	2.668	1	66	.107
	Based on Median	2.788	1	66	.100
	Based on Median and with adjusted df	2.788	1	65.352	.100
	Based on trimmed mean	2.761	1	66	.101

H0 is accepted and H1 is rejected because Table 4's significance value is 0.107 indicating that is higher than 0.05. The data are homogeneous as a result.

To compare two student groups, t-test was adopted. The findings demonstrate that mean difference of 19,000 existed between the first group of students. Students on the second class had a mean difference of 15,543 between them. The mean difference between the two groups was determined to be the most significant difference between them, and the test's significance level was 0.000.

If the probability is high (above 0.05), student performance either before or after using a flipped classroom design model cannot be distinguished It is obvious that there is a significant difference between how students performed before as well as after using

Table 5. Experiment class paired sample t-test

Paired Samples Test

			Pair 1
			Pre_test - Post_test
Paired Differences	"Mean"		−19.000
	"Std. Deviation"		9.909
	"Std. Error Mean"		1.699
	"95% Confidence Interval of the Difference"	"Lower"	−22.457
		"Upper"	−15.543
t			−11.181
df			33
Sig. (2-tailed)			.000

a flipped classroom design model if the probability is low (below 0.05). After the students completed pre- and post-tests, the researchers discovered that the flipped classroom design model significantly enhanced the students' reading comprehension classes. This demonstrates that the experimental group's students in the experimental class outperformed their reading comprehension scores compared to reading comprehension scores gained by students in the control group. Then, using the effect size, also known as eta-square, one can assess the distribution of significant effects between the experimental pre-test and post-test. Here, the difference between the pre-test and post-test scores for the experimental class is calculated.

$$\tilde{\omega}^2 = \frac{t^2}{t^2 + n - 1}$$

$$\tilde{\omega}^2 = \frac{t^2}{t^2 + n - 1}$$

$$\tilde{\omega}^2 = \frac{11.181^2}{11.181^2 + 34 - 1}$$

$$\tilde{\omega}^2 = \frac{125.014}{125.014 + 33}$$

$$\tilde{\omega}^2 = 0.791157$$

$$\text{Eta - squared} = \tilde{\omega}^2 \times 100\%$$

$$\text{Eta - squared} = 0.791157 \times 100\%$$

$$= 79.1157\%$$

Table 6. Paired sample t –test of controlled class

		Pair 1
		Pre_test - Post_test
Paired Differences	Mean	−14.824
	Std. Deviation	7.933
	Std. Error Mean	1.361
	95% Confidence Interval of the Difference Lower	−17.592
	Upper	−12.055
t		−10.895
df		33
Sig. (2-tailed)		.000

The value of eta-square (0.791157) indicated a significant effect. This demonstrates the potency of the investigated variables. The degree of correlation between the variables was calculated using the Pearson correlation coefficient (r). The correlation between variables is divided into four categories. The correlation is very weak, as indicated by the score of 0.0r0.3. The score of 0.3r0.5 denotes a weak correlation. Moderate correlation is defined as a score of approximately 0.5r0.7. Scores of 0.7 to 0.9 and r > 0.9 are regarded as having strong and extremely strong correlation, respectively. The significant correlation remains significant even if the p-value is less than 0.05.

To ascertain whether there were any differences in the students' reading comprehension achievement between the groups before and after the application of traditional method, t-test was engaged. Table 6 contains the findings.

The t-test determined that there was a 14,824-point mean difference between the two groups. This implies that the groups differ in a statistically significant way. 17,592 and 12,055 are the lower and upper difference intervals, respectively.

The results of using traditional method on students' reading comprehension before and after they engaged in their reading activities are not significantly different if the probability of significance is greater than 0.05. The results of using traditional method before and after students engaged in their reading activities are significantly different if the probability of significance is less than 0.05. This implies that the reading comprehension of students is significantly impacted by the use of traditional method. The difference in the amount of change between the groups before and after the experiment was significant based on the following method.

$$\tilde{\omega}^2 = \frac{t^2}{t^2 + n - 1}$$

$$\tilde{\omega}^2 = \frac{10.895^2}{10.895^2 + 34 - 1}$$

$$\tilde{\omega}^2 = \frac{118.701}{118.701 + 33}$$

$$\tilde{\omega}^2 = 0.78246$$

$$\text{Eta - squared } = \tilde{\omega}^2 \times 100\%$$

$$\text{Eta - squared } = 0.78246 \times 100\%$$

$$= 78.246\%$$

The relationship between the variables is strong, as indicated by the high effect associated with the eta-square value (0.78246). This denotes that there is a good chance that the eta-square value will be meaningfully associated with the variables.

4.2 Discussion

This study sought to determine how well the flipped classroom design model could boost students' achievement in reading comprehension more than a traditional classroom. The outcomes demonstrated that, compared to the control group, the experimental class using the flipped classroom design model significantly increased students' reading comprehension scores. The statistics data, which showed that the mean score for the controlled class was 19.000 while it was 14.824 for the experimental class, served as evidence for this. This suggests that flipped classroom design is more effective than traditional classroom teaching of reading comprehension.

The standard deviation measures how much variation there is in a group of data. In this study, the standard deviation for the post-tests in the experimental and controlled groups was about the same (9.909 and 7.933, respectively). This means that the groups were pretty similar, which is what we would expect if the groups were randomly chosen.

By looking at the standard error, the level of variability in sample can be ascertained. The experimental group's standard error was 1.699, while the control group's was 1.361. This shows that the experimental group more accurately reflected the population than the control group.

According to the research, flipped classrooms are more effective at teaching students to read more effectively. In the flipped classroom, this is done so that students can learn by working on relevant projects [21].

As for this study, both student groups had similar outcomes from the same experiment. The purpose of this research was to see if using flipped classrooms to teach English grammar in secondary school has any impact on students' performance, how they feel about learning English independently, and what they think of the method. It was found that after they gave a final post-test to the students, their grammar performance improved [17].

In short, flipped classrooms may have helped students improve their reading comprehension skills [18].

5   Conclusion

Students can benefit from taking flipped classroom design, according to research. Based on the findings, it can be said that flipped classroom design can be used to teach reading comprehension and produce positive results because it actively involves students in their learning. After treatment, the advantages of using flipped classrooms were obvious. Here, it can be argued that learning through flipped classrooms can help students comprehend English reading. By using flipped classrooms, students can develop their independence and learn how and where to study even outside the classroom. Students must learn to evaluate their own knowledge and skills, plan their strategies, track their progress, and modify those strategies as necessary in order to become self-directed learners. Additionally, flipped lectures give students the chance to assess, use, and discuss previously learned material while putting component skills to the test. The executive guidance based on knowledge schema created through pre-learning prior to class may have contributed to the benefits that the students in this study saw from flipped classrooms. Future research can examine how the flipped classroom approach is applied at various educational levels.

References

1. T. Oliver, "Children first?," *New Sci.*, vol. 163, no. 2194, p. 56, 1999, https://doi.org/10.4324/9781315270234-7.
2. L. Martin and D. Tapp, "Teaching with Teams: An introduction to teaching an undergraduate law module using Microsoft Teams [Enseñar con equipos: una introducción a la enseñanza de un módulo de derecho de pregrado con Microsoft Teams]," *Innov. Pract. High. Educ. J.*, vol. 3, no. 3, pp. 58–66, 2019.
3. M. Karimi and R. Hamzavi, "The Effect of Flipped Model of Instruction on EFL Learners' Reading Comprehension: Learners' Attitudes in Focus," *Adv. Lang. Lit. Stud.*, vol. 8, no. 1, p. 95, 2017, https://doi.org/10.7575/aiac.alls.v.8n.1p.95.
4. H. Obari and S. Lambacher, "Successful EFL teaching using mobile technologies in a flipped classroom," no. 2015, pp. 433–438, 2015, https://doi.org/10.14705/rpnet.2015.000371.
5. R. Vaezi, A. Afghari, and A. Lotfi, "Investigating listening comprehension through flipped classroom approach: Does authenticity matter?," *Call-Ej*, vol. 20, no. 1, pp. 178–208, 2019.
6. Dawood Al-Hamdani & Musabah Al Breiki, "the Effect of Flipped Vocabulary Learning on Achievement and Attitudes of Efl Ninth-Graders in Oman," *IMPACT Int. J. Res. Applied, Nat. Soc. Sci. (IMPACT IJRANSS)*, vol. 6, no. 10, pp. 35–44, 2018, [Online]. Available: http://impactjournals.us/archives?jname=14_2&year=2018&submit=Search&page=5
7. N. Sookoo-Singh and L. N. Boisselle, "How Does The 'Flipped Classroom Model' Impact On Student Motivation And Academic Achievement In A Chemistry Classroom?," *Sci. Educ. Int.*, vol. 29, no. 4, pp. 201–212, 2018, https://doi.org/10.33828/sei.v29.i4.2.
8. Y. N. Huang and Z. R. Hong, "The effects of a flipped English classroom intervention on students' information and communication technology and English reading comprehension," *Educ. Technol. Res. Dev.*, vol. 64, no. 2, pp. 175–193, 2016, https://doi.org/10.1007/s11423-015-9412-7.
9. B. Ayçiçek and T. Y. Yelken, "The effect of flipped classroom model on students' classroom engagement in teaching english," *Int. J. Instr.*, vol. 11, no. 2, pp. 385–398, 2018, https://doi.org/10.12973/iji.2018.11226a.

10. H. Abaeian and L. Samadi, "The Effect of Flipped Classroom on Iranian EFL Learners' L2 Reading Comprehension : Focusing on Different Proficiency Levels," vol. 3, no. 6, pp. 295–304, 2016.

11. S. L. Christenson, C. Wylie, and A. L. Reschly, "Handbook of Research on Student Engagement," *Handb. Res. Student Engagem.*, pp. 1–840, 2012, https://doi.org/10.1007/978-1-4614-2018-7.

12. J. Bergmann and Sams A, *Flipped Your Classroom*, vol. 44, no. 8. 2011. [Online]. Available: https://www.rcboe.org/cms/lib/GA01903614/Centricity/Domain/15451/Flip_Your_Classroom.pdf

13. J. F. Strayer, "How learning in an inverted classroom influences cooperation, innovation and task orientation," *Learn. Environ. Res.*, vol. 15, no. 2, pp. 171–193, 2012, https://doi.org/10.1007/s10984-012-9108-4.

14. J. L. Bishop and M. A. Verleger, "The flipped classroom: A survey of the research," *ASEE Annu. Conf. Expo. Conf. Proc.*, no. August, 2013, https://doi.org/10.18260/1-2--22585.

15. S. G. Wilson, "The Flipped Class: A Method to Address the Challenges of an Undergraduate Statistics Course," *Teach. Psychol.*, vol. 40, no. 3, pp. 193–199, 2013, https://doi.org/10.1177/0098628313487461.

16. A. Elsayed Elsayed, N. Attia Kandeel, and W. Wahdan Abd El-Aziz, "The Effect of Foot Reflexology on Physiological Indicators and Mechanical Ventilation Weaning Time among Open-Heart Surgery Patients," *Am. J. Nurs. Res.*, vol. 7, no. 3, pp. 354–361, 2019, https://doi.org/10.12691/ajnr-7-3-16.

17. S. S. Al-Harbi and Y. A. Alshumaimeri, "The Flipped Classroom Impact in Grammar Class on EFL Saudi Secondary School Students' Performances and Attitudes," *English Lang. Teach.*, vol. 9, no. 10, p. 60, 2016, https://doi.org/10.5539/elt.v9n10p60.

18. J. Enfield, "Looking at the Impact of the Flipped Classroom Model of Instruction on Undergraduate Multimedia Students at CSUN," *TechTrends*, vol. 57, no. 6, pp. 14–27, 2013, https://doi.org/10.1007/s11528-013-0698-1.

19. P. Ramakrisnan, Y. B. Yahya, M. N. H. Hasrol, and A. A. Aziz, "Blended Learning: A Suitable Framework For E-Learning In Higher Education," *Procedia - Soc. Behav. Sci.*, vol. 67, pp. 513–526, 2012, https://doi.org/10.1016/j.sbspro.2012.11.356.

20. F. S. Kirmizi, "Relationship between reading comprehension strategy use and daily free reading time," *Procedia - Soc. Behav. Sci.*, vol. 2, no. 2, pp. 4752–4756, 2010, https://doi.org/10.1016/j.sbspro.2010.03.763.

21. Ş. Uluçınar Sağır and D. Sakar, "Flipped classroom model in education," *Int. J. Soc. Sci. Educ. Res.*, vol. 3, no. 5 S, pp. 1904–1916, 2017, https://doi.org/10.24289/ijsser.348068.

Financial Reporting Practice in Pesantren: A Comparative Study of Malaysia and Indonesia

Periansya[1], Evada Dewata[1](✉), Saifulnizam Bin Zakariah[2], Noor Azira Binti Sawal[2], Edwin Frymaruwah[1], and Indriani Indah Astuti[1]

[1] Accounting of Department, Politeknik Negeri Sriwijaya, Palembang, Indonesia
evada78@polsri.ac.id
[2] Jabatan Perdagangan, Politeknik Melaka, Melaka, Malaysia

Abstract. This study is intended to identify financial reporting practices Pesantren in Indonesia and Malaysia, and to compare the level of knowledge, skills, utilization of information technology, and the implementation of pesantren accounting standards in financial reporting practices in Indonesia and Malaysia. Research was conducted at pesantren which is officially registered in the Ministry of Religious Affairs of the Republic of Indonesia and the Melaka Malaysia Islamic Religious Position in 2021. The sampling method uses purposive sampling and testing using One Sample T Test and One Way Analysis of Variance. The findings state that there were differences in financial reporting practices in Pesantren in Indonesia and Malaysia, especially in Accounting Knowledge and Utilization of Information Technology. However, when viewed from the Skills and Implementation of Pesantren Accounting Standards, there is no significant difference in financial reporting practices.

Keywords: Pesantren Accounting · Financial Reporting · Skills · Information Technology

1 Introduction

Pesantren is one of the traditional non-profit oriented islam educational institutions, both in Indonesia and Malaysia, Islamic education is able to strengthening the mentality of human resource in their respective countries. In Indonesia, there are 27,722 Pesantren spread across all provinces [1]. This number is quite large and proves that pesantren are in great demand and trusted by the public as a good choice of educational place. Pesantren in Indonesia are mostly owned by private owners foundations [2]. Although Pesantren is not profit-oriented, it must do financial management properly as revealed [3] there are three things that must be done for the existence of Pesantren, namely Quality Assurance, Autonomy, and Accountability.

Issues related to accountability practices through financial reporting are a phenomenon and criticism of some parties, because pesantren are considered closed institutions and exclusive to modern financial management practices. Some research results

R. Martini et al. (Eds.): FIRST 2022, ASSEHR 733, pp. 38–43, 2023.
https://doi.org/10.2991/978-2-38476-026-8_5

such as [4, 5] have proven that financial reporting and the presentation of information are forms of information disclosure. [6] revealed that the practice of accounting in Indonesia is still simple and financial accountability reported by the finance department is still not optimal, although financial statements have been viewed by the management of Pesantren as a very significant instrument in improving organizational accountability [7] and pesantren management has not considered the community as a stakeholder to report financial information [8].

The first Maahad Pesantren was established in Malaysia in 1966 as a result of the idea of Musabaqah al-Quran and the visit of Al-Azhar Chancellor of Sheikh Mahmud Syaltut University to the opening ceremony of the National Mosque [9]. Currently, the development of the pesantren institution in Malaysia has grown as a result of the increasing awareness of the Muslim community on the need to understand the Quran. As a result, the existence of private pesantren centers and institutions are increasing with a wide range of syllabus and governance guidance. In Malaysia, the institution of pesantren is known for two categories, namely government-based institution and private institution.

Government-based institutions are unable to cope with the high demand from parents who are interested in making the flow of pesantren education as a mainstream education for their children. In this regard, the empowerment of private institutions is significant which consistent with the current requirement that set by the government known as National Pesantren Education Policy or Dasar Pendidikan Tahfiz Negara (DPTN). [10] Pesantren have poor management governance and have not been well planned which also affects the aspect of its implementation [11].

There are accountability problems in fundraising and mismanagement of accumulated funds for Pesantren [12]. When there is misconduct in the governance of a pesantren institution, it will weaken the institution itself. According to [12] a reporting should be provided by management of non-profit organizations related to fundraising information to ensure governance and accountability for the financial management of a non-profit organization.

In the practice of preparing financial statements, pesantren have not fully adopted the accounting standards and guidelines of pesantren yet [13–15] Several contributing factors as revealed [16, 17] that there is still a lack of accounting knowledge in financial report practices, besides that the management of institutional management of pesantren is still managed traditionally.

The lack of Pesantren accounting literature is the reason for this research. So it is necessary to know how financial reporting practices compare to Pesantren in Palembang, Indonesia and Melaka City, Malaysia. Indonesia and Malaysia were chosen as the two countries compared in this study because the influence of cultural and religious backgrounds in Indonesia and Malaysia is almost the same. This study aims to compare the level of knowledge, skills, utilization of information technology and the implementation of Pesantren accounting standards in financial reporting practices in Indonesia and Malaysia. The findings are expected to make a practical contribution to regulators (government) and Pesantren as information and input in the practice of financial reporting of pesantren as well as the importance of accountability of pesantren financial reporting for internal and external parties.

2   Literature Review and Research Hypotheses

Accounting knowledge is everything that is known related to financial activities and is needed to compile financial statements, including an understanding of Accounting Standards, the process of recording financial reporting, types of financial statements, the functions of each financial statement and the components (elements) in financial statements. This accounting knowledge can be obtained through accounting education or training. The lack of accounting knowledge from financial managers can cause the non-implementation of the financial accounting information system optimally. Skills or competence is intended for a person who has extensive procedural skills demonstrated in his experience. In preparing financial reports, good and qualified skills are needed. Many skills that are not in accordance with their respective fields in accounting and financial report making will have an impact on the poor quality of financial statements and timeliness in making financial statements. Technological devices are a supporting factor to create a realization of financial responsibility reports to have the quality of financial statements in the presentation and reliable value of information in them. The development of technology makes it easier to make financial reports. The use of information technology plays a role in minimizing errors in entering data because in technology everything is arranged and neatly arranged with the existing technology system. Financial reporting of a pesantren is important to show the traceability of the use of funds received to take care of the operations of the pesantren institute. The biggest distribution faced by institutions in reporting are inputs, activities, outputs and results [12]. According to [18] financial information is very important to be presented in the financial reporting of pesantren.

3   Research Methodology

This type of research is in the form of exploratory studies using comparative research designs on Pesantren in Palembang, Indonesia and Melaka City, Malaysia. The population of this study was in Pesantren with the type of educational unit in Palembang City, Indonesia which amounted to 8 Pesantren and 8 Pesantren in Melaka, Malaysia. The samples in the study were saturated samples, namely 16 Pesantren. The respondents of this study are parties who have the authority and know about the process and procedure for preparing financial statements, namely 4 people consisting of the Caregiver of the Pesantren, the Chairman/headman of the Pesantren, the Management of the Pesantren and the Treasurer of the Pesantren. So that the total research sample was 64 respondents. The collection technique in the form of primary data with a data collection period carried out from June-August 2022. Research instruments for indicators of Accounting Knowledge and Skills refer to [19]. The data analysis technique starts from the validity and reliability test of the questionnaire, descriptive analysis and a different test is carried out using an independent sample t test if data is normally distributed, if the data is not distributed normally then using the Mann Whitney Test difference test.

4   Result and Discussion

There were 64 questionnaires for each of the 8 Pesantren in Palembang, Indonesia and Melaka City, Malaysia. It is known that the returned questionnaires were 52 questionnaires and 52 could be used. The return rate of the questionnaire (response rate) and can be used (response use) is 81.25% with details of 30 respondents from Palembang City, Indonesia and as many as 22 respondents from Melaka City, Malaysia.

The assumption of homogeneity aims to know whether the variance of the measured score is the same or not, this test is applied with multivariate, since the involvement of variables is bound together. The homogeneity test is used the Box's M test through its significance degree $= 0,05$. Decision-making is based on the criterion that if the result of its significance produces a value of more than 0,05 then the variance-covariance matrix in both classes is the same or homogeneous.

These results show a sig. (signification) is above the level of significance of 0,05, so based on the decision-making criteria on the homogeneity test, the conclusions for the variable Skills and Implementation of Pesantren Accounting Standards include Homogeneous. Meanwhile, the variables of Accounting Knowledge and Utilization of Information Technology include inhomogeneous data.

From The Difference using the Mann-Whitney Test, the signification level of 0,010 is below the significance of 0,05, this can be interpreted to mean that there are significant differences in the financial reporting practices of Pesantren in Indonesia and Malaysia in terms of their accounting knowledge. The findings of this study can be seen in each country in terms of education is different in each country, making financial reporting results and quality different, and sometimes pesantren financial employees do not come from accounting or financial backgrounds. As revealed [4] Weak knowledge of accounting by managers and implementing staff at Pesantren is one of the causes of the preparation of pesantren financial statement not in accordance with applicable standards.

The results of the Mann-Whitney Test, obtained a signification level of 0,764 above the level of significance of 0,05, this can be interpreted as there is no difference in skills in the practice of financial reporting of Pesantren in Indonesia and Malaysia. This finding proves that employees or administrative personnel at Pesantren in these two countries are qualified and already have technical skills in the field of accounting.

furthermore, a signification level of 0.000 is below the level of significance of 0.05, this can be interpreted to mean that there are significant differences in the financial reporting practices of Pesantren in Indonesia and Malaysia in the use of information technology, which may be seen in the sophistication of the technology used differently in each country including the availability of information technology facilities and infrastructure itself. The results of this study show the role of technology utilization, that the higher the technology used, the easier it will be for financial employees to compile financial reports.

The Mann-Whitney Test shows that the signification rate of 0,629 is above the level of significance of 0,05, this can be interpreted as there is no difference in the Implementation of Pesantren Accounting Standards with the financial reporting practices of Pesantren in Indonesia and Malaysia. This is because there is the same average attitude supported by the same culture in both Indonesia and Malaysia so it tends not to make the results of financial reporting different. Even though the preparation of financial reports is still not in accordance with the rules in Pesantren which can result in differences in the preparation of Pesantren financial reports, this matter is still taken seriously by the management as part of a form of accountability, it is still taken seriously by the management as part of a form of accountability.

5 Conclusion

There are significant differences in financial reporting practices in Pesantren in Indonesia and Malaysia, especially in Accounting Knowledge and Utilization of Information Technology. However, when viewed from the Skills and Implementation of Pesantren Accounting Standards, there is no significant difference in financial reporting practices. An important implication of these findings is that there are 2 challenges in implementing financial reporting practices, namely first, pesantren must have human resources who have knowledge and are competent in the field of accounting records and financial reporting. Second, maximize the use of information technology to improve efficiency. For this reason, cooperation between institutions is needed, namely between Pesantren and Islamic financial institutions, educational and training institutions, and universities.

This research has limitations, including this research only examines descriptively the practice of financial reporting in terms of 4 components. In future research, it is recommended to examine more other components such as Pesantren Accounting Standards, Competence, and Motivation. This study also only used samples from 2 cities in each country. If possible, investigations can be carried out on more samples and from more countries.

References

1. Kemenag. (2022). Jumlah Pesantren di Indonesia. Jakarta. Accessed from http://ditpdpotren. kemenag.go.id
2. Afifuddin, H. B. and Siti-Nabiha, A. K. (2010). Towards Good Accountability: The Role of Accounting in Islamic Religious Organisations. World Academy of Science, Engineering and Technology, 66 (6), 1133 -1139.
3. Sung, T. K. (2018). Industry 4.0 : a Korea Perspective. Technological forecasting and social change, 132, 40 - 45.
4. Baehaqi, A., Faradila, N, & Zulkarnain, L. (2021). Akuntabilitas Dalam Akuntansi dan Pelaporan Keuangan Pondok Pesantren di Indonesia. Liquidity, 10 (1), 44 - 53.
5. Meutia, I., & Daud, R. (2021). The meaning of financial accountability in Pesantren: The case of Indonesia. International Entrepreneurship Review, 7(2), 31-41.
6. Niati, A., Suhardjo, Y., Wijayanti, R., & Hanifah, R. U. (2019). Pelatihan Pengelolaan Manajemen Keuangan dan Pelaporan Keuangan Akuntansi Pesantren bagi Pengelola Yayasan Pondok Pesantren X di Kota Semarang. Jurnal Surya Masyarakat, 2(1), 76-79.
7. Basri, H., & Siti-Nabiha, A. K. (2016). Accounting System and Accountability Practices in An Islamic Setting: A Grounded Theory Perspective. Pertanika Journal: Social Sciences & Humanities, 24, 59-78.
8. Basri, H. & Tabrani, M. (2015). Management and Financial Transparency of Islamic Religious Organizations: The Case Study of Modern Pesantren in Contemporary Indonesia , Global Journal on Humanites & Social Sciences. 02, pp 41–49. Available from:http://www.world-educationcenter.org/index.php/pntsbs

9. Chek, Y., & Mohamad, S. (2016). Sumbangan Darul Quran Terhadap Pengajian Al-Quran Dalam Kalangan Orang Kurang Upaya Penglihatan. Al-Turath Journal of Al-Quran And Al-Sunnah, 1(2), 25-33.

10. Ridza, B. H., Jalil, R. A., Sipan, I., & Nukman, Y. (2017, November). Critical Success Factor (Csf) Service Delivery For Pesantren Institution Teaching & Learning Environment. In AIP Conference Proceedings (Vol. 1903, No. 1, P. 040003). AIP Publishing.

11. Nawi & Salleh, N. H. (2017). Pembinaan Model Pengajian Pesantren Di Malaysia. Ojie: Online Journal Of Islamic Education, 5(1), 1–11.

12. Bani H, Katan M, Noor Ahm, And Fatah Mma (2014). Applying Stakeholder Approach in Developing Accountability Indicators for Pesantren Centers. In The International Conference On Accounting Research And Education: 1–14.

13. Tania, A. L. (2021). Urgensi Pedoman Akuntansi Pesantren Dalam Pelaporan Keuangan. Adzkiya: Jurnal Hukum dan Ekonomi Syariah, 8(02), 211–232.

14. Sholikhah, Y. A. S., & Susilowati, D .(2019). Fenomena Kualitas Laporan Keuangan Pesantren Berdasar Pedoman Akuntansi Pesantren Dan PSAK No. 45. Soedirman Accounting Review: Journal of Accounting and Business 3.

15. Biduri, S., Rahayu, R.A., & Mukarromah, I. (2019). Implementasi PSAK No. 45 pada Penyusunan Laporan Keuangan Pondok Pesantren Demi Terciptanya Transparansi dan Akuntabilitas. Seminar Nasional dan The 6th Call for Syariah Paper, 222–235.

16. Rachmani, F . A. (2020). Pengaruh pengetahuan tentang pedoman akuntansi pesantren ter-hadap penyajian laporan keuangan pesantren. In Proceeding of National Conference on Accounting & Finance. Vol. 2, pp. 39-46.

17. Cahya, A. D., Fidiastuti, F., & Utama, A. S. (2021). Analisis pelaporan keuangan dilihat dari jenjang pendidikan dan pengetahuan akuntansi. Jurnal manajemen, 13 (3).

18. Zainon, S., Atan, R., Wah, Y. B., & Nam, R. Y. T. (2011). Institutional Donors' Expecta-tion of Information from The Non-Profit Organizations (NPOS) Reporting: A Pilot Survey. International Ngo Journal, 6 (8), 170-180.

19. Masliza Idani binti Mahmood, Nurul Safwanah binti Muhammad Saleh. (2018). A Financial Record for Bookkeeping Practices among Wholesale Market at Melaka Tengah. 8th National Conference in Education Technical & Vocational Education and Training

20. Aladejebi, O., & Oladimeji, J. A. (2019). The impact of record keeping on the performance of selected small and medium enterprises in Lagos metropolis. Journal of Small Business and Entrepreneurship Development, 7 (1), 28 - 40.

Capital Assets and Salai Fish Business Sustainability (Study on Panca Jaya's Business, Sungai Rengit Village, Banyuasin Regency)

Neneng Miskiyah[1]([envelope]), Marieska Lupikawaty[2], Titi Andriyani[1], and Siska Aprianti[1]

[1] Department of Business Administration, Sriwijaya State Polytechnic, Palembang, Indonesia
nenengmiskiyah@polsri.ac.id
[2] Department of Accounting, Sriwijaya State Polytechnic, Palembang, Indonesia

Abstract. The role of human, social, and financial capital in sustaining the salai fish business. The higher the educational background, the longer the business owner's experience, the higher the orientation and strategy development carried out by the business owner to improve business performance. The role of social capital in increasing the salai fish business demonstrates that by maintaining good relationships with the workforce, consumers, and patin fish producers, maintaining communication, trust, and still prioritizing honesty, tolerance, fairness, and generosity to consumers in business operations. The power of social networks can increase innovation and ease of access to information for Panca Jaya business owners. One of the challenges in running a business is a lack of financial capital; however, by utilizing access to finance, such as the business owner of Panca Jaya, namely cooperative loans, loans from relatives or friends, and additional capital obtained from the accumulation of business profits, the salai fish business can continue. Even consumers outside of Banyuasin Regency and South Sumatra Province are interested in salai fish.

Keywords: Human Capital · Social Capital · Financial Capital

1 Introduction

One of South Sumatra Province's main fish-producing regions is Banyuasin Regency. Almost all sub-districts have the potential to be used for the cultivation of freshwater fish, particularly patin fish and lele fish. In the Talang Kelapa District's, Sungai Rengit Village, there is the largest patin fish farming facility in the Banyuasin Regency. In 2020, Banyuasin Regency will produce 58,758.85 tons of catch through capture fisheries, with a total of 17,313 fishermen, and 41,490.52 tons through aquaculture, with a total of 8,412 growers. Patin fish are the primary aquaculture crop produced in Sungai Rengit village, where production averages around 20 tons per day or 7,200 tons annually [1].

It is important to make an effort so that the results of patin fish farming are not only sold in fresh form, but also in the form of preservation to make them last longer, as fishery products are products that are easily damaged or do not last long. Due to the plentiful supply of raw materials and the high demand for salai fish from both inside and outside the Banyuasin Regency region, the salai fish industry is one of the more promising ones for the locals of Sungai Rengit village.

The Sungat Rengit village community's practice of smoked fish, also known as salai fish, is categorized as traditional because it represents a legacy of knowledge and skills that have been passed down from generation to generation as evidenced by the marketing model used, the technology used, and business management as a production activity. Since many similar businesses have been run, particularly in fish-producing regions, it is necessary to be able to grow similar firms into larger and more sophisticated ones. According to research by [2, 3] the salai fish industry is still restricted by a lack of marketing channels, outdated technology, expensive production costs, and a labor shortage. The salai fish industry in Sungai Rengit village faces numerous challenges, while Panca Jaya's salai fish business also faces similar challenges. The salai fish industry won't be able to grow if this isn't fixed right away. A successful and sustainable life for the family will be affected by the increased efforts done. Although human, social, and financial capital are endogenous characteristics that individuals should be able to manage, they are still very low.

Human capital refers to the abilities and talents of workers that have an effect on the entire output of the business [4]. According to [5] fundamental theory of human capital, education and experience are major determinants of business success. People can use their knowledge and talents to be productive and effective members of society by investing in human capital. According to [6] and [7], human capital has an impact on MSME performance.

Social capital is a resource that comes from knowing other people [8], and it may offer people helpful information, knowledge, and input in both financial and non-financial aspects [9] to help them start their own businesses. Business performance is influenced by social capital, including ties to the community, trust, and a common goal [10]. Based on [11] discovered that social capital plays a role in entrepreneurial activities, but contrary to [12] findings, micro-enterprises performance is unaffected by social capital.

Financial capital refers to the sources of cash that enable them to be employed and utilized by the community in pursuit of livelihood objectives. This financial capital can take the shape of inventories or reserves that they personally or through financial institutions own, as well as a steady stream of cash [13]. Wealth, income, expenses, savings, and accounts payable are all examples of financial capital. In managing and growing a business, financial capital is crucial. Income will also rise if capital does [14]. According to the findings of the study done by [15], financial capital significantly influences the growth of microbusinesses in Kabila District, Bone Bolango.

The Talang Kelapa District's abundant patin fish output, which serves as the primary raw material for salai fish manufacturing, is actually a benefit for those who make smoked fish. The Panca Jaya salai fish business and the other salai fish business share many of the same issues. These include a lack of business capital (both still relying on their own capital), ineffective financial management, the inability to hire more workers due to financial constraints, and problems related to education, experience, and health. For the Panca Jaya fish business in Sungai Rengit village, this study will assess capital assets in order to boost output, develop an effective marketing plan, and ensure the long-term viability of the enterprise.

2 Literature Review

2.1 Business Sustainability

Every entrepreneur or businessperson who has the initiative, motivation, and ingenuity to build a business is responsible for its development. Generally speaking, businessmen must be able to recognize possibilities that others miss, take those opportunities to launch a firm, and manage that business successfully. Based on [16] divides business growth into three categories: (1) upstream or downstream expansion; (2) business diversification; and (3) selling the business.

2.2 Capital Assets

Human capital investment theory states that those with a higher education degree earn more over their lifetime than those who have a lower educational level. According to [17, 18], knowledge and expertise gained through education, training, experience, and migration are activities to increase the value of labor through investment in human capital, which is expected to increase future income. Aside from education, experience, and migration, human capital can be invested in health [19]. Health is the foundation for work productivity and the ability to improve education. Workers who are physically and mentally healthy will be more productive at work. According to [6], human capital is an important component for the creation and dissemination of knowledge capable of creating innovations or developing new products through high-quality individuals. This is in agreement with the results of [12, 20, 21] that the performance of micro-enterprises is significantly impacted by human capital. Human capital is an important component in business development in order to become a market pioneer in a competitive market.

Social capital refers to the community or community that allows for cooperation. Cooperation networks are emphasized in order to foster togetherness in a group or community in society, which is then used to improve the quality of life. Through a focus on social networks, norms, values, and beliefs that are developed from inside the group and become group norms, as well as reciprocity, social capital highlights group potential and patterns of interactions between two or more individuals and between groups [22, 23].

Thus, social capital has a broad and multifaceted definition that includes networks, norms, social trust, and local wisdom, all of which enhance social collaboration (coordination and cooperation) for the common good. This social capital must be strengthened in order to:

a) As autonomy grows, social capital becomes a community asset, allowing members to be self-sufficient and manage their own interests.
b) Cooperation strengthening, assisting communities in managing social risks and increasing community capacity to prevent or respond to shocks, cooperation strengthening
c) Strengthen social networks by having social capital community members help one another and manage risk through informal relationships.

According to the findings of [24–26], social capital influences the growth of businesses. However, contrary to [12] findings, micro-enterprise performance is unaffected by social capital.

Financial capital is a factor that affects business continuity because it is certain that if a business is going to run its business, it will require a number of funds, both from loans and personal capital. Financial capital as capital used to fund a company's daily operational activities, particularly those with a short time horizon [27]. Financial capital is essential for the smooth operation of micro-enterprises, and adequate financial management can assist micro-enterprises in maintaining their survival and growth rate in an increasingly competitive market [28]. Based on the findings of [18, 29] research, financial capital has an effect on the growth of micro-enterprises, whereas [7] stated that financial capital has an effect on the growth of micro-enterprises and the company's innovation strategy.

3 Research Methods

This study will analyze the sustainability of the salai fish business using capital assets, specifically human, social, and financial capital. Panca Jaya Salai Fish Business conducted the research, with the research location in Sungai Rengit Village, Talang Kelapa District, Banyuasin Regency. This is a field study with a qualitative approach and a case study research strategy. The descriptive and qualitative analysis techniques were used in this study [30]. This analysis was carried out to obtain a comprehensive picture of the variables observed. The results of in-depth interviews with the owner of the Panca Jaya salai fish business regarding the relationship between human, social, and financial capital were evaluated and reviewed.

4 Results and Discussion

Individual capital assets are anything that individuals own for personal or investment purposes. Human capital, social capital, and financial capital are the capital assets owned by Panca Jaya salai fish business owners, all of which have an impact on the level of individual and family welfare.

4.1 Human Capital

One of the assets of sustainable livelihoods is human capital. Education, work experience, skills, health, and migration are all indicators of human capital formation. The respondent's education is at the master's level (S2), so the respondent can easily apply the knowledge they have to do this salai fish business. Quick comprehension, as well as the ability to obtain a lot of information about the salai fish business from various sources, ultimately adds to the respondents' knowledge base, which can then be applied in this business.

The competencies of business owners influence the business's growth and sustainability. The ability to run a business and a strategic orientation to open new markets, new production, and utilize new technology are attributes of the business owner's educational background and business experience. The business owner has 9 years of experience running this salai fish business. Understanding the process of this salai fish business takes time. At first, the owner worked alone, but with patience and continued learning, the business owner was able to hire two workers who assisted in the process of making smoked fish, beginning with cleaning the fish, cutting it, and placing it on the smoking device. According to the findings of the interview, the business owner still believes in smoking fish because it requires patience for the results of smoked fish to be good.

The owner has never received any training in the processing of salai fish from the district government or any other agency while running this business. The owner's education level is high enough that he can learn on his own by trying and trying again until he finds the correct formula for making salai fish. Business owners, however, have followed technical guidance organized by the Banyuasin Regency Food Security Service for food safety.

The higher the educational background and the longer the experience of the business owner, the higher the orientation and strategy development carried out by the business owner to improve the performance of his business [18, 31]. It is clear that the salai fish business owner's level of education and work experience can support business development and the sustainability of the business being undertaken to be better and continue to grow.

4.2 Social Capital

The network of relationships is a resource that can be used to carry out daily activities. Social capital, specifically as a social connection that binds group members together, refers to the relationships developed and the rules that influence the amount and quality of community social relations throughout a broad range.

The salai fish business owner works with third parties, specifically patin fish producers, to run the business. The owner of this cooperative relationship buys fresh patin fish directly from producers in the Sungai Rengit village area. In one salai fish processing process, the owner requires up to 60–65 kg of fresh patin fish (live) purchased from fish producers. At the start of the business, the owner must construct a simple tarpaulin pond to house the purchased patin fish in order to keep it alive before processing it. This condition is ineffective; the fish are sometimes dead before they are processed. Additionally, business owners must go directly to the patin fish pond and bring their own purchased patin fish. However, because cooperative relationships with patin fish producers have been well established over time, business owners can now call and request that catfish be delivered on the day the fish processing begins.

Aside from patin fish producers, the owner establishes a network of relationships with suppliers, specifically cooperatives with the Agricultural Management Agency to sell the salai fish produced. In Sungai Rengit village, there aren't many people involved in the salai fish trade. People in Sungai Rengit mostly work as laborers for patin fish ponds, breeders, and farmers, so the only salai fish business that is currently active and continues to operate is the Panca Jaya salai fish business.

The business owner maintains positive relationships with his employees, customers, and patin fish producers. Maintain communication and trust, and continue to prioritize honesty, tolerance, fairness, and generosity to customers in business operations. The nature of the kinship that continues to exist between the business owner and his employees is that the business owner is open to communication and working relationships with the employees/laborers who work with him. As a result, business owners believe that their employees will continue to assist them in all of their tasks. Business owners who also work as agricultural extension workers find it easier to approach various parties to build trust through a friendly, warm, and personal relationship. Business owners can also socialize with the surrounding community to help their business run smoothly in a variety of ways, such as by giving donations, infaq, and alms to local residents who cannot afford it.

Many studies show that social capital is one of the capitals that can help with entrepreneurship. The combination of social and human capital can both contribute to entrepreneurial success and bridge the gap between the family business and its environment [11, 32]. The same statement was made by Fatoki that stating the existence of a significant relationship between capital assets and the performance of small and medium enterprises [24].

4.3 Financial Capital

Financial capital is one of the elements influencing business continuity because it can be determined that a business requires a number of funds, both from loans and personal capital, to run its operations. In economic terms, capital is goods or money combined with production factors such as land and labor to create new goods and services. Capital is an essential component of any business, whether small, medium, or large.

The owner starts the salai fish business with 1–2 million rupiah in personal funds. The owner only uses additional capital from business profits, cooperative loans, and borrowing from family/friends to expand the business. While running the business, the owner believes that his capital is insufficient to expand the salai fish business. Panca Jaya's gross monthly turnover is currently 7–8 million rupiah, with the owner owning 4–5 million rupiah in capital. According to the interview results, business owners are optimistic that they can continue to run their business with limited capital because of abundant raw materials, ease of obtaining them, relatively low raw material prices, and high consumer demand for salai fish. However, business owners will continue to seek additional capital to ensure that the Panca Jaya salai fish business grows and can meet consumer demand both within and outside of Banyuasin Regency.

5 Conclusion

Panca Jaya business owners' competencies have a significant effect on their business's growth and sustainability. The respondent's level of education makes the salai fish business easier to conduct. Sufficient experience enables business owners to continue innovating and developing the salai fish business.

The business owner maintains positive relationships with his employees, customers, and patin fish producers. The keys to respondents' success in running this salai fish business are maintaining communication, trust, and continuing to prioritize honesty, tolerance, and fairness toward consumers, workers, and patin fish producers. Good social skills in the surrounding community help the business run smoothly. Respondents have used various methods to maintain good relations with the surrounding community, including giving donations, infaq, and alms, particularly to the poor.

While running the business, the capital needed to develop the salai fish business is still lacking. Additional funds are obtained through the accumulation of business profits, cooperative loans, and borrowing from family and friends. Respondents are optimistic, however, that they can continue to run the salai fish business and meet consumer demand with limited capital.

Acknowledgments. Thanks to the help of many people, this research was able to be completed properly. The researchers would like to express their gratitude to the Sriwijaya State Polytechnic, the Center for Research and Community Service, Panca Jaya Salai Fish Business, and the Head of the Department of Business Administration for their support and co-operation.

Authors' Contributions. Neneng Miskiyah, Marieska Lupikawaty contributed to the concept and design of the research. Titi Andriyani, and Siska Aprianti carried out data collection. Neneng Miskiyah, Marieska Lupikawaty, Titi Andriyani, and Siska Aprianti contributed to the analysis of the results and writing the manuscript. All authors discussed the results and commented on the manuscript.

References

1. Dinas Perikanan Kabupaten Banyuasin, "Laporan Tahunan 2020," Kabupaten Banyuasin, 2021.
2. T. Sitompul, R. NIzar, and A. Putri, "STRATEGI PENGEMBANGAN USAHA IKAN SALAI LELE (Clarias gariepinus) DI KELURAHAN AIR DINGIN KECAMATAN BUKIT RAYA KOTA PEKANBARU (Studi Kasus Usaha Bapak Ahmadin Margolang)," J. Agribisnis, vol. 21, no. 2, pp. 187–198, 2019, doi: https://doi.org/10.31849/agr.v21i2.3826.
3. Hengki, "Nilai Tambah Usaha Salai Ikan Patin di Desa Sungai Rengit, Kecamatan Talang Kelapa, Kabupaten Banyuasin," Jimanggis (Jurnal Ilm. Manag. Agribisnis), vol. 2, no. 1, pp. 17–26, 2021.
4. M. Marshall and A. Samal, "The Effect of Human and Financial Capital on the Entrepreneurial Process: An Urban-Rural Comparison of Entrepreneurs in Indiana," Am. Agric. Econ. Assoc. Annu. Meet. Long Beach, Calif., no. February 2006, pp. 5–24, 2006.
5. G. S. Becker, Human Capital, Third Edit. Chicago: The University of Chicago Press, 1975.
6. I. Syarifah, M. K. Mawardi, and M. Iqbal, "Pengaruh modal manusia terhadap orientasi pasar dan kinerja UMKM," J. Ekon. dan Bisnis, vol. 23, no. 1, pp. 69–96, 2020, doi: https://doi.org/10.24914/jeb.v23i1.2521.
7. W. Sombolayuk, R. M. Yusup, and I. Sudirman, "Studi Hubungan Antara Modal Manusia, Modal Sosial, Dan Modal Keuangan Dengan Strategi Inovasi Perusahaan UKM (Studi Kerangka Konseptual)," Simak, vol. 17, no. 01, pp. 84–118, 2019, doi: https://doi.org/10.35129/simak.v17i01.69.
8. I. A. Dar and M. Mishra, "Dimensional Impact of Social Capital on Financial Performance of SMEs," J. Entrep., vol. 29, no. 1, pp. 38–52, 2020, doi: https://doi.org/10.1177/0971355719893499.

9. M. A. Roomi, "Entrepreneurial capital, social values and Islamic traditions: Exploring the growth of women-owned enterprises in Pakistan," Int. Small Bus. J., vol. 31, no. 2, pp. 175–191, 2013, doi: https://doi.org/10.1177/0266242610397403.

10. S. Gronum, M. L. Verreynne, and T. Kastelle, "The Role of Networks in Small and Medium-Sized Enterprise Innovation and Firm Performance," J. Small Bus. Manag., vol. 50, no. 2, pp. 257–282, 2012, doi: https://doi.org/10.1111/j.1540-627X.2012.00353.x.

11. Primadona, "Peranan Modal Sosial Dan Modal Manusia Dalam Wirausaha," in Seminar Nasional Ekonomi Manajemen dan Akutansi (SNEMA) Fakultas Ekonomi Universitas Negeri Padang, 2015, no. c, pp. 199–204.

12. P. C. Gainau, "DETERMINAN KINERJA USAHA MIKRO (Studi Pada Usaha Mikro di Kecamatan Wenang, Manado)," J. Bisnis Perspekt., vol. 12, no. 1, pp. 9–26, 2020, doi: https://doi.org/10.37477/bip.v12i1.

13. R. Wijayanti, M. Baiquni, and R. Harini, "Strategi Penghidupan Berkelanjutan Masyarakat Berbasis Aset di Sub DAS Pusur, DAS Bengawan Solo," J. Wil. dan Lingkung., vol. 4, no. 2, pp. 133–152, 2016, doi: https://doi.org/10.14710/jwl.4.2.133-152.

14. M. P. Yadav, V. VPRP, and R. S. Pradhan, "Impact of Financial, Social and Human Capital on Entrepreneurial Success," Int. J. Small Bus. Entrep. Res., vol. 6, no. 4, pp. 1–28, 2018.

15. A. Iasoma, S. Sofhian, and Y. Zainuddin, "Pengaruh Modal Usaha Dan Strategi Pemasaran Terhadap Pengembangan Usaha Mikro Di Kecamatan Kabila Kabupaten Bone Bolango," Finans. J. Sharia Financ. Manag., vol. 2, no. 2, pp. 45–60, 2021, doi: https://doi.org/10.15575/fjsfm.v2i2.13923.

16. Humaizar, Manajemen Peluang Usaha. Bekasi: Dian Anugerah Perkasa, 2010.

17. R. G. Ehrenberg and R. S. Smith, Modern Labor Economics: Theory and Public Policy, Eleventh E. United State: Prentice Hall-Pearson, 2012.

18. A. Kalkan, O. C. Bozkurt, and H. Bayraktaroglu, "The Effects of Human Capital , Social Capital and Financial Capital on the Performance of SMEs," Glob. J. reserach Anal., vol. 4, no. 10, pp. 241–248, 2015.

19. M. P. Todaro, Pembangunan Ekonomi di Dunia Ketiga, Edisi Ketu. Jakarta: Penerbit Erlangga, 2000.

20. D. Santoso, I. Indarto, and W. Sadewisasi, "Pola Peningkatan Kinerja Bisnis UKM Melalui Modal Sosial Dan Modal Manusia Dengan Kebijakan Pemerintah Sebagai Moderating," J. Din. Sos. Budaya, vol. 21, no. 2, pp. 152–171, 2019, doi: https://doi.org/10.26623/jdsb.v21i2.1764.

21. V. Yukongdi and J. M. Cañete, "The Influence of Family , Human , Social Capital & Government Support Services on Women Entrepreneurial Start-up Decisions : A Qualitative Study," Rev. Integr. Bus. Econ. Res., vol. 9, no. Supplementary Issue 1, pp. 307–319, 2020, [Online]. Available: http://buscompress.com/journal-home.html.

22. T. T. Vo, "Social capital and household vulnerability : New evidence from rural Vietnam," 2018. doi: https://doi.org/10.35188/UNU-WIDER/2018/609-8.

23. J. Jumirah and H. Wahyuni, "The Effect of Social Capital on Welfare in Indonesia," J. Indones. Econ. Bus., vol. 33, no. 1, pp. 65–76, 2018, doi: https://doi.org/10.22146/jieb.29219.

24. O. O. Fatoki, "The Impact of Human, Social and Financial Capital on the Performance of Small and Medium-Sized Enterprises (SMEs) in South Africa," J. Soc. Sci., vol. 29, no. 3, pp. 193–204, 2011, doi: https://doi.org/10.1080/09718923.2011.11892970.

25. T. Tedjaningsih and D. Sufyadi, "Modal Sosial dan Keberlanjutan Usahatani Mendong," Mimb. Agribisnis, vol. 6, no. 2, pp. 588–599, 2020.

26. I. Neira, M. Portela, M. Cancelo, and N. Calvo, "Social and human capital as determining factors of entrepreneurship in the Spanish Regions," Investig. Reg., vol. 26, no. 26, pp. 115–139, 2013.

27. Kasmir, Analisis Laporan Keuangan, Cetakan ke. Jakarta: PT RajaGrafindo Persada, 2014.

28. N. K. Widiastuti, "Pengaruh Sektor Pariwisata Terhadap Kinerja Keuangan Daerah dan Kesejahteraan Masyarakat Kabupaten/Kota Di Provinsi Bali," E-Jurnal Ekon. dan Bisnis Univ. Udayana, vol. 2, no. 5, pp. 292–311, 2013.

29. B. Kalac, S. Becirovic, and I. Skenderovic, "The role of financial capital in the development of small and medium enterprises," Tech. Technol. Educ. Manag., vol. 10, no. 2, pp. 262–267, 2015, [Online]. Available: http://www.swmsa.net/art/s/2333/.

30. M. Kuncoro, Metode Riset untuk Bisnis dan Ekonomi. Jakarta: Penerbit Erlangga, 2009.

31. A. A. Djatmiko, "Pengaruh Tingkat Pendidikan, Pengalaman & Orientasi Strategi Serta Pengembangan Strategi Industri Mikro (Mikro) (Sebuah Tinjauan Teori)," Inspirasi, vol. 8, no. 15, pp. 59–75, 2013.

32. M. Cano-Rubio, G. Fuentes-Lombardo, M. J. Hernández-Ortiz, and M. C. Vallejo-Martos, "Composition of familiness: Perspectives of social capital and open systems," Eur. J. Fam. Bus., vol. 6, no. 2, pp. 75–85, 2016, doi: https://doi.org/10.1016/j.ejfb.2016.12.002.

Digitalization Role of the Front Office in the Banking Business, Impact and Implementation

Paisal Paisal[1]($\boxtimes$), Afrizawati Afrizawati[1], Fernando Africano[1], M. Riska Maulana[1], and Habsah Binti Mohammad Sabli[2]

[1] Bussiness AdminstrationState Polytechnic State of SriwijayaPalembang, Palembang, Indonesia
Paisal@polsri.ac.id
[2] Polytechnic Mukah Sarawak, Mukah, Malaysia

Abstract. This study was conducted to see the impact of banking digitalization on the role of the front office (teller and customer service) in the banking business activities, as well as the implementation in the banking business. The data for this study used primary data collected through distributed of questionnaires, as well as secondary data taken from references and published data's. Meanwhile, the population used are all employees of BNI 46 in the Palembang area who work as a front office including tellers and customer service. The results of this study show that the partial test data (t test) has a significant correlation with the role of the front office BNI 46 Palembang area with a significance level of 0.032, the t-test value for X1 is 2.194, beta value is 0.184 and X2 the significance value is 0.191, t-value is -1.321., beta value -0.165 its mean digitalization has a positive influence on the role of the front office and according to the results of calculated F value of 3.269 with a signifcant value. 0.044. it indicated the F value was greater than F table 3.126 and the signification.0.044 value is smaller than 0.05. Thus H0 was rejected and the other side Ha is accepted. So it can be said the variables of the impact of digitalization and the implementation of digitalization are together significant influence on the role of the front office (teller, customer service).

Keywords: Digitalization · Front Office · Banking Business

1 Introduction

Banking digitalization is something that is an unavoidable in many partsoftheworld. (1) in his writings on digitalization in the banking sector in India concludes due to the adoption of this digitalization, banking sectors in India face some remarkable changes as well as hurdles. Now we are in the digital era, it is not possible to avoid the growth and services or digital banking. Everyone uses the modern mobile device, which is smartphone, phone cells and other comunication to access digital banking servicese. Even digital banking is the place of inevitable today but its also can make every help for banking service. So it can be concluded that the current digitalization of banking is

R. Martini et al. (Eds.): FIRST 2022, ASSEHR 733, pp. 53–61, 2023.
https://doi.org/10.2991/978-2-38476-026-8_7

not an option, but has become a must if banks want to continue to compete for available market share.

The existence of digitalization in banking is believed to increase efficiency, one of which is using the latest applied technology in running its business. The seriousness of banks in working on digital banking to improve services and quality in order to remain competitive in a competitive business environment, raises new issues or concerns in terms of Human Resources (HR). The use of technology in some banking services results in a reduction in the work done by humans. The application of banking digitalization cuts down the complicated and time-consuming bank administration process while also cutting or eliminating a number of jobs that are usually done by humans, especially front office work.

Indonesia is one of the countries with a low level of penetration of banking services. Compared to other developing countries, Indonesia is lagging behind in terms of financial inclusion. According to a World Bank (2), only 36 percent population of adult has account with formal financial institution. This point is lower than the average for East Asia and Pacific countries (69 percent), the average for lower-middle income countries (42 percent). In Southeast Asia, Indonesia even lags far behind Thailand, where 78 percent of the population has a bank account (3).

Currently, Indonesia is heading for a digital transformation in the operational implementation of its system. The Financial Services Authority (OJK) was noted that the new digital penetration rate covers 39.2 percent of the Indonesian people, so that there is still quite a lot of room for improvement in Digital Banking, especially since the potential for economic development and people's behavior is increasingly digitized. So far, the banking industry has tried to develop several parts of the transformation related to Digital Banking. The era of banking digitalization make more simple for customers to get access financial banking services, only through their hands customers can do transactions via phones cell usage diverse strategies starting from from sms banking to internet banking. The presence of utility offerings for every financal institution permits to get admission freely, while not having to return back to the branch office.

Based on from above conditions, this research need the real impact of digitalization of banking on the role of tellers and customer service in banking business activities as the front line in providing services to customers. The study will be conducted on the role of tellers and customer service at the BNI 46 bank in the Palembang area so that it can show the impact and implementation of the use of banking digitalization in the position of teller and customer service in bank business activities.

2   Literature Review

Digitalization

Digitalization is a digital communication and digital media on contemporary social life. Then, according to Gartner.com's dictionary of terms defines, digitalization as "the use of digital technology to transform a business model and provide new revenue and value-generating opportunities; this is a process of moving to digital business. And in fact, the digitization process cannot occur without digitization. Digitization is the use of digital technology and digitized data, to influence the way jobs are completed, change the way company-customers interact, and create new (digitally) revenue streams.

Research conducted by (5) shows that the banking industry in providing services must adapt to technological developments to provide the convenience desired by customers for banking services. The development of Financial Technology or known as FinTech since 2015 has made banks have to be aware of its developments if they do not want to be abandoned by their customers who can switch to other financial institutions.

Banking Digitalization

Banking digitalization is something that is unavoidable in many parts of the world. (1)In his writings on digitalization in the banking sector in India concludes "Due to the adoption of this digitalization, the banking digitalization certainly has a positive impact on banks and their customers. Transactions that are no longer limited by place and time are a significant advantage for customers, while for banks the increase in income from fee-based income and a decrease in labor costs are among other positive impacts.Banking digitalization also has several challenges in its development. (6) writes about several shortcomings of banking digitalization, namely Personal relationship between the bank officials and the customers has been minimized due to access from one place. As everything has been mobilized the security in protecting transactions has been reduced in such a case issues regarding transactions have been increased. There is a high risk in making transactions because identification of theft of encrypted software.

With the advancement of technology that causes changes in analog information into digital information, people prefer to use digital information for the following reasons:

1. Easytosearch, browse, access and use according to user needs.
2. Easytoproduce, send, receive, filter, update based on user's ability.
3. The format ofwriting and the content of the message sent is the same as the format of writing and the content of the message received.
4. Not hamperedby long distances, language differences and time differences.
5. Sending andreceivingmessages is very fast and cheap.
6. Easytostoreand process so it does not require large storage space.
7. Easytoapply in various media becausethe format ofthecontentof digital information will be the same, between one device and another (7).

Front Office

Front office at a bank are employees assigned to the front line to serve the banking needs of customers either face to face or through other communication tools such as telephone or email. This task is closely related to the Teller and Customer Service functions. (8) in their research said that Tellers and Customer Service are frontliners at Bank Negara Indonesia whotelleris a bank employee at the counter whose main task is to serve customers such as serving cash receipts or payments, de[psits accept, checks, provide other bank services to public, cashier the signature authorization is required as a valid sign of a transaction document; in financial institutions and has great responsibility for his work play an active role in serving customers with 3S, namely smile, greet, andgreeting. Tellers whose role is to transact cash deposits and withdrawals, serve BPJS deposits, serve payments and open overbooking of blocked customer account numbers, while Customer Service has a role to serve customers in opening the first account to make savings at the bank, serving customers with a friendly smile and full of patience.

Customer Service
Customer Service is an activity that is intended or intended to offer pleasure clients, through services which could meet customer activities and needs (9). Customer Service performs a completely vital position in organizations and banks. Therefore, the undertaking of Customer Service is spine of the operational activities of the banking world. So it could be concluded that the position of Customer Service is to maintain loyal customers so that they stay dependable tobe our clients via fostering nearer relationship with clientss. And additionally looking to get new clients to undergo numerous strategies and additionally persuade customers approximately the high satisfactory of the goods they have.

Teller
Teller is bank officer who is responsible for deposits accepts, cashing cheque, and provide other banking services to public, the authorize teller signature is a valid sign of a transaction document; In financial institutions, teller generally work behind the counter, in large banks the duties and functions of the cashier have been assigned as a job descriptions, for example, a teller processes deposits by mail, stores, and records all proof of deposit payments from each bank. Customer. Tellers can also be categorized as bank employees who are responsible for cash traffic. Teller is bank employee at the counter whose main task is to serve customers such as serving cash receipts or payments, deposits accept, cashing, provide other banking services to the public, the signature of the teller authorization is required as a valid sign of a transaction document; and has great responsibility for his work.

3   Results and Discussion

Validity test is used to determine the feasibility of the items in a list of questions in defining a variable. This questionnaire generally supports a certain group of variables. The validity test should be carried out on each question item in the validity test. We compare the results of rcount with r table, df score = n-2 sig 5%. If r table r count then itis valid (10).

In the Table 1, its seen that the significant value (2-tailed) 0.000 less than 0.05 then it is valid and rcount (Pearson Correlation) is greater than r table(0.1966) so that the item or valid question. Valid if the value of r count > r table, R count = correlation of total corrected item (CITC). R count = 0.2303 Reliable if the Cronbach's value is negligible > 0.6, i.e. 0.928 (Table 2).

From Table 2, it seen the value of Sig. (2-tailed) 0.000 is less than 0.05 then it is valid and r count (Pearson Correlation) is greater than r table (0.1966) so that the item or question was valid. Valid if the r count > r table, R count = corellation total corrected item (CITC) R table = 0.915 Reliable if Cronbach's value is negligible > 0.6

From Table 3, it can be seen that the value of Sig. (2-tailed) 0.000 is less than 0.05 then it is valid and r count (Pearson Correlation) is more high than r table (0.1966) so

Table 1. Test Validity and relialible X1 (*front Office*)

Item-Total Statistics

	Scale Mean if Item Deleted	Scale Variance if Item Deleted	Corrected Item-Total Correlation	Cronbach's Alpha if Item Deleted
X11	63.15	68.685	.645	.923
X12	63.03	67.666	.722	.921
X13	62.90	66.810	.789	.919
X14	63.10	68.755	.729	.921
X15	63.00	69.222	.659	.923
X16	63.27	70.896	.503	.927
X17	63.12	67.637	.736	.921
X18	63.32	69.552	.491	.928
X19	63.11	67.571	.817	.919
X110	63.07	67.481	.748	.920
X111	63.14	69.009	.748	.921
X112	63.25	71.661	.334	.933
X113	63.14	69.009	.748	.921
X114	63.19	66.518	.734	.921
X115	63.14	69.009	.748	.921
X116	63.22	72.757	.329	.932

Table 2. ValidityTestandreliability X2 (Banking Business) Statistics Total Item

	Mean Scale if Deleted Item	Variance Scale if Deleted Item	Total Item Corrected-Total Correlation	Cronbach's Alpha if Deleted Item
X21	32.96	29.262	.597	.912
X22	32.97	29.083	.551	.915
X23	32.93	26.426	.806	.897
X24	32.96	28.457	.741	.903
X25	33.07	27.065	.754	.901
X26	33.16	27.834	.712	.904
X27	33.10	27.199	.706	.905
X28	32.99	28.486	.709	.905
X29	33.07	27.870	.757	.901

Table 3. Validity TestandReability Yvariabel

	Mean Scale if Delete Item	Variance Scale if Deleted Item	Corrected Item-Total Correlation	Cronbach's Alpha if Deleted Item
Y1	42.16	34.278	.585	.904
Y2	42.04	33.596	.668	.900
Y3	41.99	32.458	.798	.893
Y4	42.12	35.165	.514	.908
Y5	42.10	34.088	.707	.899
Y6	42.03	33.721	.689	.899
Y7	42.21	34.082	.687	.900
Y8	42.12	33.304	.728	.897
Y9	42.55	31.973	.622	.905
Y10	42.60	31.271	.665	.902
Y11	41.92	34.188	.656	.901

Table 4. Partial Test Y (Role of Front Office) and X1 (Impact of Digitization)

Coefficients[a]

Model		Unstandardized Coefficients		Standardized Coefficients	t	Sig.
		B	Std. Error	Beta		
1	(Constant)	39.022	7.347		5.311	.000
	X1	.184	.084	.251	2.194	.032

a. Dependent Variable: Y

that the item or question was valid. Valid if r count > r table R count = corrected item total correlation (CITC) R table = 0.909 Reliable if Cronbach's value is negligible > 0.6

Partial testing is used to determine whether there is an influence between digitalization on the role of the front office in the banking business at Bank BNI 46 Palembang area. Partial Testing by conducting a one-on-one test between the dependent variable and the independent variable. Based on the results of SPSS 25 can to see in the Table 4.

The data results from processing above (Table 4), it can be seen that the impact of digitalization has a significant correlation to the role of the front office of BNI 46 Palembang area with a significance of 0.032 with a t-test value for X1 which is 2.194 and beta 0.184. Means the impact of digitalization has a positive affect on the role of the front office, so it can be assumed that digitalization can indirectly take over some of the roles and tasks of the front office (teller and customer service) in the future, tellers

Table 5. Y Partial Test (front office role) and X2 (digitization implementation)

Coefficients[a]

Model		Unstandardized Coefficients		Standardized Coefficients	t	Sig.
		B	Std. Error	Beta		
1	(Constant)	39.022	7.347		5.311	.000
	X2	-.165	.125	-.151	-1.321	.191

a. Dependent Variable: Y

Table 6. Simultaneous Test (Simultaneous Variables Y, X1 and X2)

ANOVA[a]

Model		Sum of Squares	df	Mean Square	F	Sig.
1	Regression	258.736	2	129.368	3.269	.044[b]
	Residual	2769.785	70	39.568		
	Total	3028.521	72			

a. Dependent Variable: Y
b. Predictors: (Constant), X2, X1

and customer service must adaption the technology according banking digitalization (mobile banking, sms banking, online banking and so on), and continue their skills so they can contend and contribute to the banking business side by side with digitalization that continues to grow in the banking world. at the moment.

The data results from processing in Table 5, it can be seen that the implementation of digitalization has a significant correlation with the role of the front office (teller and customer service) at BNI 46 Palembang area with a significance of 0.191, a t-value of -1.321 and a beta value of -0.165. Means more service features in bank digital technology will make it easier for customers access transactions without having to go through the front office which has been done so far, it is not impossible if the front office does not upgrade its professional skills as a front office, then gradually the role of the front office office will be replaced by existing digitization technology.

The F test show an analysis the effect of the independent variables simultaneously (simultaneously) test on the dependent variable. So in this study the F test serves to prove effect between the X1 variable and the X2 digitization impact variable on the front office (Y) role variable in the banking business of BNI 46 Palembang Area. Based on the estimation results of these factors (Table 6).

Based on the table above, the calculated F value is 3.269 with a sig value. of 0.044. This indicates that the calculated F value is greater than F table 3.126 and the sig.0.044 value is smaller than 0.05. Thus, H0 is rejected and Ha is accepted. So it can be concluded that the variables of the impact of digitization and the implementation of digitization together have a significant influence on the role of the front office (teller, customer service). This happens because the results of the F test show that Fcount is greater than Ftable.

Implementation of digitization on the role of the front office in the banking business at Bank Negara Indonesia 46 Palembang area

The seriousness of banks in working on digital banking to improve services and quality so that in practice they can still compete in a competitive banking business environment, digitalization in the banking sector is expected to provide one solution to improve business between commercial banks in Indonesia. The implementation of banking digitalization raises new issues or concerns in terms of Human Resources (HR). The use of technology in some banking services results in a reduction in the work done by humans. The application of banking digitalization cuts down the complicated and time-consuming bank administration process while also cutting or eliminating a number of jobs that are usually done by humans, especially front office work.

The implementation of digitalization in the banking sector has a positive influence on the role of the front office in the banking business, meaning that digitalization in every banking business process and in providing services to customers directly has a significant impact on the function of the front office, namely tellers and customer service which are the front line of the service system. Bank. In the future, this will have an impact on the number of front offices because some of the tasks of tellers and customer service can already be replaced with technology through machines and applications.

4 Conclusion

From partial data results show (t test) and F test seen that the impact of digitization has a significant correlation with the role of the front office of BNI 46 Palembang Area.means that the impact of digitization has a positive influence on the role of the front office, so that it can indirectly take over some of the roles and tasks of the front office because the digital technology services offered have the features needed for customers to transact simple banking sector services without have to go through the front office which has been done so far.

The implementation of digitalization in the banking business has a good role for the progress of the banking business where the banking business, especially for non-cash transactions, is a necessity for customers, no longer just a complementary product but has also become a lifestyle for customers to get convenience in transacting at the bank. Along with various developments in the banking business that are engaged in digital business strategies, there needs to be an accelerated transformation in the banking business. One of the acceleration developments is banking digitalization, the implementation of banking digitalization is expected to provide innovation and provide a more concrete reference for banking digitalization in the future in order to acceleration of digital transformation, as well as a policy response to mitigate various challenges and risks from banking digital transformation.

References

1. Golden AR. An Overview of Digitization in Indian Banking Sector. Indo-Iranian Journal of Scientific Research (IIJSR) [Internet]. 2017 Nov 27 [cited 2022 Sep 30];1(1):209–12. Available from: http://iijsr.com/data/uploads/1025.pdf
2. World B. The World Bank Annual Report 2014 [Internet]. 2014 [cited 2022 Sep 30]. Available from: https://openknowledge.worldbank.org/handle/10986/20093
3. DBS.com. Meningkatkan Finansial Inklusi Melalui Digitalisasi Perbankan [Internet]. [cited 2022 Sep 30]. Available from: https://www.dbs.com/spark/index/id_id/dbs-yes-asset/files/(Riset%203)%20Meningkatkan%20Finansial%20Inklusi%20Melalui%20Digitalisasi%20Perbankan.pdf
4. OJK. Ringkasan Peraturan Otoritas Jasa Keuangan Nomor 14/POJK.03/2021 Tentang Perubahan atas Peraturan Otoritas Jasa KeuanganNomor 34/POJK.03/2018 Tentang Penilaian Kembali Pihak Utama Lembaga Jasa Keuangan [Internet]. 2021 [cited 2022 Sep 30]. Available from: https://www.ojk.go.id/id/regulasi/Documents/Pages/Penilaian-Kembali-bagi-Pihak-Utama-Lembaga-Jasa-Keuangan-/Summary%20-%20POJK%2014%20-%2003%20-%202021.pdf
5. Kholis N. Perbankan Dalam Era Digital Baru. Economicus [Internet]. 2018 [cited 2022 Sep 30];12(1):80–8. Available from: file:///C:/Users/ferna/Downloads/149-Article%20Text-394–1–10–20201112.pdf
6. Sujana SVM. Digitalization in Banking Sector. International Journal of Research and Analytical Reviews (IJRAR) www.ijrar.org [Internet]. 2018;5(3):333–7. Available from: https://ssrn.com/abstract=3897629
7. Marlina A, Bimo WA. Digitalisasasi Bank Terhadap Peningkatan Pelayanan Dan Kepuasan Nasabah Bank. Jurnal Ilmiah Inovator. 2018;7(1):14–34.
8. Rahareng VJ, Relawan N. The Influence of The Academic Service Quality Toward Student Satisfaction (Study on Students of Business Administration of Telkom University). Jurnal Ad Bispreneur [Internet]. 2017 [cited 2022 Sep 30]; 2(2):125–33. Available from: http://jurnal.unpad.ac.id/adbispreneur/article/view/13164
9. Kasmir. Dasar-dasar perbankan edisi revisi. Jakarta: Rajawali Pers; 2012.
10. Sujarweni VW. Metodologi Penelitian Bisnis Dan Ekonomi. Yogyakarta: Pustaka Baru Press; 2015.

Thematic Concepts of Economic Development and Political Dimensions to Create Cultural Tourism for Kemaro Island, Palembang

Desloehal Djumrianti$^{(\boxtimes)}$, Pridson Mandiangan, Alditia Detmuliati,
and Alfitriani Alfitriani

Politeknik Negeri Sriwijaya, Jl. Srijaya Negara, Bukit Besar, Palembang, Indonesia
djumrianti@polsri.ac.id

Abstract. The main goal of study is to analysis community based tourism (CBT) concept which implement in order to develop cultural tourism in Palembang, particularly in the Kemaro Island. Primary data were collected through semi-structure interview to several key informants and observations. While, secondary data were gathered through documentations, and some literatures. By using Huber Miles and thematic and coding approaches, the study found that economic and political dimensions were more dominant rather than environment, culture, and social factors to construct Kemaro Island as a cultural destination. In the economic factor, the study disclosed job available for societies who stay in the island. They also more creative to earn money from tourism activities in their areas. Thematic concept of 'hydroponic planting on a floating village' make the place more attractive, and selling traditional foods were good model of CBT for creating cultural end. This not only impacts on the families' incomes but also to local generated-revenues. At the same time, Pagoda and Kelenteng are not only merely as Buddhism praying places but now visitor enjoy as tourist attractions. Another interesting finding was religion tolerant among Buddhists and Muslims. All locals are Muslims but they compact with Buddhists in order to keep the Buddhism praying places and doing activities in those areas. Thus, the model of CBT of cultural tourism on Kemaro Island was fairly enough contributed by those two factors above.

Keywords: Cultural Tourism · Kemaro Island · Economic Dimension · Political Dimension

1 Introduction

Today tourism is one of sectors which contributes to Indonesia's foreign exchange. South Sumatra is one of the provinces that is intensively developing its tourism industry, which is continuously improving in maximizing its tourism potential. One of the Tourist Destinations offers cultural tourism especially Palembang.

Kemaro Island, for example, can be offered as a destination for cultural tourism. This island is a small delta located in the waters of the Musi River, Palembang, with an

© The Author(s) 2023
R. Martini et al. (Eds.): FIRST 2022, ASSEHR 733, pp. 62–70, 2023.
https://doi.org/10.2991/978-2-38476-026-8_8

area of about 32 ha, located approximately 6 km from the Ampera Bridge and about 40 km from the city center of Palembang.

This island offers visitors an atmosphere of ethnic Chinese culture, and romantic. There is a Buddhist place of worship, a 9-story Pagoda lays in the middle of the island. This building was built in 2006. There is also a temple that already existed. Hok Tjing Rio Temple or better known as Kuan In Temple which was built in 1962. In front of the temple there are the tombs of Tan Bun An and Siti Fatimah side by side. The two figures are the main characters of the Kemaro Island legend. The local legend is written on a rock beside the Hok Tjing Rio Temple. Syahdan, long ago a prince from China named Tan Bun An came to trade in Palembang (Inge, 2018). The legend of love between a Prince from China named Tan Bun An and a Princess of the Sriwijaya Kingdom of Palembang origin named Siti Fatimah is a special attraction for tourists.Kemaro Island is not only a religious and cultural tourist spot, but this place is also inhabited by the community. Based on data, the island is inhabited by around 173 families, namely RT 17 and 18 Kelurahan 1 Ilir, Ilir Timur II District. Around the island there is 1 RT inhabited by about 48 families who live there.

Societies who live on the island and surroundings participate in several activities around places of worship. They do this whether they realise it or not. The involvement of the local community on this island will directly have an impact on the development of Kemaro Island itself as a destination. Locals is one aspects to be considered in the concept of creating a tourism place or attraction, and its sustainability [1].

Pre-survey results showed that the people who live on the island of Kemaro and its surroundings are involved in participating in the tourism development of this area. They work as providers of traditional boat transportation services (Getek) crossing tourists from the Intirub, Lola Mina, and Peti Kemas piers near Kemaro Island. The pier used to board and drop passengers from this place to Kemaro Island is not safe because it is too high and is very risky for accidents. Meanwhile, the pier may not change its shape or be renovated or replace the existing pier. The insecurity of the pier has an impact on the interest and number of tourists to cross from this place. Many tourists turn to the Benteng Kuto Besak (BKB) wharf which is safer even though it is further away from Kemaro Island, and the transportation service provider is not a resident or local community of Kemaro Island.

In addition, community involvement in tourism on Kemaro Island is that they act as local food sellers such as pempek, models, meatballs, chicken noodles, and young coconut ice. One to another seller similar foods, there is no division of food segments, and good characteristics of the food products made. This has an impact on the interest of tourists to enjoy culinary on the island of Kemaro is low. This is because the food can be found anywhere in Palembang, sometimes many tourists even bring their own food.

The involvement of the people of Arab descent intentionally and unintentionally in order to create Al Munawar village as a place to visit can be seen and felt. This is similar to what people in Kemaro island do, they involve themselves in tourism activities on the island with or for certain purposes.

However, tourism development efforts that were which used locals are considered for some, a few failures in their development because policy holders still thought partial, institutional ego and sectoral ego, where local communities have limited budget to handle their areas as a tourism destination [2].

In contrary, A study found that thematically there were some areas of involvement of local communities in developing destinations in remote areas in Pahawang Lampung, such as mutual cooperation among stakeholders; greater compactness of groups of local women; efficient and effective using some ladies in providing foods for visitors; other communities members were involve in the serving tourists as guiders, and private services, the most important element is a collaboration between central and local government to create the enabling environment for tourism. This shows that the level of interest of a group of people and cooperation between the government and the community has built and developed tourism in this place [3].

The development of a destination have contributing to nature, economic, and improving of locals incomes [3, 4]. Similarly, it also potential to carried out according to develop strategy so that the tourist attraction can be utilized in improving the economy of the surrounding community [5].

Various previous studies and opinions from scholars have encouraged this study, to explore how to model the right Community based tourism (CBT) that can be used for cultural tourism in Palembang, taking the case of Kemaro Island of Palembang. There has been no similar study conducted until this study will be conducted to find a CBT model that can be implemented in this destination. Previous studies explored the strengths and weaknesses of community-based potential of Kemaro Island to turn weaknesses and threats into opportunities from an economic perspective [6]. Furthermore, 50% of food and beverage traders are local people who live around Kemaro Island, and 21% of boat drivers are also people from around Kemaro Island [6].

Therefore, the problems can be formulated in this study: What are strategic and tactics of local community and other stakeholders involve in the development of Kemaro Island as Cultural Tourism that recognize as important elements of community-based tourism.

2 Introduction Critism of Some Works

2.1 Theories of CBT

Tourism is a unique sector, tourist may explore many parts of it CBT which let visitors enjoy and involve in the community to explore their traditional cultures, ritual, wisdom, and local habitats [7]. While, locals conscious that they are being the commodity of commercial for tourism purposes. To accommodate the CBT government should pay their attentions to all aspects of economic, political, environment, and social to develop a destination. So, it is clear enough that CBT is collaboration work between community government, and other parties.

In addition, community have important roles in the planning and decision making process of a place as a tourist destination [8]. The participation of community have to recognized as an important element in order to develop a destination [9, 10].

Thus, it is clearly enough that community is one of crucial elements of CBT. Heterogeneous of them are the power of themselves. Assume their respective responsibilities in the context of developing destinations around them [9].

2.2 Community Empowerment Through CBT

Community will be empowered in the development of tourism in their area. In this concept 'a form of tourism' which provides opportunities for local communities to develop and control tourism management. Their involvement on CBT have both directly and indirectly benefits for themselves [11, 20, 21].

The community in this case is seen broadly, not only residents in the sense of a group of people living in an area, but also those categorized as community leaders such as the Camat, Head of Customary Village, and Ustadz. Organisational groups such as Ibu-ibu, Karang Taruna, and Taklim Council are potential partners in community empowerment efforts, and companies with their cooperate social responsibility (CSR) or central bank collaborating work together in order to develop a destination [12].

2.3 Types of CBT

CBT is not merely about activities of community on tourism, but also about creativity and profitability. Thus, when a group of community members involve in the tourism activities in their areas and they get the profits from these activities, it called CBT. If locals take opportunities by using their assets for tourism purposes, then it also called CBT. The last type of CBT is the collaboration business between one to another family in a destination areas in the context of tourism that is CBT too [19].

Hence, the CBT is more about balancing and harmonization about locals, natural resources, tourists and environment [13].

2.4 Cultural Destination

A place is recognized as a cultural destination when it has something that used for art [14]. However, cultural old assets which available in a city also can be used for cultural tourism [15]. Thus, this indicates that a cultural destination is not merely about heritage but also including art.

While, the most important aspect should considered for a cultural destination is when it has historical evidences and assets [16]. Indicators and profile of a cultural destination when they have visitors, loyal visitors, and repeat visitor enjoy natural and manmade attractions including service and hospitality in a tourism place [17].

3 Methodology

3.1 Location and Time

The study was conducted Kemaro Island, Palembang, Indonesia and surrounding areas.

3.2 Objects of Research

Community who live in the Kemaro Island. Around 173 families who active involve in the tourism activities in Buddhism religious place. This area has two main places for Buddhists praying spaces. There is a village consists are RT 17 and RT 18. In 2021 by using from Corporate Social Responsibility (CSR) of a Fertilizer company they create 'water tourism village' on their village.

3.3 Key Informants

Informants in this study are key informants, which means people who do know in detail and in depth about the object being studied. There are nine persons, consist two person locals who sell foods, two person who sell souvenirs, housewives who are involved in the hydroponic program from Bank Indonesia. The local government, who is represented by the head of the local RT, RT 17 and RT 18 are also used as informants. In addition, to complete the data required opinions and input from the provincial government, so that 1 person from the Tourism and Creative Economy Office has been prepared.

3.4 Gathering Data Method

Data were collected through (1) Interview to 9 key informants, namely the head RT 17 and RT 18 kelurahan 32 Ilir, Kecamatan Ilir Barat 2 Palembang. The interview also to two food traders, two more souvenirs' sellers, housewives, and staff of tourism and economic creative Palembang. (2) Observation to local community also conducted to understand their habits, and activities in order to develop, control, and look after the place as a cultural destination.

Researchers also gathered secondary data from some references, such as data visitors to Kemaro Island from Tourism an Economic Creative, Palembang. It was also collected from books, journals, previous studies which related to purposes of study, particularly related to CBT.

3.5 Data Analysis Techniques

The study used Miles and Huberman; and themes and coding to analyze data obtained from interviews and observations. There are three steps, reduction; data display; and conclusion. In the first step was deleting some data which unnecessary or not related with purposes of study. After read and read, create a first notes and themes [18]. The second phase is data display. Here, data will be displayed in a table, graph, or chart. The last phase is the conclusion. It will conclude and verify at the end of the stage. Before making conclusion, the data still tested and verify for correctness, and truly accountable.

4 Results and Discussions

4.1 Data Reduction

There were several data that obtained from interviews and observations. The purposes of this phase is make simpler. This stage was repeated for many times until researchers get data required. Interviews results and field notes matched, irrelevant or unrelated data will erased and not used. Thus, data of five elements of CBT, economic, political, social, environment, and culture were grouped.

4.2 Data Display

Base on grouped of above, there were five elements of CBT.

4.2.1 Economic Factors

- Creating job opportunities for the community and creative ideas that can generate additional family income
- In general, the community in the two RTs can earn income from tourism activities around them
- Indirectly it will definitely affect local revenue (PAD)
- Focus on hydroponic planting on their house, ibu-ibu PKK get benefits to provides another attraction of their village.

4.2.2 Culture

- Make Pagodas and monasteries or Buddhist places of worship a cultural attraction
- Religious differences between visitors and the people around the pagoda in the delta are very harmonious and tolerant of each other
- Local people can also use their hospitality as a supporting part of tourist attractions

4.2.3 Social

- The people of RT 17 and RT 18 who take advantage of tourism activities on Kemaro Island and its surroundings get jobs or income and sell food, take pictures, sell souvenirs and souvenirs.
- Only a small part of the people around the Pagoda are proud of the Chinese cultural assets in the delta, this is due to the many restrictions made by ethnic Chinese who control the Buddhist place of worship.
- Tourism activities involving the community in RT 17 and 18 show a fairly balanced gender equality. PKK women from the two RTs are active in managing hydroponic and ornamental plants and selling food. Meanwhile, you are active in maintaining physical assets other than the Pagoda, such as the gazebo where the community center is located, clean water installations, mini gates, and selling dogan.

4.2.4 Environment

- There is water that can be used for toilets and drinking water in RT 17 and 18 but not in the Pagoda area
- There is a well-managed litter box
- Visitors and tourism activities do not harm the environment

4.2.5 Politic

- Fairly good community involvement on tourism activities
- Awareness of ownership of assets available from the community.
- The community has the freedom to manage the destination

To understand how much the involvement and contribution of community of RT 17 and RT 18 on tourism in Kemaro Island, as shown on the Fig. 1.

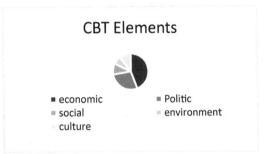

CBT Elements

■ economic   ■ Politic
■ social   environment
   culture

Fig. 1. Pie chart of CBT Elements on Cultural Tourism of Kemaro Island. Source: data processing, 2022

As shown on the Fig. 1 economic was the most of elements which implement of cultural tourism on Kemaro Island. The concept of ibu-ibu PKK created the 'hydroponic planting' and produce traditional foods to sell. It indicates that thematic concepts selected by them was appropriate to expose their contribution to tourism activities on this Island.

The second big element of CBT that applied on Kemaro Island was politic. This not regarding to the political issues on the country in general. Politic means in this study was awareness of community involve in tourism activities and maintain assets of Pagoda and Kelenteng on the island. The freedom of community managing the Kemaro Island was also an important aspect on development of this area as cultural tourism.

While three other elements (social, environment, and culture) were lesser than those elements. A unique statement from informant as below:

We have obstacles from some of Chinese people who look after the Pagoda and Kelenteng were not allow access from the area of religious to the village. They assume have to be clearly border between community live and religious.

From outside, it seems there is a harmonisation between both locals and Pagoda and Kelenteng guards, somehow, it takes times to discuss about this issue.

4.3 Economic and Politic Elements as CBT Concept to Construct Cultural Destination of Kemaro Island

As mentioned earlier, there were two most elements that important on the development of Kemaro Island as cultural destination. The Fig. 2 illustrates how those elements configure the island as cultural destination. The thematic concept of hydroponic planting and their awareness of community to involve and look after the assets were showing their power to create the place as one of favourite destinations in Palembang. Those two aspects have relationship one to another, the awareness to involve were empower them to enhance quality of live from tourism sector.

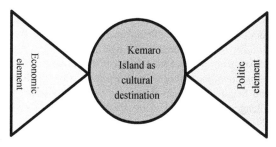

Fig. 2. Model of thematic concept of CBT on cultural tourism. Source: data processing, 2022

5 Conclusion

Community is crucial in the context of creating a cultural tourism. Kemaro Island is one of destinations in Palembang offers the religious space to visit. Locals who stay in the island have been taken benefits from tourism activities on their area.

The study found that there were two most elements, economic and politic. While three others, social, culture, and environment lesser than those. The study discover a model of CBT on cultural tourism in Kemaro Island was thematic concept of economic and politic which selected by community has been generated the village on the island as a destination which not only for praying purposes but people may enjoy it also as a cultural destination.

The next study will focus on the readiness of community to create their places as education tourism spaces.

References

1. Mtapuri, O. and Giampiccoli, A.: Towards a comprehensive model of community-based tourism development. *South African Geographical Journal = Suid-Afrikaanse Geografiese Tydskrif*, *98*(1), pp. 154-168 (2016).
2. Dangi, T.B. and Jamal, T.: An integrated approach to "sustainable community-based tourism". *Sustainability*, *8*(5), p.475 (2016)
3. Djumrianti & Osseo-Asare.: Strategies for Developing a Remote Destination: the sharing economy in local communities. *Journal of Environmental Management and Tourism*, Volume XII, Issue 1(49), Spring 2021 (2021)
4. Isdianto, A., Luthfi, O.M., Asadi, M.A., Saputra, D.K., Musalima, F.P.A., Haykal, M.F. And Adibah, F.: Pantai Kondang Merak: Bertahan Secara Ekosistem Atau Bertumbuh Secara Ekonomi. *Jurnal Education And Development*, *8*(4), pp. 224- 224 (2020).
5. Giampiccoli, A. and Saayman, M.: Community-based tourism development model and community participation. *African Journal of Hospitality, Tourism and Leisure*, *7*(4), pp. 1-27.
6. Roihan.: Analisis pariwisata berbasis masyarakat di pulau Kemaro ditinjau dari aspek ekonomi. *Skripsi*. Palembang: Politeknik Negeri Sriwijaya (2020)
7. Sin, H.L. and Minca, C.: Touring responsibility: The trouble with 'going local' in community-based tourism in Thailand. *Geoforum*, *51*, pp. 96-106 (2014)
8. Álvarez-García, J., Durán-Sánchez, A. and del Río-Rama, M.D.L.C.: Scientific coverage in community-based tourism: Sustainable tourism and strategy for social development. *Sustainability*, *10*(4), p. 1158 (2018)

 9. Kurniawan, A. R. (2020). Tantangan pengembangan pariwisata berbasis masyarakat pada era digital di Indonesia (Studi Kasus Pengembangan Pariwisata Berbasis Masyarakat di Pangalengan). *Tornare: Journal of Sustainable and Research, 2*(2), 10 (2020)
10. Björk, P.: Ecotourism from a conceptual perspective, an extended definition of a unique tourism form. *International journal of tourism research, 2*(3), 189-202 (2000).
11. Nagy, K.X.H. and Segui, A.E.: Experiences of community-based tourism in Romania: Chances and challenges. *Journal of Tourism Analysis: Revista de Análisis Turístico, 27*(2), pp. 143-163 (2020).
12. Jaafar, M., Md Noor, S., Mohamad, D., Jalali, A., & Hashim, J. B.: Motivational factors impacting rural community participation in community-based tourism enterprise in Lenggong Valley, Malaysia. *Asia Pacific Journal of Tourism Research, 25*(7), 799-812 (2020).
13. Suganda, A. D. (2018). Konsep Wisata Berbasis Masyarakat. *I-ECONOMICS: A Research Journal on Islamic Economics, 4*(1), 29-41 (2018).
14. Atsız, O., Leoni, V. and Akova, O.: Determinants of tourists' length of stay in cultural destination: one-night vs longer stays. *Journal of Hospitality and Tourism Insights* (2020).
15. Boukas, N., Ziakas, V. and Boustras, G.: Towards reviving post-Olympic Athens as a cultural destination. *Current issues in Tourism, 15*(1-2), pp. 89-105 (2012).
16. Kladou, S. and Kehagias, J.: Assessing destination brand equity: An integrated approach. *Journal of Destination Marketing & Management, 3*(1), pp. 2-10 (2014).
17. Atsız, O. and Akova, O.: Cultural destination attributes, overall tourist satisfaction and tourist loyalty: First Timers versus Repeaters. *Advances in Hospitality and Tourism Research (AHTR), 9*(2), pp. 268-291 (2021)
18. Mezmir, E. A.: Qualitative data analysis: An overview of data reduction, data display, and interpretation. *Research on humanities and social sciences, 10*(21), 15-27 (2020).
19. Ping, W.J. (No Date) Community-Based Ecotourism and Development in Northern Thailand. pp. 1–15. Accessed from http://www.asianscholarship.org/asf/ejourn/articles/jianping_w.pdf
20. Mohamad, N. H., & Hamzah, A. .: Tourism cooperative for scaling up community-based tourism. *Worldwide Hospitality and Tourism Themes* (2013)
21. Gutierrez, E.L.M., 2022. Participation in tourism Cases on Community-Based Tourism (CBT) in the Philippines. *Ritsumeikan Journal of Asia Pacific Studies, 37*(1), pp. 23-36 (2018).

The Awareness Review of Muslim Friendly Tourism Map Through Utilization of Promotional Media

Sari Lestari Zainal Ridho[1(✉)], Habsah Binti Haji Mohamad Sabli[2],
Mohammad Fardillah bin Wahi[2], Suhaimi bin Sibir[2], Ummasyroh[1],
and Fernando Africano[1]

[1] Politeknik Negeri Sriwijaya, Jalan Srijaya Negara, Palembang 30139, Indonesia
sarilestari@polsri.ac.id
[2] Politeknik Mukah, KM 7.5, Jalan Oya, OYA, 96400 Mukah, Sarawak, Malaysia

Abstract. The purpose of this study is to describe or review the results of the evaluation of efforts to increase awareness of halal tourism through the design of a Muslim friendly culinary tourism map, which is implemented in one of the traditional culinary of micro, small and medium enterprises in the city of Palembang. The research method is carried out with a qualitative descriptive research method approach by using an indicator of the number of Muslim friendly culinary tourism map coverage to measure awareness. The results of this study indicate the extent to which messages about Muslim friendly culinary tourism are spread. It is hoped that through the spread of this Muslim friendly culinary tourism map, more tourists are interesting in visiting the Palembang city.

Keywords: Muslim Friendly Tourism · Small and Medium Enterprises · Tourist

1 Introduction

1.1 Background of Study

This research is purposed to describe or review the results of the evaluation of efforts to increase awareness of halal tourism through the design of a Muslim friendly culinary tourism map, which is implemented in one of the traditional culinary of micro, small and medium enterprises in Palembang city.

The design of Muslim friendly tourism map purpose was to promote and guide tourist to halal Palembang culinary through social media, i.e.: Instagram. This purpose in line with the effort to support Muslim friendly tourism in Indonesia (generally) and to develop Muslim friendly tourism in Palembang, as promotion and guidance is two activities that cannot be separated from tourism industry.

Promotion. It can define as one of a marketing strategy communication form [1]. Marketing approach is needed in every enterprise, generally, and within tourism industry, specifically. Since it has significant positive contribution to the tourism destination of a country [4]. It is agreeable that now day social media is has been used as the new form of word of mouth promotion, that enable a person to share his experience to others [3].

R. Martini et al. (Eds.): FIRST 2022, ASSEHR 733, pp. 71–75, 2023.
https://doi.org/10.2991/978-2-38476-026-8_9

Guiding. The need for Guidance in the tourism industry is a challenge. Tourists need guidance, education and information, both in certain specific tourism business units [6], as well as in general. Hence it is understandable why in a Destination Management Organization, Guiding Service is one of the activities that its existence requires [5].

2   Research Methods

2.1   Methodology

This study uses a qualitative descriptive research method. This method is also called the interpretive method because the research data is related to the results of interpretation based on the philosophy of data found in data collection. The research method is carried out with a qualitative descriptive research method approach by using an indicator of the number of Muslim friendly tourism map coverage to measure awareness.

The Method of Qualitative Descriptive Research. The qualitative descriptive research method analyzes more on the surface of the data with the aim of explaining the situation, and by using this method the data collected can be analyzed, explained and described using the delivery of analytical sentences. In other words, a group of data that has been obtained will be analyzed and developed in the form of a series of evaluation sentences so that they can be presented in a way that expresses the overall results of the research easily read and understood. After the data is analyzed, it will be discussed further by displaying pictures, data and tables of observations and drawing conclusions from data analysis. Data analysis consists of three streams of activities that occur simultaneously, namely: first, data reduction, second, data presentation/analysis, and third, drawing conclusions [2].

3   Result and Discussion

3.1   Feature Insight Instagram

Instagram social media accounts can be used as promotional media and location indicators. One of the differences in using Instagram account settings as a professional account or a business account is the availability of the insights feature. After activating an Instagram business or professional account, the insights feature can be used which contains content, social media activity and viewers or account followers who see posts from a business or professional Instagram account earlier.

The Instagram Insights feature can provide information on the number of audience numbers within a set time. For example, as shown in Fig. 1, that in the last 30 days, there are as many as 281 accounts that have been reached, 37 of which are non-follower viewers.

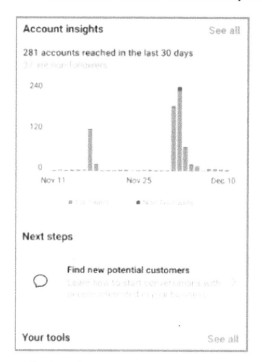

Fig. 1. A figure of Feature Insight Instagram

Table 1. Instagram Post Insight

Like	Comment	Save
69	**2**	**3**

Feature View Insight Instagram. In addition to the Insight feature in general, there is a View Insight feature which can provide information including the number of viewers who like a post, the number of comments on a post and the number of viewers who saved the post. Based on Fig. 2, it can be seen the activity in the Instagram post insight feature.

Table 1 displays tabulated information from Instagram's Featured View Insights from Muslim Friendly Tourism Map posts. Based on the table, the number of viewers who liked Muslim Friendly Tourism Map posts was 69 viewers, 2 viewers commented on the post and 3 viewers saved the post.

The data above show that the results of this study indicate the extent to which messages about Muslim friendly culinary tourism are spread. It is hoped that through the spread of this Muslim friendly culinary tourism map, more tourists will be interested in visiting Palembang city. The purpose of this study is to describe or review the results of the evaluation of efforts to increase awareness of *halal* tourism through the design of

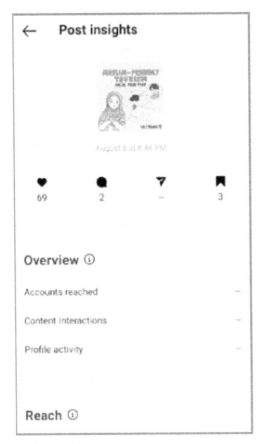

Fig. 2. A figure Feature View Insight of Muslim friendly Palembang culinary tourism map post on Instagram.

a Muslim friendly culinary tourism map, which is implemented in one of the traditional culinary of micro, small and medium enterprises in Palembang city.

4 Conclusion

In the beginning it has been discussed that the purpose of this research is to describe or review the results of the evaluation of efforts to increase awareness of halal tourism through the design of a Muslim friendly culinary tourism map, which is implemented in one of the traditional culinary of micro, small and medium enterprises in Palembang city. Based on the results and discussion, it can be concluded that the result of this study indicate the extent to which messages about Muslim friendly culinary tourism are spread. It can be said that the purpose of the Muslim Friendly map as the promotion and guiding tool to the halal tourism facility has been achieved. It is hoped that through the spread of this Muslim friendly culinary tourism map, more tourists are interesting in visiting the Palembang city. The Muslim friendly map publication and implementation to the small, medium culinary enterprises is effective as a tool to increase awareness of tourist by providing guiding of *halal* tourism facility culinary destination.

References

1. Alexandrescu, M.-B., Milandru, M.: Promotion as a form of Communication of the Marketing Strategy. L. Forces Acad. Rev. 23, 4, 268–274 (2018). https://doi.org/10.2478/raft-2018-0033.
2. Ibrahim: Metodologi Penelitian Kualitatif: Panduan Penelitian Beserta Contoh Proposal Kualitatif. ALFABETA, Bandung (2015).
3. Santi, I.N., Fadjar, A.: The Function of Social Media as a Promotion Tool for Tourism Destinations. 135, Aicmbs 2019, 130–132 (2020). https://doi.org/10.2991/aebmr.k.200410.020.
4. Seturi, M.: About the Importance of Tourism Promotion Policy (Georgian Case). In: International Scientific Symposium "Economics, Business & Finance." pp. 76–81 Institute of Researches and International Simposiums Alkona, Jurmala (2018).
5. Strange, J. et al.: Tourism Destination Management: Achieving Sustainable and Competitive Result. US Agency for International Development, Washington DC (2010). https://doi.org/10.1016/j.ypmed.2017.06.020.
6. Yamada, N.: Why tour guiding is important for Ecotourism: Enhancing guiding quality with the Ecotourism promotion policy in Japan. Asia Pacific J. Tour. Res. 16, 2, 139–152 (2011). https://doi.org/10.1080/10941665.2011.556337.

The Use of Webqual 4.0 and Importance Performance Analysis (IPA) Method for Sriwijaya State Polytechnic International Office Website Quality

Tiur Simanjuntak[1]([✉]), Beni Wijaya[1], Evi Agustinasari[1], Yusri Yusri[1], and Qingjian Li[2]

[1] Department of English, Politeknik Negeri Sriwijaya, Palembang, Indonesia
`tiursimanjuntak@polsri.ac.id`
[2] College of International Exchange, Shandong University of Science and Technology, Qingdao, China

Abstract. Digital flows allow the dissemination of information to be carried out borderless. The world of education also takes advantage of this. Nowadays, a website has become the face of the institution and the mean of promotion for international students. Therefore, doing evaluations from various aspects is very important to maintain satisfaction and attract user interest. It is utmost importance to analyze the performance of the Sriwijaya State Polytechnic International website to find out whether it has met the expectations of society towards the campus. There are two methods used in analyzing the website quality in this study. The first method is the Webqual 4.0 method using 23 questions from three dimensions (information, usability, and interaction). The second method is Importance-Performance Analysis (IPA) to identify the three dimensions that require improvement. This research was conducted on 177 domestic and international respondents using a questionnaire. The analyses revelaed that the website quality had an average gap (GAP) of -0.01 indicated the low performance level. Then, the results of the quadrant analysis in IPA required an increase in the priority quadrant: indicator number 5 about an attractive appearance, indicator number 6 about design according to the type of web information system, indicator number 15 about information presented in accordance with the format (shape, font, color, etc.), multimedia features, and indicator number 23 about the overall website.

Keywords: webqual · IPA · website · international office

1 Introduction

Information and communication technology continues to develop rapidly in the present. The era of computerization development continued and developed until the 1990s, giving birth to internet technology which is utilized in various forms. One of which is web technology. With the rapid development of it, Sriwijaya State Polytechnic also uses web

R. Martini et al. (Eds.): FIRST 2022, ASSEHR 733, pp. 76–84, 2023.
https://doi.org/10.2991/978-2-38476-026-8_10

technology in promoting the campus. The website for a university is the face of the university in the virtual world. Sriwijaya State Polytechnic also has its own national and international official website as a promotional medium. The existence of these two websites is a forum for information about profiles, study programs, facilities, and so on to internet users both from within and outside the country so that it is easier to introduce and promote the campus without having to come directly to the campus. In this study, researchers prefer to analyze the website quality for international internet users.

One of the countries that have several foreign students far above Indonesia is Malaysia. According to the report [9], "the number of foreign students in Malaysia in 2014 has exceeded 108,000 with a target of 250,000 by 2025". Based on this statement, international students can improve and revive the economy of a country, and not only that, the presence of foreign students is expected to improve quality and bring benefits to universities. Based on this information, the international website should provide clear, concise, interesting, and not excessive information to attract foreign students to continue their education in Indonesia, especially at the Sriwijaya State Polytechnic. Hence, it is in the best interest to analyze the performance of the Sriwijaya State Polytechnic International website to find out whether it has met the expectations of society towards the campus as a promotion medium by using two methods; Webqual 4.0 and Importance-Performance Analysis.

2 Literature Review

2.1 Website Quality

A website serves to provide information to internet users. As claimed by [17], a website can be interpreted asa collection of pages used to display textual information, moving images, animations,sounds,and/orcombinations of all, both dynamic innature,forming a series of interconnected buildings, each islinked by theweb of pages.As stated by [15], a website is a collection of pagesof information availableon the Internetforworldwideaccess, as long as connected to the Internetnetwork.The quality of a website must be considered to support the image of an institution. [8] states that An institution's web site is the image of the institution in cyber space, so web site quality is an important factor for the institution to consider. [4] mentions that a good website is a website whose main focus is the content of the website, which is the main factor that causes users to return to visit a website. The quality of the website greatly affects how user perceptions and user satisfaction are supported by several features of a website. As reported by [10], auser'sperception of the quality of a website is based on the features available on the website, which can meet theuser's needs and highlight the advantages of the website itself. This is also supported by [1] who state that websites can affect user satisfaction and influence users to use the website.

2.2 Websites for Higher Education

Education websites can be used as a parameter for campus responsiveness in dealing with the development of the era of technology and information. Following an attractive website design style or trend, with easy-to-use navigation can increase the interest of many visitors and students to access the website [19]. This opinion is supported by [8] who states that the university website is a reflection of the campus image so its appearance needs to be considered. Students often pay attention to the physical appearance of a website.

2.3 Webqual 4.0 and Importance-Performance Analysis

Webqual (website quality) is a method of how to measure a website according to the user perceptions [12]. According to [14], webqual 4.0 consists of three dimensions as follow:

a) Usability quality: a quality related to website design, such as Website appearance, usability, navigation, images displayed to users, etc.
b) Information quality: the content quality on the website, whether or not it is appropriate for information to be conveyed such as accurate information, format, and relevance.
c) Service interaction quality: the quality of service interaction that a user experiences while browsing a website to see the reputation and easy communication with the campus.

[16] Argues that IPA isa simple and convenient technique foridentifyingservice-provider attributes that need improvement or deprioritization.As stated by [6], IPA can be used to set attributes based on the level of implementation, which will later be useful in developing a website by measuring the gap.

2.4 Previous Related Studies

In the past two years, there have been several studies discussing website evaluation for various user needs, ranging from educational institutions to E-commerce companies, one of which was focused on the analysis of website quality with Webqual 4.0and IPA methods by [2]. This studywas intended to evaluate the performance provider company platform Tokopedia. With 100 respondents, the quality of the Tokopedia website has a WebQual Index with a score of 0.85 which can be concluded as a good quality because it was close to 1.00. Indonesia's e-commerce map showed that in the first quarter of 2022, the highest number of website visitors in Indonesia was ranked 1st by Tokopedia [2]. This shows the effectiveness of these two methods in evaluating the website because they have results that are linear with the facts on the ground. However, the results of the 4 quadrants of the IPA method indicate that there is a need to improve performance in quadrant 1, namely on usability parameters related to the ease of operating the Tokopedia Website. This is what makes the Tokopedia website not perfect.

As e-commerce interacts with users through platforms, it is not surprising that the Tokopedia website shows good performance. On the other hand, websites for universities are generally only considered supporting facilities so they require more attention [4]. In his research on the website evaluation for the new student admission, [3] evaluated the Ahmad Dahlan University Website for new student admissions. Conducted with

250 respondents, this study shows that there is a need for improvements to the variable "information that is easy to understand". For websites that are intended for new student admissions, the ease of understanding information is a very important variable to pay attention to.

3 Methodology

Questionnaire was used as the data collection technique which consisted of 3 dimensions with 23 question indicators. Then, this questionnaire was given to 177 respondents from several countries with the status of students. This questionnaire was distributed indirectly through the link of google form distributed via social media (Whatsapp and e-mail). Before the questionnaire was given to the respondents, the researcher conducted testing on the three dimensions of the questionnaire. In this study, n (number of respondents) = 177 people, and there are three research variables, so to calculate the value of the r table $df = n - 2 = 177 - 2 = 175$, with a significant level of 0.05, the r table obtained is 0.148. Each indicator of the Webqual on Performance or the level of the website is declared valid. All webqual on performance in this study are also declared reliable. It is shown that each research instrument has a very high level of average reliability since *Cronbach's alpha*(r) > 0.06.

After collecting data, the analyses were conducted. In this quantitative study, the data were analyzed by using the two methods; Webqual 4.0 and Importance-Performance Analysis (IPA). This IPA analysis can be carried out by using several steps. Management in a company has a good level of service if the value of the gap is getting smaller [7]. Gap analysis can be done by finding the average value of each variable in terms ofimportance and performance on the Webqual 4.0 indicators. After getting the average importance/performance on 3 variables of Webqual 4.0, it was followed by getting the average value of the gap (GAP) using the following equation:

$$Qi\ (GAP) = Performance\ (i) - Importance\ (i)$$

The level of conformity is explained in three parts by 0–32% (users are very dissatisfied), 33–65% (users are not satisfied), and 66–99% (users are satisfied). Then the analysis of IPA quadrant with cartesian diagram was conducted. According to [10], the Cartesian diagram consists of four parts of a building bounded by two perpendicularly intersecting lines at point (X, Y) where X is the average of the Performance average number divided by the number of respondents and Y is the average of Importance average number.

4 Result and Discussion

4.1 Webqual 4.0 Analysis

The gap on the website shows a negative result (<0) which is -0.01 as shown in Tables 1, 2 and 3.

Based on the conformity analysis, the website has an attractive appearance, while the lowest rank on the indicator regarding the competence of the author in creating the website.

Table 1. Results of Webqual on Performance

Number	Answer	Likert Scale	Frequency	Percentage
1	Strongly Disagree	1	14	0.34%
2	Disagree	2	115	2.82%
3	Neither Agree nor Disagree	3	668	16.41%
4	Agree	4	1692	41.56%
5	Strongly Agree	5	1582	38.86%

Table 2. Results of Webqual on Importance

Number	Answer	Likert Scale	Frequency	Percentage
1	Strongly Disagree	1	8	0.20%
2	Disagree	2	128	3.14%
3	Neither Agree nor Disagree	3	598	14.69%
4	Agree	4	1763	43.31%
5	Strongly Agree	5	1574	38.66%

Table 3. Results of Webqual on Importance

Number	Indicator	Performance	Importance	Percentage
1	Usability	4.18	4.17	-0.01
2	Information	4.28	4.27	-0.01
3	Service Interaction	-0.01	4.05	4.06

4.2 Importance-Performance Analysis

The details of the quadrant mapping from IPA analysis are shown in Fig. 1.

Quadrant I contains metrics that website users considerimportant, however, website developers fail to meet user expectations, so the users feel dissatisfied. The following are indicators that are included in quadrant I.

a) Indicator number 5 shows that the international website has an attractive appearance or feature.
b) Indicator number 6 indicates that the international website has a design according to the type of web-based information system.
c) Indicator number 15 describes the information presented on the international website in the appropriate format (shape, font, color, and multimedia features).

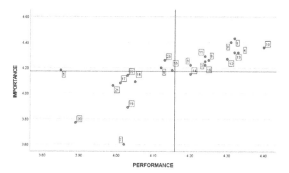

Fig. 1. Quadrant of IPA Analysis

d) Indicator number 23 shows that the overall appearance of the international website is good.

Indicators in quadrant II show the service attributes on the website affect user satisfaction and need to be maintained because all of these indicators make the website outstanding. The followings are indicators that are included in quadrant II.

a) Indicator number 1 shows that the users find it easy to learn the operation of the international website.
b) Indicator number 2 describes that the users are easy to understand the international website.
c) Indicator number 3 shows that the international website has clear navigation and instructions.
d) Indicator number 4 gives information that users feel is easy to access on the international website.
e) Indicator number 8 states that the international website has a positive influence or experience.
f) Indicator number 9 shows that the international website provides information that is quite clear and there are no errors in the delivery of information.
g) Indicator number 10 indicates that the information presented on the international website can be trusted.
h) Indicator number 11 describes that the information provided international website on time or up-to-date.
i) Indicator number 12 shows that informationposted on the internationalwebsite is relevant to theneedsofusers.
j) Indicator number 13 describes that accurate information is presented by the international website.
k) Indicator number 16 shows that the website has a very good reputation for the users.

Quadrant III is considered less important by users with its actual implementation, so repairs with low priority can be made. The followings are indicators that are included in quadrant III.

a) Indicator number 7 shows that the international website has complete facilities or features.
b) Indicator number 17 indicates that users feel safe when interacting with the international website.
c) Indicator number 18 shows that users feel that their personal information is stored safely on the international website.
d) Indicator number 19 describes that the international website provides space for user personalization.
e) Indicator number 20 shows that the international website gives spaces for the community.
f) Indicator number 21 is the international website gives access to communicate with the campus.
g) Indicator number 22 shows that the website guarantees a highlytrusted information for the users.

In quadrant IV there is an excessive performance by website managers, even though the use of these indicators is less important and the website needs to reduce the level of implementation and resources used in this indicator can be allocated to other factors of concern or priority. There is only one indicator that is included in quadrant IV, namely indicator number 14 which contains information on the international website of the Sriwijaya State Polytechnic which is presented in detail.

5   Conclusion

Based on the gap analysis results, the gap values were negative, which was -0.01. This shows that the website performance is not in the interests of users. On the other hand, the results of the total level of conformity are 89.73%. These results is <100%, which indicates the users' dissatisfaction with the performance of this website. Resultsof the IPA quadrant shows Quadrant 1 with instruments number 5, 6, 15, and 23, and Quadrant 3 with instruments number 7, 17, 18, 19, 29, 21, 22 need to be improved.

Acknowledgments. All the researchers would like to express their gratitude to the Center of Research and Community Service and the Head of the International Office of Sriwijaya State Polytechnic for their support and cooperation.

Authors' Contributions. Tiur Simanjuntak and Beni Wijaya contributed to the concept and design of the research. Evi Agustinasari and Yusri carried out data collection. Tiur Simanjuntak, Beni Wijaya, and Qingjian Li analyzed the data and wrote the manuscript. The overall results were discussed by all authors. They also commented on the manuscript for the finishing touch of the publication.

References

1. A. Hanifah, I. Ali, F. Aldyan, D. Ghifari, and M. Fatwa, "Analisis Metode Webqual 4.0 dan Importance Performance Analysis (IPA) pada Kualitas Website E-Health Surabaya (Studi Kasus: E-Health Surabaya),"*Journal Information System and Artificial Intelligence*, vol. 2, no. 2, 2022.
2. A. Ihsan, U. Hidayati, and Mardinawati, "Analisis Kualitas Website dengan Metode Webqual 4.0 Dan Importance Performance Analysis,"*Keunis*, vol. 10, no. 2, pp. 29-40, 2022.
3. A. Putra and D. Yulianto," New Student Admission Website Evaluation Using WebQual 4.0 and Importance-Performance Analysis," *Jurnal Nasional Teknik Elektro dan Teknologi Informasi*, vol. 11, no. 3, pp. 161-167, 2022.
4. A. Setiawan and R. Widyanto,"Evaluasi Website Perguruan Tinggi Menggunakan Metode Usability Testing,"*Jurnal Informatika: Jurnal Pengembangan IT (JPIT)*, vol. 3, no. 3, pp. 295-299, 2018.
5. Advernesia (2022, July 15),"Cara Uji Reliabilitas SPSS Alpha Cronbach's Data Kuesioner,". Retrieved from advernesia.com.
6. D. Apriliani, M. Fikri, and M Hutajulu, "Analisa Metode Webqual 4.0 dan Importance Performance Analysis (IPA) Pada Kualitas Situs Detik.com,"*JurnalIlmiahMerpati*, vol. 8, no. 1,pp. 34-45, 2020.
7. D. Dafit and D. Novita,"MetodeWebQual 4.0 UntukAnalisisKualitas Web Pembelajaran,"*Jurnal Teknologi Komputer dan Sistem Informasi*, vol. 1, no. 2, pp. 17-20, 2018.
8. D. Napitupulu, "Analysis of Factors Affecting the Website Quality Based on Webqual Approach (Study Case: XYZ University)," *International Journal on Advanced Science Engineering and Information Technology*, vol. 7, no. 3, pp. 792-798, 2017.
9. Education Malaysia Global Service," Malaysia Tertiary Education International Students Applications Statistics," *Ministry of Education*. 2015.
10. G. Mandias, Y. Septiawan, and M. Bojoh,"AnalisisKualitas Website Menggunakan Metode Webqual 4.0 dan IPA Terhadap Situs Sla Tompaso," *Gogito Smart Journal*, vol. no. 2, pp. 396-406, 2021.
11. Mashadi, E. Nurachmad, and M. Mulyana,"AnalisisDeskriptifPenilaian Website PerguruanTinggi,"*Jurnal Analisis Sistem Pendidikan Tinggi*, vol. 3, no. 2, p. 97-106, 2019.
12. M. Hanifah, I. Ali, F. Aldyan, D. Ghifari, and M. Fatwa, "Analisis Metode Webqual 4.0 dan Importance Performance Analysis (IPA) pada Kualitas Website E-Health Surabaya (StudiKasus: E-Health Surabaya)," *Journal Information System and Artificial Intellegence*, vol. 2, no. 2, pp. 1-8, 2022.
13. N. Kamilah, "Universitas Pendidikan Indonesia: Pengaruh Keterampilan Mengajar Guru Terhadap Hasil Belajar Siswa Pada Mata Pelajaran Akuntansi," 2015. Retrieved from S_PEA_1005771_Appendix7.pdf(upi.edu).
14. S. Barnes and R. Widgen, "WebQual: An Exploration of Web-Site Quality,"*Communications,* vol. 1, pp. 298-305, 2000.
15. S. Dwipuspita, Mulyana, & Elita. Pengaruh Penggunaan Website terhadap Keputusan Pembelian. Students e-Journal, 1(1), 26, (2012). Retrieved from http://jurnal.unpad.ac.id/ejournal/article/view/1799.
16. S. Ormanović, A. Ćirić, M. Talović, H. Alić, E. Ješleković, and D. Čaušević, "Importance Performance Analysis: Different Approaches," vol. 2, pp. 58-66, 2017.
17. Triyono, "Strategic of Education in Information System," *SENSI*, vol. 4, no. 1, p. 23, 2018.
18. WikiElektronika.com (2022, July 28),"R tabel PDF danUjiValiditas. Retrieved from WikiElektronika.com.
19. Z. Ilka and M. Hasan, "Web-Based Applications in Calculation of Family Heritage (Science of Faroidh)," *Journal of Information Systems*, vol. 1, no. 1, pp. 50-60, 2017.

SWOT Analysis as a Basis for Identifying Risks to the Going Concern of the "Waring Jaya" Palembang Catfish Farm

Muhammad Husni Mubarok(✉), Maria Maria, Indra Satriawan, and Eka Jumarni Fithri

Accounting Departement, Sriwijaya State Polytechnic, Palembang, Indonesia
mhusnimubarok@polsri.ac.id

Abstract. This study aims to identify risks using the SWOT analysis technique. This technique provides information about the potential strengths, weaknesses, opportunities and threats in the "Waring Jaya" catfish farm in the Ilir Barat I sub-district of Palembang. This research was conducted in June 2022 in the "Waring Jaya" business group which has 10 members. Data was collected through observation and interviews with group members as the informan. Furthermore, the data was compiled and analyzed using the SWOT analysis technique. Based on the results of the research, information was obtained that the strength aspect value was 3.6, the business weakness aspect value was 3.9, the business opportunity analysis aspect value was 3.6 and the business threat aspect value was 3.6. This shows that the Waring Jaya Business has potential strengths that are slightly smaller than weaknesses and opportunities that are greater than threats. Furthermore, according to the results of the business quadrant calculation, information is obtained that the x-axis value is -0.3 and the y-axis is 0.9, so it can be concluded that the Waring Jaya Business is in quadrant III. From the results of the SWOT analysis, a number of strategic issues were identified that could threaten the sustainability of the business in the future. These issues are limited business capital, regeneration of human resources in the livestock business, increasingly expensive PUR seed and feed prices which have the potential to pose a risk to business continuity in the future.

Keywords: SWOT Analysis · Risk · Going Concern

1 Introduction

Currently the world economy is still moving slowly. The Covid-19 pandemic has paralyzed the world's economy, causing widespread social restrictions around the world. The company closed office activities, and carried out work at home activities through Work From Home. Including community business activities are also limited. Restaurants, retail centers are closed during the Covid-19 pandemic. Efforts to limit and provide mass vaccinations in the world in the span of 2020–2022 are starting to give positive results. The number of Covid-19 sufferers is decreasing and can be controlled. Economic activity is slowly starting to grow and develop, this is in line with the loosening of a number of

R. Martini et al. (Eds.): FIRST 2022, ASSEHR 733, pp. 85–93, 2023.
https://doi.org/10.2991/978-2-38476-026-8_11

social restrictions rules for the community so that offices and business centers begin to actively operate again while prioritizing health protocols.

Not yet after the Covid-19 pandemic, the world was again shaken by an energy crisis. The increase in global oil prices was caused by the lack of world oil supply which was triggered by the war in Ukraine. This has an impact on global inflation. World oil prices skyrocketed, and there was a massive energy crisis around the world. The impact of rising world oil prices has also affected the Indonesian economy. The 2022 State Revenue and Expenditure Budget (APBN) is burdened by the swelling fuel subsidy spending. The government then raised the price of fuel and had an impact on inflation. According to Financial Analysis, the general inflation rate at the end of 2022 could reach 6.1% (www.nasional.kontan.co.id). This has become an additional burden for companies and the public, including small and medium-sized businesses, which triggers an increase in the price of raw materials for production and operational costs. The catfish farm business, which has just restarted fish farming activities, was also affected by the increase in fuel prices.

The Waring Jaya business is one of the catfish farmer groups that are still surviving during the pandemic. This business sells its fish products to markets and catfish pecel traders around Palembang. The rapid growth of the catfish pecel culinary industry in Palembang has helped to revive the business continuity of catfish farmers. According to Siregar et al. (2020), adaptation in the Covid-19 period is a very valuable lesson for people involved in the organizational environment.

For this reason, in the midst of an unstable economy, entrepreneurs need to make a strategic plan based on an analysis of market potential, opportunities and threats. SWOT analysis helps organizations identify appropriate business strategies and risks that can threaten the economic resilience of business actors. Economic resilience is a dynamic condition of the nation's economic life that contains tenacity and resilience that contains the ability to develop strength in the face of all threats, obstacles, disturbances and challenges directly or indirectly to ensure the survival of a nation's economy (Marlinah, 2017, p. 258).

2 Literature Review

According to (Hanafi, 2006) Risk is a danger, consequence or consequence that can occur as a result of an ongoing process or future events. Risk can be interpreted as a state of uncertainty, where if an undesirable situation occurs, it can cause a loss. This analysis is a form of assessment of the results of situation identification in order to categorize conditions as strengths, weaknesses, opportunities or threats (Syaeful Bakhri, et al., 2019, p. 71).

According to Rangkuti (2013), the SWOT analysis is divided into four main quadrants which have different strategies for each quadrant. The following is an explanation of the 4 (four) quadrants in the SWOT analysis:

- Quadrant 1. It is a very favorable situation. The company has opportunities and strengths so that it can take advantage of existing opportunities. The strategy that must be applied in this condition is to support an aggressive growth policy (Growth oriented strategy).

- Quadrant 2. Despite facing various threats, the company still has strength internally. The strategy that must be applied is to use strength to take advantage of long-term opportunities by means of a diversification strategy (product/market).
- Quadrant 3. The company faces a huge market opportunity, but on the other hand, it faces several internal constraints/weaknesses. The focus of this company's strategy is to minimize the company's internal problems so that it can seize good market opportunities.
- Quadrant 4. It is a very unfavorable situation, the company faces various internal threats and weaknesses

There are several things that can disrupt the company's sustainability, including (McKeown et al., 1991):

1. The company experiences negative trends, such as repeated operating losses, less working capital, negative cash flow, and significant poor financial ratios.
2. Other indications are related to the possibility of financial difficulties, for example failure to fulfill debt agreements/obligations, dividends in arrears, suppliers refusing to purchase on ordinary credit, debt restructuring, the need for alternative financing/funding methods, or assets that are mostly sold.
3. Internal problems, for example employees who go on strike or poor labor relations, the company depends on the success of the project, the existence of long-term commitments that do not provide economic value added, and there is a significant need for operational improvements.
4. External problems that are being faced by the company, such as lawsuits against the company, difficult rules or regulations, loss of patents, licenses or franchises, missing major customers and suppliers, and major disasters resulting in losses.

According to Ni Luh (2021) company bankruptcy can be studied both from internal factors and external factors. These internal factors include:

1. Management inefficiency, which has implications for repeated losses until the company has difficulty paying off its obligations (Fauzia, 2017; Putri et al., 2018).
2. Capital that is not balanced with the amount of debts. If the amount of debt is high, then this will be followed by a high amount of interest expense that must be paid by the company, resulting in the erosion of company profits, and even losses. If the receivables are too large, then it is also not good because there are too many assets that are idle and not generated into cash.
3. Moral hazard committed by management, which is included in the form of fraud. The fraud in question can be in terms of corruption, misinformation that misleads users of financial statements.

Furthermore, according to Ni Luh (2021), when viewed from the side of external factors, business bankruptcy can come from the following factors:

1. Customers experience changes in needs or desires that have not been previously predicted by the company, so buyers look for other companies that are able to fulfill their desires, and this has an impact on decreasing revenues.
2. Suppliers cannot provide raw materials needed by the company for production activities.
3. Debtor's failure to make payments, or taking too long to make repayments so that many assets are idle for too long and the company does not get cash flow.
4. Does not have a harmonious relationship with creditors.
5. Strict business competition with other companies.
6. Global economic conditions, for example the COVID-19 pandemic, are conditions that affect the global economy

According to (Tuanakota, 2015) there are several factors that cause auditors to issue a going concern opinion including:

1. Negative trends, such as recurring operating losses, working capital deficiency, negative cash flow and poor key financial ratios.
2. External problems, such as new laws that threaten the existence of the company, pending litigation, loss of major franchises or patents, loss of major customers and suppliers and uninsured losses.
3. Miscellaneous problems, such as default on loans, inability to pay dividends, debt restructuring, violations of laws and regulations and inability to purchase from suppliers on credit.
4. Court cases, lawsuits or similar issues that have occurred that could jeopardize the company's ability to operate.

3   Research Methods

This study is a descriptive study with a qualitative approach, namely through data analysis obtained through direct field observations regarding the strengths, weaknesses, opportunities and threats of catfish farming. Sources of data used by researchers in this qualitative research is primary data sources obtained directly from catfish farmers. In this study, the data used in the form of interviews, observations. Interviews with informants who have been determined by researchers in the form of interviews and recordings as well as identification of SWOT analysis data. This research was conducted in June 2022 in a group of "Waring Jaya" in the Ilir Barat I sub-district of Palembang which has 10 members. Data was collected through observation and interviews with group members as the informan. Researchers also use secondary data sources that come from literature studies that are related to research problems. Supported by identity and fish farming business license, as well as documentation in the form of pictures or photos taken directly in the field.

In this study, researchers used 3 (three) types of data analysis, namely data sorting, data presentation, and drawing conclusions and verification (Susanto, 2017, p. 3):

1   Sorting primary and secondary data obtained during observation and selecting data that can provide a clear and relevant picture to the research topic.

2 Presentation of data by describing the relationship between data. Data is presented in the form of tables, graphs and text.
3 Drawing conclusions and verification that can answer the formulation of the problem in research.

The location of the research was carried out in the "Waring Jaya" Palembang Business group, precisely in the Sei Hitam area, Bukit Lama village, Ilir Barat I District, Palembang.

4 Results and Discussion

Based on the results of observations and interviews, researchers obtained information about the strengths, weaknesses, opportunities and threats in the "Waring Jaya" business. In the strength section, the author identifies as many as 5 potential strengths of the Waring Jaya business which consists of having experienced human resources with a value of 0.8, having regular customers with a value of 1.2, sufficient knowledge of fish farming with a value of 0.8, mastering feed processing methods alternative with a value of 0.6, and has a network with stakeholders with a value of 0.2. Of the five potential strengths obtained a total value of 3,6 (Table 1).

Based on Table 2, information is obtained that there are 2 potential weaknesses in this business, namely the lack of capital with a value of 3.6 and the regeneration of livestock human resources which is lacking with a value of 0.3. The total value of weakness is 3.9. Based on the results of interviews, the human resources in this business already have 35 years of experience in fish farming, so they have loyal customers from time to time. This shows the main strength.

Based on Table 3, information is obtained that there are 2 potential opportunities in this business, namely The increasing number of catfish pecel businesses in Palembang City with a value of 3.2 and the demand for catfish from outside Palembang with a value of 0.4. The total score on the weakness aspect is 3,6. This is supported by the results of field observations, the installed production capacity or the capacity of the pond is able to produce 5,000 kg of fish per month, but only 3,000 kg of catfish are cultivated per month or 60% of installed production. Meanwhile, in terms of demand for catfish from

Table 1. Strength Analysis

No	Description	Weight	Rating	Score
1	Experienced HR	0.20	4.00	0.80
2	Have regular customers	0.30	4.00	1.20
3	Sufficient knowledge of fish farming	0.20	4.00	0.80
4	Alternative Feed Processing Method	0.20	3.00	0.60
5	Have a network with stakeholders	0.10	2.00	0.20
	Amount	1.00	17,00	3.60

Table 2. Weakness Analysis

No	Description	Weight	Rating	Score
1	Limited capital	0.90	4.00	3.60
2	Lack of HR regeneration	0.10	3.00	0.30
	Amount	1.00	7.00	3.90

Table 3. Opportunity Analysis

No	Description	Weight	Rating	Score
1	More and more catfish pecel businesses in Palembang City	0.80	4.00	3.20
2	There is a demand for catfish from outside Palembang	0.20	2.00	0.40
	Amount	1.00	7.00	3.60

Table 4. Threat Analysis

No	Description	Weight	Rating	Score
1	Competitors for large-scale catfish farming are starting to emerge	0.10	2.00	0.20
2	The price of catfish seeds is getting more expensive	0.40	3.00	1.20
3	The price of catfish PUR feed is getting more expensive	0.30	3.00	0.90
4	Government aid is dwindling	0.20	2.00	0.40
	Amount	1.00	10.00	2.70

new customers, it reached 6,000 kg per month. There is still a potential of 33% for fish that can be cultivated in ponds.

Furthermore, based on Table 4, information is obtained that there are 4 (four) potential threats to this business, namely large-scale catfish business competitors starting to appear with a value of 0.2, the price of catfish seeds is getting more expensive with a value of 1.2, then the price of PUR feed catfish is getting more expensive with a value of 0.9 and government assistance is decreasing with a value of 0.4. The total score on the threat aspect is 2.7.

Based on Table 5, information is obtained that the "Waring Jaya" business is in quadrant III. This business faces a huge market opportunity, but on the other hand, it faces several obstacles. Opportunities to meet the demand for catfish are quite high, but the main obstacle for this business is limited working capital. Before the pandemic, the Regional Government was very concerned about breeders and provided assistance for catfish seeds, so that farmers could be helped when the price of catfish seeds was expensive.

This business needs to formulate several strategies in overcoming a number of obstacles in its business, including:

Table 5. Calculation of X and Y Axis in 4 Quadrant Analysis

No	Description	Score X Axis	Score Y Axis
1	Strength	3.60	-
2	Weakness	3.90	-
3	Opportunity	-	3.60
4	Threat	-	2.70
	Amount	-0.3	0.90

1 Fostering cooperation with BUMN/BUMD in terms of partnerships by utilizing CSR funds.
2 Improving communication with relevant agencies to seek opportunities for financial assistance for fish farmers.
3 Utilizing ponds that are not used to breed catfish brooders for the availability of catfish seeds.
4 Looking for alternative feeds other than chicken intestines, such as snails and golden snails to anticipate the spike in the price of PUR and Intestines.

Furthermore, from the SWOT analysis above, the author also identifies several potential problems or risks that can disrupt business continuity in the future, including:

1 The regeneration of catfish farmers' human resources can be a threat to the "Waring Jaya" business, this is because the potential strength of this business will be lost and will indirectly threaten the sustainability of the business in the future.
2 The risk of business losses, which is triggered by the increase in the price of seeds and feed due to the increase in fuel prices. This needs to be anticipated by looking for alternative feed that is economical, or if possible, farmers can increase the selling price of catfish, although this policy cannot continue to be carried out due to limited people's income and can lead to a decrease in demand for catfish in the market.
3 Risks from large-scale business competitors, which have adequate capital and technological equipment. so being able to compete with more economical selling prices will also pose a threat in the long run. For this reason, joint efforts by catfish farmers are needed by forming a community of fish farmers with a wider area coverage, holding discussions or fish farmer forums to find sustainable solutions to a number of problems faced by farmers in the future.

5   Conclusion

Based on the discussion above, the author can conclude several important things related to the discussion of the SWOT analysis on the "Waring Jaya" business:

1. The "Waring Jaya" business is in quadrant 3 where this business has the opportunity to fulfill a fairly large market potential, plus pond land resources that have not been fully utilized due to limited capital and try to take several strategies to overcome business weaknesses and threats.
2. There are several potential problems or risks detected from the SWOT analysis above, which can be a disruption to business continuity in the future. For this reason, it is necessary to anticipate by handling risks with risk mitigation, risk transfer and risk sharing approaches.

References

Hanafi, Mamduh. (2006). Manajemen Resiko. Yogyakarta: Unit Penerbit dan Percetakan Sekolah Tinggi Ilmu Manajamen YKPN.

Marlinah, L. (2017). Meningkatkan Ketahanan Ekonomi Nasional Melalui Pengembangan Ekonomi Kreatif. Dalam Jurnal Cakrawala Humaniora Universitas Bina Sarana Informatika Vol. 17, No. 2 258-265. https://ejournal.bsi.ac.id.Diakses pada 9 Juli 2020.

McKeown, J. C., Mutchler, J. F., & Hopwood, W. (1991). Toward An Explanation of Auditor Failure to Modify The Audit Reports of Bankrupt Companies. Auditing: A Journal of Practice & Theory, Supplement, 1–13.

Ni Luh Putu Uttari Premananda. (2021). Prediksi Keberlangsungan Perusahaan Sub Sektor Hotel, Restoran Dan Pariwisata Di Era Pandemi Covid-19. Pariwisata Budaya: Jurnal Ilmiah Agama Dan Budaya, 6(2), 153–159.

5. Siregar, H., Rahayu, A., Wibowo, L. A., & Indonesia, U. P. (2020). Manajemen Strategi Di Masa Pandemi Covid 19. Jurnal Ilmiah Manajemen, 1(2), 40–58.

Susanto, R. I. (2017). Analisis Strategi Pengembangan Bisnis Pada PT. Patrinsaka. AGORA, Vol. 5, Nomor 1.1–7. https://media.neliti.com.Diakses pada 27 Juni 2020.

Syaeful Bakhri, dkk. (2019). Analisis SWOT Untuk Strategi Pengembangan Home Industry Kue Gapit Sampurna Jaya Kabupaten Cirebon. Dalam Jurnal Dimasejati Vol. 1 No. 1, 64- 81. www.shekhnurjati.ac.id. Diakses pada 8 Juli 2020.

Rangkuti, Freddy. 2014. Teknik Membedah Kasus Bisnis Analisis SWOT Cara, Perhitungan Bobot, Rating dan OCAI. Jakarta: Gramedia Pustaka Utama.

Tuanakota. (2015). Audit Kontemporer (1st ed.). Jakarta: Salemba Empat.

https://nasional.kontan.co.id/news/5-dampak-dari-kenaikan-harga-bbm-yang-bakal-dirasakan-langsung-masyarakat. Diakses tanggal 20 September 2022.

The Employer Satisfaction Study on Graduates from TVET Institution

Nur Riana Binti Abdul Rahim[1]([✉]), Juhaidie Zamani Bin Jamaludin[2],
and Habsah Binti Haji Mohamad Sabli[1]

[1] Department of Commerce, Polytechnic Mukah, Mukah, Malaysia
`riana@pmu.edu.my`
[2] Department of Civil Engineering, Polytechnic Mukah, Mukah, Malaysia

Abstract. The quality of education has been questions in the country due to many polytechnic graduates are still unemployed and work outside the field studied while in polytechnics. Some blame the graduates themselves and others blame the polytechnics for not providing a curriculum that is in line with the requirements of the employer. Therefore, this study was conducted to look at the problem whether among graduates or otherwise. This study aims to identify the level of skills and knowledge among employers toward Malaysian polytechnic graduates. A total of 151 students who graduated in 2014/2015 participated in this study, which also used descriptive statistics. Overall, the results for skills and knowledge in high level. The results of this study are expected to support the Ministry of Education Malaysia in general, the Department of Polytechnic Education and Community Colleges, Ungku Omar Polytechnic especially in the planning of the program. It can also be used as a benchmark for the formulation of the curriculum in polytechnics especially the elements of employability skills. The industry can also use the results of this study for knowledge of employability skills requirements among employees employed to increase work productivity and thus increase the productivity of the company.

Keywords: skill · knowledge · graduates · polytechnic · students

1 Introduction

Currently, the Malaysian government is geared towards National Transformation 2050 (TN50). TN50 is setting up a 30-year target which is an effort to shape Malaysia's future for the period 2020 to 2050. The formation of TN50 is a follow-up to the New Economic Policy (1971–1990) and the vision of 2020 (1991–2020). The purpose of TN50 is to achieve the goals of National Transformation 2050 (TN50). Knowledge is seen as an important asset and reference to guide towards planning, implementation, and monitoring. Thus, the management of knowledge and information is an element that needs to be emphasized by the government to guide knowledge and information used optimally. TN50 also requires a community with technical and vocational skills to meet the needs of the country by 2050. Thus, the Technical and Vocational Education and Training System (TVET) is an education system that can help to achieve the government's

R. Martini et al. (Eds.): FIRST 2022, ASSEHR 733, pp. 94–104, 2023.
https://doi.org/10.2991/978-2-38476-026-8_12

aspiration to produce graduates who are able to fulfill the needs of industry 4.0 and TN50. The Prime Minister in the presentation of the national development plan for the period 2016 to 2020 in the Dewan Rakyat stressed that the Technical and Vocational Training Programme (TVET) is an important platform to increase the skill workforce in preparation for Malaysia towards a developed country by 2020. A total of 1.5 million new jobs will be created through the 11th Malaysia Plan (11MP) and 60 percent of them will require skilled manpower in TVET-related fields. Thus, the Malaysian Education Development Plan 2013–2025 was designed to develop a system that not only focuses on the normal academic pathway but also emphasizes the TVET pathway.

In order to become the institution of choice in technical and vocational education, the management of the polytechnic should strive to make the polytechnic a premier institution, and subsequently, the graduates produced to meet the needs of the employer as well as the job market today. The graduates that employers currently want are a workforce with technical skills and employability skills. Thus, this research aims to examine the employability skills of Malaysian polytechnic students according to the employer's glasses. However, there is a mismatch of skills and knowledge among graduates which are the gap between the criteria required by the industry and the education that graduates are going through [1, 2]. Based on [1], there is an insufficient amount of theoretical and practical knowledge among students at a university while they are undergoing industrial training. The findings of the [3] showed that a mismatch of technical skills and marketability skills were among the causes of unemployment among graduates.

Past studies have found it is difficult to show a clear consensus on which skills contribute to market ability [4]. Although there are employers who make interpersonal communication, and team skills their choice, there are also employers who give preference to information technology abilities. As for [5], generic and non-generic skills play an equally important role in determining the employability of graduates. Hence, there is a need to identify the level of skills and knowledge for polytechnic graduates. Therefore, the objective of this study is to identify the level of skills and knowledge among employers of Malaysia polytechnic graduates. The scope of this study is limited to graduates of Ungku Omar Polytechnic. The respondents included graduates of Ungku Omar Polytechnic who graduated in the 2014/2015 session. Only two types of instruments were used which are interview and questionnaire protocols. The interview and questionnaire protocol are focused on the level of skills and knowledge based on the employer's perception of polytechnic graduates. Based on the review of the literature, employability skills are a very influential area of skill in ensuring the success and progress of a company or industry in general. Human resources that are competent and skilled in carrying out their entrusted responsibilities are the dream and hope of the training center for its trainees. The ability of the trainees to provide satisfaction to employers and the good acceptance of the employers of the workforce produced is a good sign for the programme implemented at Ungku Omar Polytechnic. The results of this study are also useful to employees or graduates who venture into the field of employees to research and apply the elements of employability skills studied in this study. They are more willing to compete and adapt to a changing environment of work due to the k-economy and globalization. As a result, graduates are more confident and competent and able to earn lucrative rewards from employers. This study contributes to the easing of new epistemology in employability skills towards sustainable development. This opens up a new dimension in the field of knowledge among researchers in the future. Therefore, this study is urgently needed to be carried out due to the factors discussed.

The findings of this research are also useful for those who are involved in the field of employment to make comparisons and assessments on the elements of employability skills that employers desire and that everyone must have before they venture into a particular field of employment. This effort is expected to help them get a job more easily as well as earn a salary based on the knowledge and skills they have. Finally, the findings of this study are expected to contribute ideas, understanding of concepts as well as development in the field of knowledge related to employability skills as well as their importance to the world of work today.

2 Literature Review

Based on the review of the literature, it was found that employers want employees with a wide range of job skills including soft knowledge and skills. The employability of the graduates produced is also a yardstick to the success of the polytechnic and the program followed by the students. This study is expected to provide information and improve the elements of employability that should be emphasized in implementing the program of study in polytechnics as well as the elements of employability in terms of knowledge and skills required by employers and industry inlinewiththeideaoftheIndustrialRevolution4.0. Unemployed graduates area serious phenomenon that occurs nowadays. Labor market statistics show that the output of local institutions of higher learning is still unable to cope with job vacancies even though the output of a group of workers exceeds the demand of employers. Among the main factors of the occurrence of this phenomenon is that the resulting graduates are still unable to meet the requirements of today's employers.

Employability is defined as someone capable of obtaining the skills and knowledge toper form multiple jobs at any one time, not only are they able to perform those tasks quickly but they can perform tasks without further training [6]. Whereas [7] state this employability refers to the specific personality of individuals acquired and used in their career profession. [8] stated that employability is a set of attitudes, knowledge, and skills that potential employees need to have to ensure they have the ability in the workplace. Besides that, employability skills the basic skill needed for one to get job and enable the individual to carry out duties well [9].

According to [10] skills training is an employee who can optimally use new technologies and materials as well as effectively use inventiveness and innovation. For this purpose, a country must develop a work force that not only has high academic and technical qualifications but acquires a diversity of skills and knowledge using ICT. A person with great skills will be able to increase employers or the work place productivity [11]. A work force with employability skills can cope with social change and ever-changing economic conditions [12]. Some employers consider academic competence alone insufficient and begin to ask higher education institutions to produce graduates equipped with various elements of employability. Scholars in the field of knowledge sharing also mention a variety of definitions of knowledge. Knowledge may also be described as an individual's experience and understanding that is transformed into a meaningful form and used by the individual to complete a task. Individuals can speak, formulate, write, draw and collect newly acquired information, according to [13]. This information can be preserved in a variety of formats, including papers, photos, and videos. There are two types of knowledge: implicit and explicit knowledge. Implicit knowledge is personal information derived from personal experience and includes intuition, personal values, and beliefs [14]. Implicit knowledge created by academics and imprinted in their minds, for example, is a store house of intellectual capital in Higher Education Institutions.

In Malaysia, a higher education institution now offers students the opportunity to put their classroom learning into reality through industrial training. The six-month training period attempts to acquire knowledge in line with the abilities required by the sector, and it appears that this will play an essential part in ensuring a quality and professional workforce in the future [15]. When it comes to teaching staff, knowledge is an issue that should be present. Knowledge is an important aspect of improving development and productivity. Based on the [16] states that there are two important criteria in ensuring that economic development in Australia is constantly improving, namely by further improving the skill and knowledge level in employment in the present or future. A knowledge-driven economy will add sources of growth through activities that can increase value-added and thus contribute to the Overall Productivity Factor. To achieve this level, employees need to be equipped with skills and knowledge that in turn will enhance creativity and innovation to bear the brunt of economic improvement in the era of globalization and liberalization [17]. The employees must have the ability to generate knowledge, share existing knowledge, and apply organizational-related knowledge to a new atmosphere is critical [16].

The bigger challenge is to provide the human capital that the industry needs and meets the satisfaction of employers. [18] stated that, there are mismatch between the need of industry and education in institutions. The gap occurs will not be able to fulfill the skills needed by the industry. It is often raised about graduates who do not have enough skills and do not meet the requirements of the industry they are about to venture into. According to [19], the problem of unemployment among university graduates is often associated with the issue of shortage and weakness of most graduates of higher institution. The curriculum in local educational institutions is also said to not meet the needs and demands of the private sector job market which provides 90 percent of the job opportunities in the country. The fundamental problems faced by local university graduates to get a job are the lack of communication in English, using computers, interacting with other races, working as a team, and their willingness to work outside of office hours of duty.

Now, employers are not only looking at academic qualifications but also looking at the ability or skills of graduates from the spiritual and entrepreneurial aspects [19] discussed the issue of skills that graduates need to have as well as having good academic qualifications. The findings of their study found that graduates with high soft skills such as self-employment, information technology skills, leadership, adaptability, and intellectual skills have helped graduates to get a job in a short period. According to [17], the employ ability of graduates refers to skills that include personality, interpersonal skills, and even good attitudes and behaviors. It states that in the ever-changing world of work, industry employers need workers who are more creative, flexible, and have high interpersonal skills.

3 Methodology

This study was conducted through the quantitative research approach method using survey forms conducted on 331 people in the industry sector throughout Malaysia. Quantitative methods use descriptive statistical analysis using SPSS Ver23 software. In this study, the population was 331 listed in the tracking directory of Malaysian poly-technic graduates. Studies were conducted quantitatively by conducting surveys on the sample of employers of polytechnic graduates. We used random sampling techniques in the selection of study samples. The selection of this method was made to ensure that the study sample can represent the employer population in a polytechnic. The total employer size is based on a sample size determination table by [20] with a confidence level of 95%. Thus, this study will use 331 employers who have been chosen at random. This is to ensure that the selected samples represent the actual industrial population. For qualitative data collection through interview techniques, this study uses purposeful sampling which is a non-probability sampling technique that selects samples based on the importance and purpose of the study. This technique is suitable for emphasizing variable control [21]. According to [3], this technique is similar to the strata sampling technique. The selection of suitable respondents is necessary for an assessment to meet the required information needs i.e. stakeholders. Questionnaire studies formed from the previous section are used as a data collection tool. The questionnaire used for the study contains three main sections. Part A consists of the company's background information, Part B of the general information of polytechnic graduates and Part C is more about assessing the aspects of skills, knowledge, and soft skills. The questionnaire was sent and emailed to the employer and followed up via a phone call to ensure that the employer received the instrument that had been sent. Stamped and self-addressed envelopes are also provided for the re-delivery of completed questionnaires. To ensure that the find-ings from the questionnaire remain consistent, feedback and comments from structured interviews will also be taken into account in support of the findings of the questionnaire.

The instruments used in this study were questionnaires adapted from [22], [24] and [19]. The language and arrangement of items however have been modified based on the suitability of the local environment. The new item was purified because the previous study instruments were found to be non-exhaustive in the aspect of item measurement. The questionnaire was formed by taking into account all the variables discussed in the study of the literature. Before the collection of data and actual studies were carried out, the introduction of the purpose of the study is stated together in the questionnaires that have been distributed. Respondents were also told that during the course of the study, other relevant information would also be collected. Respondents were given confidence that the information provided will be used only for research purposes. Respondents were asked to give honest and voluntary answers. Their participation contribution was highly appreciated and also important for this study. The instrument used in this study was a questionnaire containing three constructs with 10items. Part A of the questionnaire includes background information of the company or respondent containing four items.

Part B is related to the general information of graduates and has seven items. Part C related to skills and knowledge has a total number of items of 10. This questionnaire item was measured using the Likert Scale. The use of the Likert Scale was chosen because it has high reliability and validity [4]. The Likert scales used are (1) Very Low, (2) Low, (3) Medium, (4) High, and (5) Very High.

4 Data Analysis and Interpretation

Table1 shows a total of 331 questionnaires were sent and emailed to employers through-out Malaysia. They were 151 respondents gave feedback, and the feedback rate was 45.62%.

Table 2 shows the reliability analysis of each variable in the study. The findings of the reliability analysis of the variables and dimensions of the study found that the Alpha Cronbach coefficient had a value of 0.956. This suggests that the questionnaire instrument has high reliability.

Table 3 shows the demographic analysis of the study looked at the number of respondents (employers), the type of organization, the number of respondents by field, and the starting salary offered by the employer to polytechnic graduates. The graduates by field of Mechanical Engineering total 16 (10.6%), Electrical Engineering total 7 (4.6%), Civil Engineering total 31 (20.5%), Shipping Engineering total 2 (1.3%), Information Technology total 11(7.3%), Trade total 49 (32.5) and others total 35 (23.2%). Most graduates earn between RM1,001 and RM1,500 (88.7%), followed by a total salary ranging from RM1,501 to RM2,000 (11.3%).

Table 4 shows the mean score and standard deviation of the skills of PUO graduates based on the perception of the employer. On the whole, employers agree that the level of perception of graduates of PUO is high (Mean = 4.14). The highest mean are the skills of using a computer in information processing (Mean = 4.18) and the skill of choosing equipment/technology (Mean = 4.18). The second highest mean is for the

Table 1. Questionnaire Sent, Feedback Received, and Feedback Rate

Questionnaire	Sum	Feedback Rate
Sent/email feedback	331	
received	151	45.62%

Table 2. Reliability Analysis

Constructs	Item numbers	Alpha
Skills	6	
Knowledge	4	45.62%
Sum	10	0.956

Table 3. The Demographic Background of the Respondents

Respondent Profile		n	(%)
Organization	Private	144	95.4
	Government	7	4.6
Field	Mechanical Engineering	16	10.6
	Electrical Engineering	7	4.6
	Civil Engineering	31	20.5
	Shipping Engineering	2	1.3
	Information Technology	11	7.3
	Trade	49	32.5
	Others	35	23.2
Salary	RM1,001–RM1,500	134	88.7
	RM1,501–RM2,000	17	11.3

Table 4. Mean Score and Standard Deviation of Graduate Skills

Item	Skills	Mean	S.D	Rank
C01	Information management skills	4.14	0.622	3
C02	Skills of using a computer in information processing	4.18	0.644	1
C03	Proficiency in choosing equipment/technology	4.18	0.612	2
C04	Creative and innovative thinking skills	4.12	0.652	5
C05	Decision-making skills	4.09	0.615	6
C06	Problem-solving skills	4.13	0.592	4
	Average Mean Score	**4.14**	**0.513**	

level of information management skills (Mean = 4.14).The lowest mean is for decision making skills (Mean = 4.09).

Table 5 shows the mean score and standard deviation of knowledge of PUO graduates based on the perception of the employer. On the whole, employers agree that the level of perception of graduates of PUO is high (Mean = 4.11). The highest mean is for the level of knowledge of PUO graduates to be related to knowledge related to the field of duty (Mean = 4.13) followed by the level of knowledge of graduates of PUO related management about the organization (Mean = 4.12).The lowest mean is for technical knowledge based on work requirements (Mean = 4.08).

Table 5. Mean Score and Standard Deviation of Graduate Knowledge

Item	Skills	Mean	S.D	Rank
C07	Technical knowledge based on work needs	4.08	0.627	4
C08	Knowledge of applying technology	4.10	0.630	3
C09	Management knowledge of the organization	4.12	0.610	2
C10	Knowledge relating to the field of duty	4.13	0.574	1
	Average Mean Score	**4.11**	**0.520**	

5   Discussion and Conclusion

The skills of PUO graduates are non-leaning variables and the results of the analysis show the overall mean is high (Mean = 4.14). This means that the majority of employers agree that PUO graduates have the necessary skills and that the overall level of work performance of polytechnic graduates is good. Based on the results of the analysis, the majority of employers agree that PUO graduates have high skills in using computers for information processing purposes (Mean = 4.18) and skills in choosing equipment/technology (mean = 4.18). The results of this analysis are in line with the previous researchers, [13] who stated that employers would prefer to hire graduate that have analytical skills.

   Therefore, PUO graduates have technical skills relevant to current developments and PUO always provides a hands on educational approach to ensure that its graduates can compete in the real industry world. It is also in line with [3] who also stated that a workforce with employability skills can cope with any social changes and ever-changing economic conditions Referring to this study, knowledge is a non-dependent variable and the results of the analysis show that the overall mean of employers' perception of the knowledge of PUO graduates is high (Mean = 4.11). Most employers agree that the level of knowledge of graduates of PUO in the areas of work carried out in the industry is excellent (Mean = 4.13). The findings of this quantitative and qualitative study are parallel where core knowledge skills play an important role in determining the opportunities for graduates to get jobs whether in small, large, or medium sized organizations.

   Empowering the technical field of polytechnic graduates is a challenge of higher education and is the basis of polytechnics to ensure that graduates from polytechnics have skills in the field that are involved while in polytechnics. This effort also meets the requirements of the Department of Polytechnic Studies policy which set 10 surges on this challenge, among which is the 2nd surge of quality TVET graduates and the 10th surge of producing holistic graduates. Therefore, the mobilization of all parties in implementing this policy should be integrated and supported by outsiders, namely the industry. In other words, polytechnic graduates must at least have a technical skills certificate, a Malaysian skills certificate, a certificate of competency, and a professional certificate to enable them to compete in the external market. In this regard, Polytech Knowledge Linkages to Industry (PKLI) was created to help polytechnic students improve their technical skills by implementing a PKLI structured program while undergoing six months of Industrial Training (LI) in the industry.

This program involves the institutions and industries. Institutions can establish a relationship of understanding through Notes of Understanding and opportunities to exchange information and experiences through the invitation of industry speakers. In addition, the PKLI program also provides opportunities and benefits for lecturers to improve their skills through up skilling and reskilling. To further enhance the employability of polytechnic graduates, the programs offered must meet the current needs of the market with a focus on the thrust areas that have been set. In addition, polytechnic graduates need to have sufficient skills, employability skills, and sufficient entrepreneurial skills to maintain the ability of polytechnic graduates to seize job opportunities in the industry. A new approach is needed for the construction of skills and the application of an entrepreneurial culture among students. In addition, the offering of new programs should involve the cooperation and recognition of various parties such as industry and professional bodies to meet the current needs of the industry.

The relationship between the PUO and the employers in the industry can be established by inviting industry representatives to the PUO every semester to participate in dialogue sessions and deliver seminars to lecturers and students. In addition, lecturers at PUO are encouraged to undergo a thorough menu of the industry to gain the latest knowledge, skills, and experience to be shared with the students. Therefore, this can further strengthen the relationship between the PUO and the industry. The exchange of knowledge and experience in the industry sector can have a long-term positive impact on the teaching, learning, and management style at PUO. PUO has not forgotten the industry and employers who have contributed a lot to the progress of the PUO by inviting industry representatives to the PUO convocation every year. In this way, the openness of opportunities and prospects of PUO graduates can be highlighted during the convocation. The students' excellent activities in the academic and co curricular fields are exposed by giving appreciation and contribution to the successful students. Therefore it can to some extent reveal the skills of graduates of PUO.

The findings showed that the employability of PUO graduates was high at 94.6% (graduate tracking data). This indicates that employers are willing to hire PUO graduates to work in private or government organizations. This is because employers' perception of employability skills for polytechnic graduates is high at 86.3%. The overall results of the analysis showed that the majority of employers agreed that PUO graduates have excellent skills and knowledge and overall mean achievement is high. The study was conducted on employers with PUO graduates who had graduated in 2014 and 2015. This study is also limited to organizations/companies located in Malaysia. Organizational/company information is obtained from the data of PUO graduates working as a result of the graduation tracking studies conducted. Further studies from the perspective of polytechnic graduates should be carried out in the future as feedback from employer is very important as a basis for formulating policies and strategies for the success of the Polytechnic Transformation Direction. Through this strategy, it can also indirectly help each polytechnic to create action plans and initiatives that can improve the employability of graduates, and improve the needs of R&D and curriculum.

References

1. Bilal, M. N. M., & Ummah, M. S. A Case Study on the Impact of Internship Training in Finding Successful Job Placements: With Special Reference to South Eastern University of Sri Lanka. In *Proceedings of International HR Conference* (Vol. 3, No. 1) (2016).
2. Wesley, S. C., Jackson, V. P. & Lee, M. The perceived importance of core soft skills between retailing and tourism management students, faculty and businesses. Employee Relations, 39(1), 79-99 (2017).
3. Franchak, S. J., & Smiley, L. L. Evaluating Employer Satisfaction: Measurement of Satisfaction with Training and Job Performance of Former Vocational Education Students. Research and Development Series No. 210 (1981).
4. Suleman, F. Employability skills of higher education graduates: Little consensus on a much-discussed subject. Procedia-Social and Behaviora lSciences, 228,169-174(2016).
5. Kwok, D., Gujral, M., & Chan, J. Work readiness: A study of student intern's self-perception and supervisor evaluation. In *International Conference on Teaching & Learning in Higher Education* (Vol. 1, No. 3) (2014).
6. Little, Brenda M. *Employability for the workers: What does this mean?*. Education and Training,53(1):pp.57–66(2011).
7. Lowden, K., Hall, S., Elliot, D., & Lewin, J. Employers' perceptions of the employability skills of new graduates. *London: Edge Foundation, 201126*(2011).
8. Botman, H.R. Employability in a developmental context for a just dispensation (2011).
9. Robinson, J.P. *What are employability skills*. The workplace, 1(3), 1-3(2000).
10. Pegg, Ann, Waldcock, Jeff, Hendy-Isaac, Soniaand Lawton, Ruth. *Pedagogy for Employability*. York: Higher Education Academy (2012).
11. Lange, F., & Topel, R. The social value of education and human capital. *Handbook of the Economics of Education, 1*, 459-509 (2006).
12. Clark, W. Employability skills in action? Evaluating the Career Development Centre Skills Award. In Learning and Teaching Symposium 2011: Learning Futures (2011).
13. Office for Standards in Education, Children's Services and Skills (OFSTED). *Good practice in involving employers in work-relate dedication and training* (2010).
14. Rosenberg, Stuart, Heimler, Ronald, and Morote, Elsa-Sofia. *Basic employability skills: A triangular design approach*. Education and Training, 54(1): pp. 7–20 (2012).
15. Omar, M.Z., Kofli, N.T., Mat, K., Darus, Z.M., Osman, S. A., Rahman, M.N. A., & Abdullah, S. *Employers' evaluation on attributes obtained during industrial training*. In Proceedings of the 7th WSEAS International Conference on Education and Educational Technology (EDU'08) (pp. 259–263) (2008).
16. Marchante, A.J., Ortego, B. and Pagan, R. *An Analysis of Educational Mismatch and Labor Mobility in the Hospitality Industry*. Journal of Hospitality and Tourism Research.299–318 (2011).
17. Gunn, V., Bell, S., & Kafmann, K. Thinking strategically about employability and graduate attributes: Universities and enhancing learning for beyond university. QAA Scotland. Retrieved June 11, 2017. (2010).
18. Mohamed, A., Isa, F. L. M., & Shafii, H. Kemahiran di kalangan graduan sebagai kriteriapenting pasaran tenaga kerja: kajian kes graduan fakulti kejuruteraan, UKM.In SeminarPendidikan Kejuruteraan dan Alam Bina (2007).
19. Krejcie, R. V., & Morgan, D. W. Determining sample size for research activities. *Educational and psychological measurement, 30*(3), 607-610 (1970).
20. Cohen, M. Research Methods in Education. Routledge; 7edition (April 28, 2011) (2011).

21. Creswell, J., & Clark, P. Designing and Conducting Mixed Methods Research (2nd edition). SAGE Publications, Inc. (2011).
22. Jones, W. Education and Employment .Expectations and Experiences of Students, Graduates and Employers. Lawrence Verry, Inc., River Road, CT06255 (1981).

Fraud Prevention in Government Procurement of Goods and Services

Maria Maria[1]([✉]), Muhammad Husni Mubarok[1], Jamaliah Said[2],
Darusalam Darusalam[2], Desi Indriasari[1], and Sarikadarwati Sarikadarwati[1]

[1] Accounting Department, State Polytechnic of Sriwijaya, Palembang, Indonesia
`mariamardjuki@polsri.ac.id`
[2] Accounting Research Institute & Faculty of Accountancy UiTM, Puncak Alam, Selangor,
Malaysia

Abstract. This study explores the prevention of government procurement fraud in Palembang city, which is thought to be related to the competency of the government apparatus and Internal Control System (SPI). This research was conducted empirically by involving 50 government units with an analysis of procurement actors (budget user powers, commitment-making officials, procurement officials, and election working groups. The data were analyzed by multiple regression techniques. The result, prevention of procurement fraud was influenced by the competency of government apparatus and SPI. Partially, the competency of the government apparatus did not influence the prevention of fraud.

Keywords: Fraud · Prevention · Goods and Services · Government

1 Introduction

One of the government's crucial roles is to ensure the availability of good facilities and infrastructures in fulfilling the community's needs. The government carries out goods and services procurement activities (PBJ) both at the central and regional levels with APBN/APBD funding and grants. At the regional level, the government holds goods and services through regional devices (OPD) ranging from planning, implementation, and reporting until goods can be utilized. A regulation related to the PBJ in Indonesia is [1], an update from [2].

Data Anti-Corruption Agency (KPK) until mid-2021 shows that the number of corruption cases in the procurement ranks the highest in bribery. According to KPK's report, in 2021 the most corruption cases occurred in the South Sumatra region with 30 cases [3]. The findings [4] indicated that PBJ related to Covid-19 in Indonesian handling was not performed in detail from the perspective of the budgeting aspect as well as its utilization. This condition didn't rule out the possibility of fraud.

Fraud as a global phenomenon universally has penetrated both the private as well as public sectors and no country that justifies this action [5]. Someone commits fraud to make a profit in various illegal ways including many kinds of intentional irregularities [6]. This has an impact on economic, legal, and human values aspects [7]. The number

R. Martini et al. (Eds.): FIRST 2022, ASSEHR 733, pp. 105–112, 2023.
https://doi.org/10.2991/978-2-38476-026-8_13

of fraud cases in the PBJ process surely indicates that internal control is very necessary to be conducted. Aside from that, the competency of government apparatus also holds a crucial role in preventing fraud.

Internal control has an important role in preventing fraud. This is as stated in [8], SPI is a process carried out by a group of people in an entity designed to provide adequate confidence. An effective SPI can prevent and complicate fraud. Examples are in the form of policies, personnel, planning, and procedures while soft control is in the form of integrity and ethical values. In the study result [9], a weak SPI can cause fraud. A better SPI for the government will make it easier to detect the occurrence of fraud. This study focuses on SPI and the competency of local apparatus in fraud prevention. This study is conducted in all local government agencies of Palembang city with the consideration that all local government agencies anywhere are involved in the procurement implementation.

2   Literature Review and Research Hypotheses

According to Basel Committee on Banking Supervision [7], fraud consists of internal and external fraud. Internal fraud happens when employees commit fraud in their organization. External fraud involves various schemes, including vendors, customers, or theft by the third-party [10.] Fraud prevention is an effort to reduce the chances of fraud occurring, decrease the opportunity for the occurrence of fraud, reduce pressure on the employees so that they can fulfill their needs, and remove excuses that justify or rationalize fraud being committed [11]. Furthermore, [11] defined fraud as an integrated effort to suppress the occurrence of factors that cause fraud, which is an opportunity, encouragement, and rationalization. Therefore, fraud prevention generally is a preventive effort performed intensively and integrated to prevent and minimize factors that may cause fraud. The fraud triangle [12], is stated that fraud occurs due to pressure, opportunity, and rationalization.

Fraud just like corruption in Indonesia has reached a critical point and this condition places Indonesia in a low position with a corruption perception index. Procurement fraud in the government may lower the public trust in the government. Fraud in procurement has spread widely all over the world, especially in developing countries [13, 14] Procurement by the government forces of the economy. Budget absorption through procurement is an important matter and is an area prone to corruption.

SPI is an approach aiming to ensure that the intended objective, goal, and mission are achieved for an organization [15]. Structured policies and actions an involved in ensuring the transactions are conducted correctly without loss, theft, or damage. Internal control ensures that the policy set by the management will improve data completeness and accuracy. In [16], it is stated that there are control environment, risk assessment, control activities, information, and communication, to monitoring activities.

SPI prevents/reduces occurrence of fraud in government procurement. SPI is a basic requirement that must be considered by every procurement entity in its management structure. The conducted studies [17] internal control has a positive correlation with fraud prevention. [18] concludes, fight fraud activities, presence of control is necessary. However, it is different from the results of the studies conducted by [19] and [20] that show SPI doesn't affect fraud prevention. Fraud happens because of the presence of opportunities.

Internal control ensures that the procurement process is carried out by following established rules [21]. Therefore, fraud prevention can be performed by minimizing the risk of fraud loss, through internal control design for someone who has the potential to commit fraud. Fraud cannot be entirely prevented but it can be detected in certain cases by implementing internal control.

H_1: SPI influences fraud prevention in the procurement

[22] stated that competency is an individual who knows (education, experience, skill) and ethical behavior in a creation. The competency of government apparatus and fraud prevention is based on the stewardship theory approach. This theory explains the interrelation between manager and owner (society), who trusted the public service manager to have good integrity; trusted, responsible, and honest. This theory views government as managers that possess the ability are ready to act, and the best function to provide the society's needs.

The concept in this theory is the trust an authorized party so that the government (steward) in an entity act as a good steward [23]. In this case, the government as the procurement agent will do its best to not commit any fraud in the procurement, thus resulting in procurements that are honest, fair, transparent, and free from fraud. As mandated in [24], competency is the ability of everyone's effort which includes: knowledge, skill, and attitude to work according to the set standard. The competency of government apparatus according to the [1] is that procurement officials, commitment officials, and selection working groups should have a certification (certified).

The competency of government apparatus becomes a vital component considering the ability of someone is the internal factor in performance achievement. Therefore, procurement requires skill or accountability of the government in managing the finances according to the mandate given to them. Government procurement agents are expected to be capable of handling their job, being honest, and not abusing their position.

H2: The competency of government apparatus influences fraud prevention in procurement.

3   Research Methodology

The study population is all regional devices in the Palembang city government totaling 51 regional devices. This study used a saturated sample technique. However, the data that can be processed (complete) is only 50 regional devices for analysis. The observation units are the powers of budget users, commitment-making officials, procurement officials, and election working groups.

The independent variable consists of the SPI and competency of the government apparatus. Dependent variable: fraud prevention. The competency of government apparatus consists of three dimensions: knowledge, experience, and skill [22]. Dimensions for SPI refer to [16] which consists of five components.

Fraud prevention dimensions include a legal framework, a transparent procedure in opening a tender, and evaluation in offering delegation of authority referring to the concept from [25]. This research uses an "ordinal" measurement scale with a 5-points

Table 1. Multiple Correlation Between SPI and Competency of Government Apparatus

Model Summary [b]				
Model	R	R2	Adjusted R2	Std. Error of the Estimate
1	.353[a]	.125	.087	2.00154

Likert scale. The Likert scale uses assessment which is summarized in "the interval data category" [26].

The result of multiple linear regression equation ICS and competency of government apparatus on fraud prevention:

$$Y = 12.146 + .541SPI + .038CGA$$

Y = Fraud Prevention (FP)
CGA = Competency of government apparatus
SPI = Internal Control System
α = Constant
β_1, β_2 = Regression coefficient of each variable that influences fraud prevention
ε = Other factors that are not studied.

4   Result and Discussion

From the result of the questionnaire distribution to 50 local agencies in the government of Palembang city, 229 respondents participated in this research. The age of the respondents was an age of 40–50 years (38.9%), with the last education averaging S_1 (58%). Length of work in the procurement field 3–4 years (30.13%.).

The result of the multiple correlation coefficient between SPI and the competency of government apparatus simultaneously on fraud prevention in the procurement government is as follows (Table 1).

Multiple correlations (R) in Table 1 show the low relationship (0.353) between SPI and competency of government apparatus simultaneously on fraud prevention in the procurement.The results of SPSS versus 25 assisted data processing (multiple regression):

Referring to Table 2, the regression equation form of the variable SPI and competency of government apparatus on fraud prevention is as follows:

$$Y = 12.146 + .541SPI + .038CGA$$

The results of the F test showed (3.349) > (3.20) in the F table with an α of 5%, SPI and competence together had a significant effect (0.044) with a positive direction towards fraud prevention.

After the test, the result of multiple correlations between SPI and competency of government apparatus simultaneously on fraud prevention is shown in Table 1. R value

Table 2. The Result of Multiple Regression Analysis

Coefficients [a]

Model	Unstandardized Coefficients		Standardized Coefficients	T	Sig.
	B	Std. Error	Beta		
(Constant)	12.146	5.426		2.239	.030
T.SPI	.541	.210	.359	2.579	.013
T.CGA	.038	.130	.041	.296	.768

of SPI and competency of government apparatus simultaneously on fraud prevention are 0.353. The determination coefficient of 12.5% indicates that SPI and the competency of the government apparatus simultaneously give a 12.5% effect on fraud prevention, while the rest of 87.5% is the effect of other factors aside from SPI and the competency of the government apparatus. The value is 2.01174 obtained from table t where $\alpha = 0.05$ with 47, df is for two-way testing. Testing criteria used: if the absolute value of t count > t table then H0 is rejected. If the absolute value of t count $\leq$ t table, then H0 is accepted.

T count the influence of SPI on fraud prevention in the procurement is 2.579, a significance of 0.13. Value t table is 2.01174, thus in an $\alpha = 5\%$ it is decided to accept Ha so that H0 is rejected. The result of the t-test for the competency of government apparatus on fraud prevention is 0.296 with a significance of 0.768. T count < t table, then an α 5%, is decided to accept H0 so that Ha is rejected. It can be concluded that the competency does not influence fraud prevention.

a. The Effect of SPI and Competency of Local Government Apparatus, on Fraud Prevention
   Simultaneously, SPI and competency of government apparatus contribute to fraud prevention in The procurement in Palembang city government with a percentage of 12.5%. Hypotheses testing shows a value (3.349) > (3.20). Therefore, simultaneously two components above significantly influence fraud prevention. However, the contribution of the SPI and the competence of the government apparatus is a low relationship with the interval of the correlation coefficient of 2%-39.9% being in a low category.

b. The Effect of SPI on Fraud Prevention
   Test result (table 3) shows a value of t count SPI on fraud prevention (2.579) > t table (2.01174). At α of 5%, it was decided to accept Ha. These results, SPI has a positive effect on fraud prevention. SPI with a grand mean of 3.568 means that the SPI for the procurement supports efforts to prevent fraud. The most dominant dimension of SPI is information and communication as well as the dimension of the control environment.

   The result of answer categorization shows that respondents answer high in the dimension of control environment with 64%, and very high 4%. On the dimension of information and communication, respondents' answers on the scale of high are 72%.

It proves the dominance of a controlled environment, information, and communication are strong dimensions. The result of this study is the same as the statement of [9], that if internal control is weak, it can cause fraud. The result of this study also by following the previous study [17], internal control has a positive and significant correlation with fraud prevention.

c. Effect of Competency of Government Apparatus on Fraud Prevention

The testing result (table 3) that the value t count competency of government apparatus on fraud prevention in the procurement of goods and services (0.296) lower than the t-table (2.01174) with a significance of 0.768. The result of this test shows that the competency of local government apparatus does not give a effect on fraud prevention. The competency of apparatus does not give an effect. Knowledge, experience, and skill of an individual does not reduce the occurrence of fraud. This is in line with a theory [12] that fraud is committed due to the presence of pressure, opportunity, as well as rationalization. The Bad condition of ethica culture can trigger the occurrence of fraud. The competency of individuals does not prevent them from fraud.

5   Conclusion

The SPI and competency of the local government apparatus are proven to give a influence on fraud prevention in the procurement in the Palembang city government. The result of this study contributes to the policymaker so that fraud in the procurement (legal framework, transparent procedure, opening tender documents, evaluation of an offer, a delegation of authority) can be anticipated as soon as possible. The procurement agents as government apparatus are expected to carry out their duty and function honestly, be sensitive to a community issue, and be responsible for the trust given by the public. The competency of local government apparatus needs to be improved in prioritizing ethical culture and implementation of culture from the aspects of assessment activities (policy and procedure) and information as well as communication (design in the performed operation).

References

1. Peraturan Presiden Republik Indonesia Nomor 12 Tahun 2021 tentang Perubahan atas Peraturan Presiden Nomor 16 tahun 2018 tentang Pengadaan Barang/Jasa Pemerintah.
2. Peraturan Presiden Republik Indonesia Nomor 16 Tahun 2018 Tentang Pengadaan Barang/Jasa Pemerintah.
3. V. A. Dihni, "Sumatera Selatan, Provinsi dengan Kasus Korupsi Terbanyak pada 2021," *Katadata*, Mar. 07, 2022. Accessed: Oct. 02, 2022. [Online]. Available:https://databoks.kat adata.co.id/datapublish/2022/03/07/sumateraselatan-provinsi-dengankasus-korupsi-terban yak-pada2021#:~:text=Sumatera%20Selatan%2C%20Provinsi%20dengan%20Kasus%20K orupsi%20Terbanyak%20pada%2021Poltik&text=Menurut%20laporan%20Komisi%20P emberantasan%20Korupsi,Selatan%20dengan%20jumlah%2030%20kasus.
4. W. Alamsyah, "Laporan Pemantauan Tren Penindakan Kasus Korupsi Semester I 2020," Indonesia Corruption Watch, Jakarta Selatan, Indonesia, 2020.

5. E. I. Okoye and D. O. Gbegi, "Forensic Accounting: A Tool for Fraud Detection and Prevention in the Public Sector. (A Study of Selected Ministries in Kogi State)," *International Journal of Academic Research in Business and Social Sciences*, vol. 3, no. 3, pp. 1–19, 2013, [Online]. Available: www.hrmars.com/journals

6. M. Kalubanga and P. Kakwezi, "Value for Money Auditing and Audit Evidence from a Procurement Perspective: A conceptual Paper Value for Money Auditing and Audit Evidence from a Procurement Perspective-A Conceptual Paper," vol. 2, pp. 5–115, 2013, [Online]. Available: www.managementjournal.info

7. A. Abdallah, M. A. Maarof, and A. Zainal, "Fraud detection system: A survey," *Journal of Network and Computer Applications*, vol. 68. Academic Press, pp. 90–113, Jun. 01, 2016. https://doi.org/10.1016/j.jnca.2016.04.007.

8. Peraturan Pemerintah Republik Indonesia Nomor 60 Tahun 2008 Tentang Sistem Pengendalian Intern Pemerintah.

9. R. Hamdani and A. R. Albar, "Internal controls in fraud prevention effort: A case study," *Jurnal Akuntansi & Auditing Indonesia*, vol. 20, no. 2, pp. 127–135, Dec. 2016, https://doi.org/10.20885/jaLi.vol20.iss2.art5.

10. S. Chen and A. Gangopadhyay, "A Novel Approach to Uncover Health Care Frauds through Spectral Analysis," in *2013 IEEE International Conference on Healthcare Informatics*, Sep. 2013, pp. 499–504. https://doi.org/10.1109/ICHI.2013.77.

11. IND-Pusdiklatwas BPKP, "Fraud Audit 2008," Badan Pengawasan Keuangan dan Pembangunan, Bogor, Indonesia, 2008.

12. D. R. Cressey, *Other people's Money: A Study in the Social Psychology of Embezzlement*. Montclair, New Jersey: Patterson Smith, 1973.

13. M. S. Iqbal and J.-W. Seo, "E-Governance as an Anti Corruption Tool: Korean Cases," *Journal of Korean Association for Regional Information Society*, vol. 11, no. 2, p. 5178, 2008, https://doi.org/10.22896/karis.2008.11.2.003.

14. V. Kumar, B. Mukerji, I. Butt, and A. Persaud, "Factors for Successful e-Government Adoption: a Conceptual Framework," *The Electronic Journal of e-Government*, vol. 5, no. 1, pp. 63–76, 2007, [Online]. Available: www.ejeg.com

15. Z. Rezaee, "What the COSO report means for internal auditors," *Managerial Auditing Journal*, vol. 10, no. 6, pp. 5–9, Aug. 1995, https://doi.org/10.1108/02686909510088350.

16. Committee of Sponsoring Organizations of the Treadway Commission (COSO), "Internal Control-Integrated Framework," Committee of Sponsoring Organizations of the Treadway Commission, Durham, UK, 2013.

17. O. N. Joseph, O. Albert, and J. Byaruhanga, "Effect of Internal Control on Fraud Detection and Prevention in District Treasuries of Kakamega County," *International Journal of Business and Management Invention*, vol. 4, no. 1, p. 4757, 2015, [Online]. Available: www.ijbmi.org

18. T. W. Singleton and A. J. Singleton, *Fraud Auditing and Forensic Accounting*, Fourth. New Jersey: Wiley, 2010. https://doi.org/10.1002/9781118269183.

19. A. Pandu Wicaksono, D. Urumsah, and F. Asmu, "The Implementation of E-procurement System: Indonesia Evidence," *SHS Web of Conferences*, vol. 34, p. 10004, Feb. 2017, https://doi.org/10.1051/shconf/20173410004.

20. K. M. Zakaria, A. Nawawi, and A. S. A. Puteh Salin, "Internal controls and fraud-empirical evidence from oil and gas company," *J Financ Crime*, vol. 23, no. 4, pp. 1154–1168, 2016, https://doi.org/10.1108/JFC-04-2016-0021.

21. J. M. Rendon and R. G. Rendon, "Procurement fraud in the US Department of Defense," *Managerial Auditing Journal*, vol. 31, no. 6/7, pp. 748–767, Jun. 2016, https://doi.org/10.1108/MAJ-11-2015-1267.

22. R. H. Cheng, J. H. Engstrom, and S. C. Kattelus, "Educating Government Financial Managers: University Collaboration between Business and Public Administration," *Journal of Government Financial Management*, vol. 51, no. 3, pp. 10–15, 2002.

23. R. Bernstein, K. Buse, and D. Bilimoria, "Revisiting Agency and Stewardship Theories," *Nonprofit Manag Leadersh*, vol. 26, no. 4, pp. 489–498, Jun. 2016, https://doi.org/10.1002/nml.21199.
24. Undang-undang Rapublik Indonesia Nomoe 13 Tahun 2003 Tentang Ketenagakerjaan.
25. T. M. Tuanakotta, *Akuntansi Forensik dan Audit Investigatif*. Jakarta: Salemba Empat, 2010.
26. D. R. Cooper and P. S. Schindler, *Metode Penelitian Bisnis Edisi 12 Buku 1*, 12th ed. Jakarta: Salemba Empat, 2017.

Implementation of Promotional Videos in the Tourism Industry: Is It Possible to Increase Local Revenue in the Digital Economy?

Riana Mayasari[1]($\boxtimes$), Indri Ariyanti[2], Fithri Selva Jumeilah[3],
and Indriani Indah Astuti[1]

[1] Department of Accounting, Politeknik Negeri Sriwijaya, Palembang, Indonesia
`riana.mayasari@polsri.ac.id`
[2] Department of Informatics Management, Politeknik Negeri Sriwijaya, Palembang, Indonesia
[3] Departement of Computer Engineering, Politeknik Negeri Sriwijaya, Palembang, Indonesia

Abstract. This research was aimed to see the contribution of tourism sector local revenue to total LOSR. This research is applied research to consolidate previous research to solve a problem. Data collection techniques were carried out through documentation, interviews and observation. The data obtained were quantitative and qualitative data. Documentation was done by calculating the potential of LOSR in the tourism sector, interviews were carried out with the government of the city of Pagaralam, observations were made at the data collection location with real conditions. The results of this study showed that Pagaralam City's LOSR was 116.27% for the 2019–2021 period. The average contribution of the Tourism sector to LOSR was 3,63% in 2019, 1,80% in 2020, and 4,15% in 2021 with an average 3,19%. in three years. The small contribution of the tourism sector is due to the absence of good and digital-based tourism promotion activities. a strategy to increase local revenue is through promotional innovations using media with motion graphic techniques. It is expected that this applied research will be a solution to the problems experienced by the government of Pagaralam in increasing LOSR from tourism sector.

Keywords: motion graphic · tourism · local revenue · video

1 Introduction

Tourism is one of the sectors that can encourage economic improvement in an area. Tourism has a significant impact on the development of a region, particularly in increasing domestic and foreign tourists who visit various tourist destinations in Indonesia such as mountains and seas which are known for their many natural beauties. Not only that, tourism in Indonesia is also known for its friendly community and various kinds of customs and cultures.

According to some, the pariwisat world is the best way to increase profits for both local and regional governments. This is in line with Law No. 10 of 2009 on Tourism

R. Martini et al. (Eds.): FIRST 2022, ASSEHR 733, pp. 113–125, 2023.
https://doi.org/10.2991/978-2-38476-026-8_14

which states that the implementation of tourism aims to increase national income for the well-being and prosperity of the people, expand employment opportunities, promote regional development, introduce and take advantage of tourism objects and attractions in Indonesia and foster community spirit, love of the country and strengthen ties between nation.

In Indonesia, Pagaralam City is a popular tourist destination in the province of South Sumatra. The tourism industry is a top priority for the Pagaralam City Government. It is anticipated that this industry will be able to boost local Own-Source Revenue (LOSR). The city of Pagaralam has sources of LOSR that come from various sources. The tourism industry is one of the LOSR Pagaralam's sources. The restaurant tax, hotel tax, entertainment tax, levies for recreation and sports facilities, and fees for lodging/restaurants/villas all contribute to LOSR in the tourism industry. According to the Pagaralam Town Budget Realization Report, the average contribution of LOSR in the tourism industry during the previous three years, the contribution of LOSR in Pagaralam Town to the total LOSR has not yet had the intended impact. 3.0 years, not to exceed 2.5 percent of the entire LOSR.

Badung Regency is one of the comparisons for tourism districts/cities in Indonesia that have a high LOSR in the tourism sector. In 2010, the contribution from the trade, hotel, and restaurant sectors was 45.68% of Badung Regency's GDP, and in 2016, the tourism sector accounted for more than 70% of Badung Regency's LOSR. According to the distribution of the nine sectors in PDRB, Badung Regency's primary industry is tourism [1].

The lack of promotion of the tourism sector in Pagaralam Town is the main obstacle. A proper promotional strategy is needed to overcome these obstacles. Promotion and publicity aims to increase the number of visitors who come to Pagaralam, in addition, tourists can also get an overview related to Pagaralam tourism, get information about support facilities, and as a communication tool between tourists and managers of the Pagaralam tourism sector. One of the effective digital promotion media is the motion graphics tourism promotion video. In this regard, the media should be able to provide information that can reach all lines so that tourists are aware of Kota Pagaralam's potential as a tourist destination. From the background description above, it can be seen the importance of tourism promotion innovation with motion graphics techniques to become a forum to promote mountain tourism, historical sites, waterfalls, and even the culinary art of Pagaralam city, which leads to an increase in the tourism sector's LOSR contribution.

According to [2] the original income of the district is the income obtained by the district from the receipt of district taxes, district levies, profits of district enterprises, and others that are legal. In addition, the entire tourism-related activity is multidimensional and multidisciplinary, expressing the requirements of every nation and individual, as well as the interactions between tourists, other tourists, the government, and locals, as well as between tourists and the community. This is the concept of tourism. entrepreneurs and the government [3]. In addition, the Logical model is a performance measurement tool to explain and evaluate the effectiveness of the organization's work program [4]. Also, the Logical model discusses the relationship between organizational resources such as resources, activities, outputs, outcomes related to special situations. In addition, in his last assignment stated that motion graphics are pieces of visual media that are time-based and combine film and graphic design to generate interest and revenue [5]. This can be achieved by incorporating music, video, film, typography, illustration, 2D and 3D animation, and other elements. In addition, the goal of promotion is to educate, persuade, and remind potential customers about the business and its marketing strategy [6]. The purpose of this creative design is to influence the audience that uses motion graphic media so that the required aesthetics involve the senses of hearing and vision that are designed as attractively as possible so that the information conveyed can be fully understood by the target audience.

According to the problem's formulation, the question posed in this study is, "What strategy will the Government of Pagaralam City use in an effort to increase LOSR through tourist attractions?" and how can motion graphics-based promotional innovations contribute to an increase in local tourism revenue? The evaluation of the use of tourism promotion videos in motion graphics is the subject of this study's proposed scope. This research is limited to the tourism area of Kota Pagaralam. The tourism industry, which has an impact on the Pagaralam Regional Finance Agency's management of local revenue, is the primary focus of this study. This study aims to evaluate the Pagaralam City Government's tourism sector programs and activities using a logic model, and design strategies and project promotional innovation strategies that can increase Pagaralam City's local revenue. The problem's formulation from the perspective of the background and the objectives of the study show that this study is very important, because this study is able to review the condition of Pagaralam City, especially regarding the use of tourism promotion videos with motion graphics techniques to improve Pagaralam. City LOSR.

2   Literature Study

2.1   Local Revenue of the Tourism Sector

The study conducted [7] aims to determine how the tourism industry region's financial performance is affected by and the health of the district/city community in Bali Province (2001–2010). Secondary data from the Financial Bureau of the Bali Provincial Secretariat and this study made use of the Bali Province's Central Statistics Agency (BPS). Path analysis and factor analysis are the methods of analysis employed. This study concludes that the travel industry area altogether affects the monetary presentation of the locale and the prosperity of the region/city local area in Bali Territory in the years 2001–2010. Additionally, this study revealed that the district/city community's well-being is significantly influenced by the region's financial performance in Bali Province. Through path analysis, It is common knowledge that Bali Province's districts' and cities' financial performance is influenced by the tourism industry, which has an indirect effect on people's well-being.

2.2   Motion Graphic

According to [8] visual media today have an undeniable role in society, and here with the target audience, the development of motion graphics as a new tool coincides with the growing importance of media like television, film, and the internet. Along with

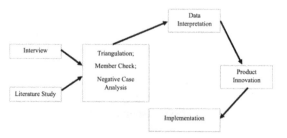

Fig. 1. Research Flow Chart

the development of industries such as advertising, cinema, games and music, motion graphics has strengthened its position in these industries and faced expectations. Taking advantage of the special techniques and properties of motion graphics to achieve useful communication is very important and justifies the need for research on motion graphics. In recent years, the network with visual media orientation and audience appeal has grown rapidly, additionally, motion graphics play a role in the fields of culture and art, and they have evolved into brand-new works of art. Considering the role of motion graphics as a brand-new means of communication, this study tries to answer this question so that whether the study is effective. Regarding the importance of this subject, evaluate and analyze the role of motion graphics as a new subfield of graphic design for enhancing visual communication efficiency (Fig. 1).

3 Research Methodology

3.1 Research Rationality

Rational research uses case study methods that look for meaning, investigate procedures and acquire a comprehensive comprehension of people, groups, or circumstances. This study took place in Pagaralam City in South Sumatra. One of the cities that was established as a result of Law No. 8 of 2001 (State Gazette of the Republic of Indonesia Year 2001 Number 88, Supplement to the State Gazette of the Republic of Indonesia Number 4115) is Kota Pagar Alam, which is found in the South Sumatra Province. Before this, Kota Pagar Alam was a part of the Lahat Regency as an administrative city. Kota Pagar Alam is a town in the Province of South Sumatra.

3.2 Types of Research

This type of research is a type of applied research. This research is a research that is the research that was carried out is applied research. This study aims to find a solution to a problem that is directly faced by the community [9]. This research aims to answer specific questions aimed at solving practical problems [10]. This applied research is called empirical, because it tries to apply the knowledge obtained with the idea of unifying knowledge to solve a situation [11]. That is, it is anticipated that the study's findings will be implemented immediately. An evaluation study is a type of applied research design like this one, this research is research that has the purpose of doing evaluation at every stage carried out in the research, starting from planning, implementation, to results [12].

3.3 Data Collection

This activity is conducted through Observation, Documentation, and Interviews. Observation activities are carried out by filling in the observation blanks. Documentation will be done by taking financial data from regional financial agencies. Expert informants were questioned in depth and semi-structured during the interviews.

This study uses several techniques to collect data, including:

Interview

An interview is a method of gathering data in which data is directly obtained from data sources through conversation. [13]. An in-depth interview is the method of the interview. Utilizing expert/face analysis techniques to select interviewees, which are people or experts who are directly involved in the preparation of programs and activities [14].

Documents

A record of past events is a document. Reports can be as compositions, pictures, or fantastic works from somebody that fits the exploration topic [15]. Interview findings will be more reliable if they are backed up by previous documents. The Local Government Realized Budget (LGRB) is the document used in this study.

3.4 Data Validity Test

This study's data were checked for validity by:

Credibility Test

A test of credibility that also measures accuracy. Credibility is a measure of how true the collected data are. It shows how well the researcher's ideas match the study's findings. The completeness of the data gathered from a variety of sources is used to assess the credibility of the data [16].

Triangulation

Triangulation is a method of collecting data that combines various approaches and data sources. Using a variety of approaches and data sources, the objective is to collect data and validate its veracity.

Source Triangulation

The process of obtaining data from multiple sources using the same method is known as source triangulation. In this study, the Head of the Financial Agency for the Kota Pagaralam Region will be the subject the data test. The researcher's examination of the data will lead to a conclusion that is confirmed by the three data sources.

Triangulation Technique

The process of applying various data disclosure techniques to data sources is known as technical triangulation. Various triangulation methods can be used to assess the data's veracity [17].

Time Triangulation
Data credibility testing is done by time triangulation by collecting data at different times [16].

Member Review
The process of rechecking the data with respondents regarding the validity of the obtained data to determine the extent to which the obtained data is consistent with what was provided by the data provider is referred to as checking the credibility of the data by member checking. If the data provider agrees with it, the data is valid [16].

Transferability Test
Transferability is external validity in quantitative research. External validity shows the level of accuracy and applicability of the findings of the study to the population from which the sample was taken [15].

Data and Information Analysis Techniques
Quantitative Data Analysis Techniques
Analysis of quantitative data is used in this study to assess the region's financial independence based on the acquisition of LOSR resources in the tourism sector to the total LOSR. The assessment of regional financial independence is also used as a tool to see the effectiveness of the realization of the planned LOSR targets.

Qualitative Data Analysis Techniques
Data analysis techniques use logical models to analyze correlations between resources, activities, outputs, results related to special situations. In addition to using a logical model, this study also uses the four-quadrant-friedman analysis performance measurement approach. Friedman's four-quadrant analysis is a combination of two different perspectives to produce categories [18].

A thematic analysis approach was used as the data analysis tool to examine the interview results in relation to the preparation of the Pagaralam City Government's programs and activities for empowering the tourism sector. Data can be analyzed, identified, and thematic patterns can be reported using the method of thematic analysis [19].

3.5 Techniques for Interpreting and Drawing Research Conclusion

Techniques used in interpreting and drawing conclusions using coding techniques. The use of coding techniques to process qualitative data from interviews. The researcher uses the coding method to collect and draw conclusions from the psychological analysis of the obtained data, as well as to get an overview of the facts as a qualitative data analysis unit [20]. Examples of data formats include email correspondence, Field notes, documents, literature, artifacts, photographs, videos, websites, and interview transcripts from participant observation the three coding techniques utilized are as follows: selective coding, open coding, and axial coding [21] (Fig. 2).

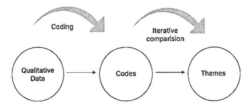

Fig. 2. Level of Thematic Analysis

Qualitative data obtained from students' written answers were analyzed using thematic analysis techniques. Thematic analysis was carried out through six stages, namely (1) getting familiar with the data; (2) create initial code; (3) build themes; (4) examining the themes produced; (5) define.

3.6 Data Analysis

Data analysis is done using a mixed method that is by combining quantitative and qualitative methods. Quantitative data analysis by measuring the gap ratio in the region's financial capacity and independence, the documents analyzed is LGRB. Qualitative data analysis by using logical models to analyze the relationship between resources, activities, outputs, decisions related to special situations. In addition to using a logical model, this study also uses another performance measurement approach, which is the four-quadrant-Friedman analysis. Examination of the meeting results utilizing topical examination which is to dissect the subjects in the meetings connected with the readiness of projects and exercises of the Pagaralam Regional Government in engaging the travel industry area.

4   Results and Discussion

4.1 Results

Contribution of the Tourism Sector
Based upon the 2019–2020 Budget Realization Report of the Kota Pagaralam Government later the realization of LOSR receipts obtained results as shown in Table 1.

According to Table 1, the Pagaralam City LOSR income realization is 116.27% for the period 2019–2021. In 2019 the average LOSR income realization is 122.81%, in 2020 by 113.26% and in 2021 by 112.73%. LOSR is divided into Provincial Tax Revenue, Provincial Retribution Revenue, Revenue from Separate Regional Wealth Management and Other Legal LOSR.

LOSR Pagaralam is divided into several sectors, one of which is the travel industry. LOSR contribution of the tourism sector to the realization of Pagaralam City LOSR as shown in Table 2.

Table 2 shows that the contribution of the tourism sector to LOSR is still not able to support the operations of the Pagaralam City government. The average contribution

Table 1. Percentage of Regional Revenue Realized by the Pagaralam City Government 2019.2021 Period

Description	Years		
	2019	2020	2021
Local Own-source Revenue-Realized Budget	122,81%	113,26%	112,73%
Local Tax Revenue-Realized Budget	105,45%	97,52%	99,70%
Region Retribution Income-Realized Budget	116,45%	127,74%	94,93%
Revenue from Separated Regional Wealth Management - Realized Budget	100,00%	100,10%	113,54%
Other Legitimate of LOSR- Realized Budget	131,34%	120,71%	118,24%

Sources: processed data, 2022

Table 2. Contribution of Tourism Sector Income to Total LOSR

Description of LOSR in the Tourism Sector	Comparison of Total LOSR		
	2019	2020	2021
Hotel Tax	0,82%	0,29%	0,65%
Restaurant Tax	0,31%	0,21%	0,45%
Entertainment Tax	0,05%	0,02%	0,06%
Advertisement Tax	0,22%	0,17%	0,35%
Retribution for Use of Regional Wealth	1,83%	0,80%	0,37%
Special Parking Retribution	0,11%	0,08%	0,17%
Retribution for Lodging and Villa	0,00%	0,00%	1,68%
Recreational and Sports Place Retribution	0,24%	0,18%	0,36%
Retribution for Sales of Regional Business Production	0,05%	0,04%	0,06%

Sources: processed data, 2022

of LOSR in the tourism sector to the total LOSR is 3.63% in 2019, 1.80% in 2020 and 4.15% in 2021. In the period 2019.2021 the average obtained is 3, 19% contribution of the tourism sector to the total LOSR.

Interview Analysis

Interviews were conducted with state civil servants working in the Pagaralam City government. In the interview, informants who know directly related to tourism and regional finance were selected. The data of the informants who were interviewed are described in Table 3.

Informants were selected by prioritizing triangulation

The region's low income is due to the low number of tourist visits. This is expressed in the following interview results:

Table 3. Informant Data for Interview

Latest Education	Working Experience	Age	Gender	Informant Number
Master Degree	15 Years	39 y.o	Men	Informant 1
Master Degree	20 Years	50 y.o	Men	Informant 2
Bachelor Degree	12 Years	40 y.o	Women	Informant 3

Sources: processed data, 2022

"Yes, bud, so far the local income of Bandar Pagaralam is quite low, especially from the tourism sector. The reason is that tourist visits to tourist attractions in Pagaralam are not too many" (Informant 1)

The results of the interview of informant 1 above show that the level of achievement of the tourism sector in Pagaralam Town is still not optimal. This is because tourist visits at various tourist sites in Pagaralam Town are still low.

The opinion of informant 1 above is reinforced by the opinion of informant 2. That is:

"Hmmm. The Regional Native Income in Pagaralam is now declining sharply, right Riana. So far, it's been quite good, but after this epidemic it has become very bad. Because there are no visitors in our tour". (Informant 2)

The results of the interview with the second informant confirmed that the LOSR contribution of the Tourism Sector in Pagaralam Town tends to be low. Especially during the pandemic, so the government thinks it is still far from the targeted amount.

While the results of the 3rd informant's interview show that it is in line with the opinions of informants 1 and 2, namely:

"As far as I can see bro. Pagaralam Town's local income in the tourism sector tends to be low because tourism promotion is relatively minimal. We feel that we really need qualified tourism promotion to cover a wider market" (informant 3)

The results of this interview with the third informant show that the Pagaralam City tourism sector still needs a breakthrough in tourism promotion and a good tourism promotion media. This is believed to be able to increase tourist visits to Pagaralam Town in the future.

In addition to interviewing the three informants regarding the low arrival of tourists in Pagaralam Town. Researchers too conduct an interview process related to the need for a promotional video to increase LOSR Kota Pagaralam, which is as follows:

"Ehhhhh, tourist visits so far only depend on word-of-mouth promotion and IG postings from the public. We do not have special tourism promotion media yet. I think if there is promotional media through tourism promotion videos, it is very good" (Informant 1)

Based on the above-mentioned interview results with informant 1, the Tourism Sector of Pagaralam City is in dire need of promotional media in the form of promotional videos. It is anticipated that this will be able to boost both the number of tourist visits and the LOSR contribution to the Pagaralam City tourism industry. The results of the next interview were conducted with the second informant, where the opinion of the second informant was also in line with the opinion of the first informant. namely:

"Yes, personally, I really want a promotional video for this special Pagaralam tour. Hehehehe. If I say a tourism promotion video, it is faster to spread information about our tourism location throughout Indonesia, not just in South Sumatra." (Informant 2)

In view of the consequences of the meeting above, stating the need for tourism promotion videos is considered quite urgent. The implementation of a tourism promotion video in Pagaralam City is believed to be able to increase tourist visits, whether local or national based on the interview with the third informant's findings. Showing the need for tourism promotion videos in the Pagaralam the travel industry area is supposed to have the option to increase tourism LOSR contributions. That is as follows:

"We have been planning for a long time to create various digital tourism promotion media, but until now that matter has not been realized. Hehehehe. I wonder why. This is because our human resources have not focused on that yet. For example, if there is a human resource, especially if it is assisted by the university, it will be very useful. The benefits are many, of course there will be more tourist visits and certainly our LOSR will increase." (Informant 3)

Both are related to the low contribution of, according to the findings of the interviews with the three informants LOSR in the tourism sector and the need for tourism promotion media in the form of promotional videos showing the need for the implementation of motion graphics tourism promotion. Video is very necessary and quite urgent to support and increase tourist visits at various tourist sites in Pagaralam Town. Increase in tourist visits in various. This tourist location is believed to be able to increase LOSR contribution from the Pagaralam tourism sector.

4.2 Discussion

The collection of LOSR carried out by the local government in Pagaralam City based on the data in this study has been carried out well. The average income of the tourism sector in this study shows that it is still not able to contribute much to LOSR. This study is in accordance with the aftereffects of the review led by [22] with the review area in Bali. A similar study, titled "Community involvement and tourism revenue sharing as a contributing factor to the United Nations Sustainable Development Goals in Jozani–Chwaka Bay National Park and Biosphere Reserve, Zanzibar," was also carried out by [23]. which has similar similarities. results to the results of this study so that these two studies as a reinforcement of the results obtained.

The tourism sector in Pagaralam City contributes to the total local income of around 3.19% of the total in the period from 2019 to 2021. The total income of the tourism sector for the period from 2019 to 2021 is Rp6.120.044.853,-. The contribution of the tourism sector is very small because the Pagaralam City Government does not systematically promote tourism in accordance with the digital economy era. 17 years since Pagaralam became a tourist destination: How can the tourism industry help local governments make more money? also has the same result, which is a small contribution of the tourism sector to LOSR. In addition, this research is also supported by previous research titled Tourism Development Strategy in the Context of Increasing Natural Income of the District in Kuningan Regency which was studied by [25].

The results of the interviews in this research can be used as the main theme, which is that the development of the regional tourism sector needs to be supported with good promotional activities. One thing that can be done is to use digital marketing in the form of videos that can represent superior tourism in Pagaralam City. Through promotional videos, the public will learn about interesting tourist destinations, historical sites and local wisdom to visit. The findings concur with the research. titled Promotional Video Design About Tourism Information In Karimun conducted by [26]. In addition, this study is also supported by a previous study conducted by [27] related to the Making of Promotional Videos of Educational Tourism Objects with a research site in Meru Betiri National Park.

The amalgamation of previous studies related to tourism promotion by [28] agreed on the importance of tourism promotion. Promotion through video is one of the good forms of promotion according to [29]. Motion graphic is a moving graphic media that can be used as a video explanation that can explain a situation [8]. Referring to previous studies, the use of motion graphics as tourism promotion media in Pagaralam City is one of the best choices that has been carried out by in-depth scientific studies.

5   Conclusion

In light of the outcomes and conversation of this review, it tends to be presumed that the Pagaralam City Government already knows how to optimize the income of the tourism sector through the use of promotional videos. The promotional technique used is making tourism videos with motion graphics techniques that are claimed to be able to represent superior tourism in Pagaralam town. The implications of this study are expected to optimize regional income. Future research is recommended to examine tourism promotion techniques from various digital points of view.

Acknowledgments. This research can be carried out through the Innovation Task Research funding scheme which is sourced from State non-tax revenue at the national level Fund of Politeknik Negeri Sriwijaya and the contribution of research partners, namely the Local Government Finance Office of the Pagaralam City. All forms and conclusions in this study are the responsibility of the research team and are not representations, views or attitudes of Politeknik Negeri Sriwijaya and the Research Partner of the Kota Pagaralam Regional Financial Agency.

References

1. "Badung Regency Central Bureau of Statistics," Badung, 2012.
2. J. Machmud and L. I. Radjak, "Pendapatan Asli Daerah, Dana Alokasi Umum Dan Dana Alokasi Khusus Terhadap Kinerja Keuangan Pemerintah Kabupaten Gorontalo," *J. Account. Sci.*, 2018, [Online]. Available: http://ojs.umsida.ac.id/index.php/jas/article/view/1106.
3. W. Purnomowati and Ismini, "Konsep Smart City Dan Pengembangan Pariwisata," *J. JIBEKA*, 2014.
4. M. E. Kalu and K. E. Norman, "Step by step process from logic model to case study method as an approach to educational programme evaluation," *Glob. J. Educ. Res.*, vol. 17, no. 1, pp. 73–85, 2018.

5. J. Febriantoko and H. Rotama, "Evaluasi Potensi Penerimaan Pendapatan Asli Daerah Bidang Pariwisata di Indonesia," *Ekuivalensi*, vol. 4, no. 2, pp. 1–15, 2018, [Online]. Available: http://ejournal.kahuripan.ac.id/index.php/Ekuivalensi.

6. R. Yung, C. Khoo-Lattimore, and L. E. Potter, "Virtual reality and tourism marketing: Conceptualizing a framework on presence, emotion, and intention," *Curr. Issues Tour.*, vol. 24, no. 11, pp. 1505–1525, 2021.

7. K. Widiastuti, "Pengaruh Sektor Pariwisata Terhadap Kinerja Keuangan Daerah Dan Kesejahteraan Masyarakat Kabupaten/Kota Di Provinsi Bali," *J. Ekon. dan Bisnis Indones.*, vol. 02, 2012.

8. S. M. Rozaq, E. Poerbaningtyas, and R. Nurfitri, "Perancangan Motion Graphic Wisata Edukasi Di Desa Sumbergondo Dengan Teknik Penggabungan Animasi 2d Dan 3d," *MAVIS J. Desain Komun. Vis.*, vol. 4, no. 01, pp. 33–46, 2022.

9. G. Guest, E. E. Namey, and M. L. Mitchell, *Collecting qualitative data: A field manual for applied research.* Sage, 2013.

10. M. Baimyrzaeva, "Beginners' Guide for Applied Research Process: What Is It, and Why and How to Do It," *Univ. Cent. Asia*, vol. 4, no. 8, 2018.

11. T. A. Brown, *Confirmatory factor analysis for applied research.* Guilford publications, 2015.

12. R. A. Krueger, *Focus groups: A practical guide for applied research.* Sage publications, 2014.

13. J. F. Gubrium and J., Holstein, "SAGE: The SAGE Handbook of Interview Research: The Complexity of the Craft: Second Edition: 9781412981644," in *The SAGE Handbook of Interview Research: The Complexity of the Craft*, 2012.

14. P. J. Elmer and D. M. Borowski, "Expert Analysis: System of S&L Bankruptcy," *An Expert Syst. Approach to Financ. Anal.*, 2011.

15. P. D. Sugiyono, "Metode Penelitian Bisnis: Pendekatan Kuantitatif, Kualitatif, Kombinasi, dan R&D," *Penerbit CV. Alf. Bandung*, 2017.

16. Satori dan Komariah, "Metodologi penelitian kualitatif," 2009.

17. N. K. Denzin, "Triangulation 2.0*," *J. Mix. Methods Res.*, 2012, doi: https://doi.org/10.1177/1558689812437186.

18. M. Friedman, *Trying Hard is Not Good Enough : How to Produce measurable Improvements for Customers and Communications.* FPSI Publishing, 2009.

19. V. Braun and V. Clarke, "Thematic analysis," *J. Posit. Psychol.*, 2016, doi: https://doi.org/10.1037/13620-004.

20. M. Baralt, "Coding Qualitative Data," in *Research Methods in Second Language Acquisition: A Practical Guide*, 2012, pp. 222–244.

21. M. B. Miles, A. M. Huberman, and J. Saldana, "Qualitative data analysis: A methods sourcebook." triveniturbines.id, 2014, [Online]. Available: https://triveniturbines.id/sites/default/files/webform/qualitative-data-analysis-a-methods-sourcebook-matthew-b-miles-a-michael-huberman-johnny-saldaa-pdf-download-free-book-dc0f646.pdf.

22. I. P. Anoma, I. Mahaganggab, and I. B. Suryawanc, "Emerging transdisciplinary theory on tourism research: A case from Bali," *practice*, vol. 11, no. 1, pp. 390–404, 2020.

23. F. Carius and H. Job, "Community involvement and tourism revenue sharing as contributing factors to the UN Sustainable Development Goals in Jozani–Chwaka Bay National Park and Biosphere Reserve, Zanzibar," *J. Sustain. Tour.*, vol. 27, no. 6, pp. 826–846, 2019.

24. J. Febriantoko and R. Mayasari, "17 Years of Establishment of Pagaralam as a Tourism City: How is the Tourism Sector's Ability to Increase Original Local Government Revenue ?," *Int. J. Sci. Eng. Sci.*, vol. 2, no. 9, pp. 61–64, 2018, [Online]. Available: http://ijses.com/wp-content/uploads/2018/10/98-IJSES-V2N9.pdf.

25. R. Masruroh and N. Nurhayati, "Strategi Pengembangan Pariwisata dalam Rangka Peningkatan Pendapatan Asli Daerah di Kabupaten Kuningan," in *Prosiding Seminar Nasional IPTEK Terapan (SENIT) 2016 Pengembangan Sumber Daya Lokal Berbasis IPTEK*, 2016, vol. 1, no. 1.

26. M. Siahaan and O. Oktavina, "Promotional Video Design About Tourism Information in Karimun," in *CoMBInES-Conference on Management, Business, Innovation, Education and Social Sciences*, 2022, vol. 2, no. 1, pp. 200–205.

27. P. W. P. Wardani, "Making A Video Promotional Of Educational Tourism Object In Meru Betiri National Park." Politeknik Negeri Jember, 2020.

28. P. Kumar, J. M. Mishra, and Y. V. Rao, "Analysing tourism destination promotion through Facebook by Destination Marketing Organizations of India," *Curr. Issues Tour.*, vol. 25, no. 9, pp. 1416–1431, 2022.

29. X. Chenchen, Z. Yurong, H. Die, and X. Zhenqiang, "The impact of tik tok video marketing on tourist destination image cognition and tourism intention," in *2020 International Workshop on Electronic Communication and Artificial Intelligence (IWECAI)*, 2020, pp. 116–119.

Evaluation of Tourism Business Activities and Multi-sectoral Income Optimization: Case in Pagaralam City, South Sumatra

Jovan Febriantoko[1]([✉]), Desi Indriasari[1], M. Sang Gumilar Panca Putra[2], and Rio Marpen[2]

[1] Department of Accounting, Politeknik Negeri Sriwijaya, Palembang, Indonesia
`jovan.febriantoko@polsri.ac.id`
[2] Department of Civil Engineering, Politeknik Negeri Sriwijaya, Palembang, Indonesia

Abstract. The motivation behind this assessment study was to learn the variables that assistance or block the enhancement of nearby income in the travel industry area, both formal and casual, in Pagaralam City by deciding the utilization of room and the spatial construction of the district. This study is significant because it examined the state of Pagaralam, particularly its use of space and spatial structure, with the goal of increasing income in both the formal and informal sectors. Initial observation, data collection, data analysis, and drawing conclusions were the stages of the study. This study utilized the contextual analysis strategy. This kind of research used a combination of quantitative and qualitative methods. Methods used to collect data include: techniques for in-depth, semi-structured interviews, the selection of informants, and expert analysis. The Financial Ratio and BMC were the methods of data analysis that were utilized in this study.The results showed that the comparison average of LOSR in the tourism sector to total LOSR was 0,0040 for the 2019 period, 0,0020 for the 2020 period and 0,0046 for the 2021 period. The solution can be drawn for optimizing regional income through the creation of a comprehensive tourism with scientific modeling of GIS.

Keywords: BMC · LOSR · tourism · GIS

1 Introduction

The Covid-19 pandemic has impacted all aspects of life, especially for Indonesia. Many sectors have been affected by the Covid-19 pandemic, one of which is the economic sector. The economy as the driving wheel of people's lives is supported by various aspects, one of which is SMEs. Small and medium-sized organizations (SMEs) in Indonesia have been seriously impacted by the Coronavirus pandemic, especially in the travel industry.This sector is experiencing decline in both small and large entrepreneurs due to unstable income.

One area that is very likely to support the economy of a region is tourism. In improving the region's economy, of course independence from the surrounding community is essential so that the achievement targets that have been set can be achieved. The tourism

R. Martini et al. (Eds.): FIRST 2022, ASSEHR 733, pp. 126–136, 2023.
https://doi.org/10.2991/978-2-38476-026-8_15

sector is now showing a very significant development, It is evident from the large number of individuals who consider traveling to be an essential need that must be satisfied.

The community and the government will benefit greatly from the growth of tourism in a region. However, the development will encounter a number of issues that make it challenging and even harmful to the community if it is not properly planned and managed. Endeavors to guarantee that travel industry can foster well and reasonably and carry advantages to people as well as limit the pessimistic effect that might emerge, the travel industry improvement should be gone before by a top to bottom review that is by leading examination on all wellsprings of help.

The intended resources consist of natural resources, cultural resources, and human resources. Kota Pagaralam is one of the most attractive tourist areas in Indonesia, Kota Pagaralam is part of the South Sumatra region. The main target of the community when visiting Pagaralam City is to travel. Based on the beauty of the landscape, it is hoped that Pagaralam City will have good income growth in the formal and informal sectors. The growth of the tourism industry contributes to an increase in Pagaralam City's LOSR resources in terms of hotel, entertainment, restaurant and hotel taxes retribution. The Realized Budget (RB) shows that Pagaralam Town is contributed by the tourism sector and it is also proven that the average LOSR contribution in Pagaralam Town's tourism sector over the past three years is not too high which is only 2.5%.

The writer's formulation of the problem that will be presented is based on the above description of the background, (1) how is the Utilization of Space and Structure of the City of Pagaralam implemented?; (2) which aspects of Kota Pagaralam's formal and informal sectors support or hinder regional natural income optimization?

The scope of research proposed in this study is related to the Evaluation of Space Use and Regional Spatial Structure in the form of Geographical Information Systems. This research is limited to the administrative area of Kota Pagaralam Government. The tourism industry, which influences Pagaralam City Regional Finance Agency's management of local revenue, is the primary focus of this study. The objectives of this innovation assignment study are (1) to evaluate the City of Pagaralam Government's use of space and regional spatial structure; (2) Recognizing the aspects of Pagaralam City's formal and informal sectors that both help and hinder the optimization of the Tourism Sector District's natural income.

Seen from the background, the study's formulation of the problem and objectives demonstrate its significance because this study is able to review the condition of Kota Pagaralam, especially regarding the use of space and the structure of the region in order to be able to increase income in the formal and informal sectors. Subsequent paragraphs, however, are indented.

2   Literature Review

2.1   Local Own-Source Revenue (LOSR)

Local income in accordance with Law No. 28 of 2009 is a regional financial source extracted from the relevant region which consists of regional tax revenue, regional retribution revenue, revenue from the management of separate regional wealth and other legitimate regional income. Sources of district income according to the Law of the

Fig. 1. Example of GIS [3]

Republic of Indonesia No. 32 of 2004, namely local tax revenue; regional retaliation results; the results of regionally owned companies and separate regional wealth management results; other valid regional income [1]. The following items which are included in regional original income in the field of tourism are restaurant taxes; hotel tax; entertainment tax; compensation for tourism/sports venues; accommodation compensation, and villas.

2.2 Geographic Information System (GIS)

Globally, GIS is a rapidly expanding system. GIS or in Indonesian called GIS (Geographical Information System) is not a system that only works to create maps, but is an analytical tool capable of solving spatial problems automatically, quickly and accurately, because it is made to collect, store, and study things and phenomena where the location of the object is important [2]. GIS is also a system/tool to create a digital map by inserting attribute data/information/table data from the map, so that from each map there is a link to its attribute data. Various types of attribute data can be created according to our needs such as area size, land cover type, population density, home/office address, if necessary the name of the village head and its RT can also be included in the attribute data (Fig. 1).

2.3 Business Model Canvas

The Business Model Canvas (BMC) is a business model that aims to map a strategy for building a strong business out of nine blocks of activities, so that it can win the competition and be successful in the long term [4]. The BMC scheme is described as follows:

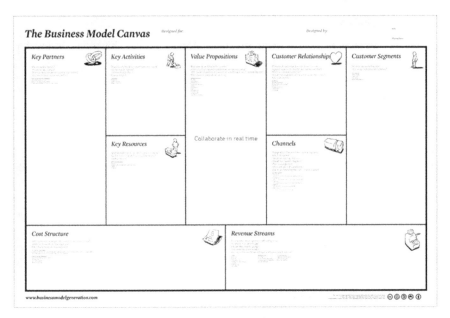

Fig. 2. Schematic of BMC [5]

This line of research began by looking at the concept of tourism as a form of observation. Based on this data, it can be evaluated using BMC and financial ratios on LOSR. The results of the assessment can be used as urban planning using the Geographical Information System (Fig. 2).

3 Research Method

The government of Pagaralam City conducted this study. The focus of this study is, among other legitimate provincial revenues, on provincial tax revenues, provincial levies, revenues from provincially owned companies and segregated provincial wealth management. Research financial document data provided by Pagaralam City.

Regional Finance Agency.The research design uses the case study method. Types of Research This type of research combines qualitative and quantitative methods. [6]. Methods of quantitative research are methodical scientific investigations of parts, phenomena, and their connections. Qualitative research methods are methods used to conduct research on the state of natural objects and make the researcher the main instrument [7]. The research stage of this innovation assignment begins with the following activities:

3.1 Stage of Data Collection

This activity is conducted through Observation, Documentation, and Interviews. Observations are made with blank observations. Documentation is carried out by taking financial data at the regional Finance agency. Expert informants were questioned in depth and semi-structured during the interviews.

3.2 Stage of Data Analysis

Data analysis was conducted using the Business Model Canvas. This model is developed with the integration of spatial planning to determine the problem to be evaluated.

3.3 The Conclusion Stage

This stage is done by drawing conclusions from the results of data analysis. The results of this conclusion will be explicitly included in the targeted output. The technique and process of data collection in this study uses several techniques to collect data, among them (1) Interview In this study, the method of interviewing was a semi-structured interview [8]. Determining the subject to be interviewed and the location of the study using expert analysis techniques [9]; (2) Documentation, the documents used in this research are City Spatial Data, Realized Budget (RB); (3) Observation, observation is done by directly observing the research object. A data collection tool that can be used in conducting observations is to use an observation form with an open observation type [10].

3.4 Technical Data Analysis

Geographic Information System (GIS). GIS is a database system that has the unique capability of working with a set of work operations and spatial reference data (spatial). to put it another way, a geographic information system, also known as a gis, is an information system that was created to work with data representing spatial reference or coordinates. [11]. All basic geographic data is first converted to digital data, before being entered into the computer. There are two basic types of geographic data, namely spatial data and attribute data. information from GIS is displayed in the form of maps, tables, charts, pictures, graphs and calculation results (Fig. 3).

Business Model Canvas. The business model canvas (BMC), a business model, is made up of nine blocks of business activity areas. It works well because it maps out a plan for building a strong company that can beat the competition and stay in business for the long haul. As a model to evaluate [13]. Visually bmc can depict the relationship of each business component. The business model canvas has 9 model blocks that make up a business unit.

3.5 Interpretation Techniques and Drawing Research Conclusions

Techniques used in interpreting and drawing conclusions using coding techniques. The use of coding techniques to process qualitative data from interviews. The researcher uses the coding method to get a complete picture of the data using qualitative data analysis and methods for collecting and making inferences from the psychological analysis of the data. [14]. Email correspondence, field notes from participant observations, journals, documents, literature, artifacts, photographs, videos, websites, and interview transcripts are all examples of data formats. Coding is a step between collecting data and more general data analysis because of this. As a result, coding is a step between data collection and more general data analysis [15]. The three methods of coding used are as follows: selective coding, open coding, and axial coding.

Fig. 3. Spatial Planning [12]

4   Result and Discussion

4.1   Results

LOSR Analysis. The results of this applied research data analysis show the results as in Table 1.

Table 1 shows that the LOSR realization research in Pagaralam City is classified as good because it has an average of more than 100% of the set target. The percentage of realization in detail is 171.74% in 2019, 141.67 in 2020 and 109.97 in 2021.

When compared to other LOSR sources, the tourism industry's overall contribution to LOSR is still very small. Table 2 shows a comparison between the description of the LOSR in the tourism industry and the total LOSR, as well as a comparison between the details of the LOSR and the total LOSR.

Based on the display in Table 2, information is obtained that the average comparison with the total LOSR is 0.0040 in 2019, 0.0020 in 2020, and 0.0046 in 2021. This comparison shows a small contribution to the total LOSR.

BMC Analysis. In BMC analysis, this research can produce 9 related components in bmc. The components that can be analyzed are:

Customer Segments. The Customer Segment component refers to the users and users to be served in the program. Through the results of observation it is known that the tourism business that will be served are tourists. Tourists usually come from outside Pagaralam City. This customer segment generally does not have a good understanding of information about the main destinations and tourist accommodation that can be chosen in Pagaralam City.

Table 1. Realization of LOSR in the Tourism Sector

Description of Local Own-sources Revenue in the Tourism Sector	Percentage of Local Own-sorce Revenue Realization		
	2019	2020	2021
Hotel Tax	141,27%	171,48%	92,23%
Restaurant Tax	152,88%	155,99%	129,25%
Entertainment Tax	95,33%	140,17%	140,18%
Advertisement Tax	99,36%	153,99%	100,32%
Tax Average	122,21%	155,40%	115,49%
Retribution for Use of Regional Wealth	733,08%	157,77%	83,40%
Special Parking Retribution	91,25%	100,00%	133,33%
Retribution for Lodging/Villa	0,00%	0,00%	102,05%
Recreational and SportsPlace Retribution	111,65%	258,83%	107,98%
Retribution for Sales of Regional Business Production	120,80%	136,80%	101,00%
Average of Retribution	211,36%	130,68%	105,55%
Average of Local Own-source Revenue Realization	171,74%	141,67%	109,97%

Sources: Processed Data, 2022

Table 2. Comparison of LOSR acquisition in the tourism sector for the period 2019–2021

Description of LOSR	Comparasion of LOSR					
	2019		2020		2021	
Hotel Tax	0,2270	0,0082	0,1625	0,0029	0,1564	0,0065
Restaurant Tax	0,0842	0,0031	0,1182	0,0021	0,1096	0,0045
Entertainment Tax	0,0140	0,0005	0,0133	0,0002	0,0134	0,0006
Advertisement Tax	0,0593	0,0022	0,0973	0,0017	0,0851	0,0035
Retribution for Use of Regional Wealth	0,5048	0,0183	0,4435	0,0080	0,0884	0,0037
Special Parking Retribution	0,0302	0,0011	0,0455	0,0008	0,0407	0,0017
Retribution for Lodging/Villa	0,0000	0,0000	0,0000	0,0000	0,4045	0,0168
Recreational and SportsPlace Retribution	0,0666	0,0024	0,0981	0,0018	0,0870	0,0036
Retribution for Sales of Regional Business Production	0,0139	0,0005	0,0216	0,0004	0,0150	0,0006
Average Value	0,1111	0,0040	0,1111	0,0020	0,1111	0,0046

Sources: Processed Data, 2022

Value Proposition. This component can be interpreted as a product or solution to be delivered to the customer that has benefits or benefits. Good information about the tourism profile and accessibility will attract tourists because it will reduce misinformation for tourists. Tourists need software that can support their tourism activities starting from transportation, culinary, accommodation and the tourist destination itself.

Channels. Channels will explain how to deliver the Value Proposition to consumers. In this case, the information user is a tourist. The dissemination of GIS facilities and use can be done through YouTube and social media owned by the community and local government.

Customer Relations. The relationship that is expected to be established with tourists is an emotional relationship through display on GIS and clarity of coordinates. Through good geographic information and common urban spatial proposals, it will be a good tourism experience for users that in the long run will increase the income of various sectors.

Revenue Streams. The income channel that will be generated from customers who will travel is more tourists, more people need information about the geography of Pagaralam City. Through high tourist visits then hopefully the economy of Pagaralam City will improve.

Keys Resources. The resources needed to produce Value Propositions are to collaborate outside the Pagarlam City Government, namely with the private sector, universities and human resource training owned by the Pagarlam City Government.

Keys Activities. This component contains activities that support the creation of institutional cooperation, provide human resources Value Propositions. The possible actions, as determined by the outcomes of interviews and observations, are to establish to manage and implement the design of the main activities.

Major Partners. Key Partners describes partners and suppliers who play a role in the process of creating a product or solution. In this component, the city government needs to collaborate with other parties that have the capabilities and technology related to GIS manufacturing.

Cost Structure. The cost structure that arises during the production process of this product if collaboration between universities is carried out is relatively minimal and does not even incur costs. This is because universities need partners to implement knowledge for their students and the City Government can act as a beneficiary

4.2 Discussion

According to the aforementioned data analysis, the tourism industry's contribution to LOSR results is not significant. This is because the nominal income is small. The reason for the tourism sector's lack of acceptance of LOSR is due to the lack of proper management. In addition, the fencealam city also does not have a geographic information system that tourists can use to obtain adequate information. Information in tourism, especially top destinations is very important. This is also supported by a study conducted by [16] with the purpose of the study so that tourists can easily obtain tourism information in the city of Bandung, a web-based geographic information system was created using Google Maps API and PHP. GIS in tourism has benefits as a channel that provides comprehensive information about an area. Research with almost identical results was conducted by [17]. The study revealed that GIS is used to manage tourism promotion in sub-Saharan Africa. BMC as an assessment tool in business can be used as an approach in strategy implementation at Mt. Merbabu National Park. The same thing was also stated in the results of the study conducted by [18]. Tourism management analyzed by BMC in this study results in an analysis of 9 components that can be used as a reference for tourism development. Other researchers who have used BMC as an evaluation model are [19]. This research was conducted to design an E-platform for sailing tourism. This applied study's findings are supported by those of the previous study.

The geographic information system is an effort to solve the problem of disinformation related to a region [20]. GIS can be a solution to optimize income in the tourism sector. The same research that has been done by GIS can be a solution to optimize income in the tourism sector. A similar study was conducted by [21] The result of the study is that GIS can be used to facilitate access to tourist accommodation. Based on the discussion in this study, GIS is a solution that can be applied as an effort to optimize tourism sector income and use urban spatial planning in Pagaralam Town.

5   Conclusion

Through fund analysis and discussion review, it can be concluded that efforts to utilize space and regional space planning have been implemented by the Pagaralam City Government. Nevertheless, the acceptance of LOSR in the tourism sector in Pagaralam Town is still not optimal due to the absence of GIS. Pagarlam City Government has the opportunity to improve management by using GIS in collaboration with universities as an information solution for leading tourist destinations. Through GIS applications, it is hoped that the government will be able to take advantage of spatial planning and urban tourism areas more optimally. Implications of future studies are expected to increase the acceptance of Pagaralam City's LOSR.

Acknowledgments. This research was carried out with State non-tax revenue at the national level funds from Politeknik Negeri Sriwijaya through the Innovation Assignment Research scheme in 2022. The partner involved and assisted in this research is the Pagaralam City Government.

References

1. J. Febriantoko and H. Rotama, "Evaluasi Potensi Penerimaan Pendapatan Asli Daerah Bidang Pariwisata di Indonesia," Ekuivalensi, vol. 4, no. 2, pp. 1–15, 2018, [Online]. Available: http://ejournal.kahuripan.ac.id/index.php/Ekuivalensi.

2. R. S. A. Usmani, I. A. T. Hashem, T. R. Pillai, A. Saeed, and A. M. Abdullahi, "Geographic information system and big spatial data: A review and challenges," Int. J. Enterp. Inf. Syst., vol. 16, no. 4, pp. 101–145, 2020.

3. J. M. Magige, C. Jepkosgei, and S. M. Onywere, "Use of GIS and remote sensing in tourism," Handb. e-Tourism, pp. 1–27, 2020.

4. H. Junaidi and D. Yulianti, "Business Model Canvas Sebagai Alat Evaluasi Potensi Ekonomi Pariwisata Studi Pada Kota Pagaralam," J. EKUIVALENSI, vol. 5, no. 2, pp. 31–44, 2019.

5. P. Giourka et al., "The smart city business model canvas—A smart city business modeling framework and practical tool," Energies, vol. 12, no. 24, p. 4798, 2019.

6. P. Sugiyono, Metode penelitian kombinasi (mixed methods), vol. 28. 2015.

7. N. Carter, D. Bryant-Lukosius, A. DiCenso, J. Blythe, and A. J. Neville, "The Use of Triangulation in Qualitative Research," Oncol. Nurs. Forum, 2014, https://doi.org/10.1188/14.onf. 545-547.

8. J. F. Gubrium and J. . Holstein, "SAGE: The SAGE Handbook of Interview Research: The Complexity of the Craft: Second Edition: : 9781412981644," in The SAGE Handbook of Interview Research: The Complexity of the Craft, 2012.

9. P. J. Elmer and D. M. Borowski, "Expert Analysis : System of S & L Bankruptcy," An Expert Syst. Approach to Financ. Anal., 2011.

10. W. Olsen, "Observation Methods," Data Collect. Key Debates Methods Soc. Res., 2012, https://doi.org/10.4135/9781473914230.n20.

11. Rastuti, L. A. Abdillah, and E. P. Agustini, "Sistem Informasi Geografis Potensi Wilayah," 2015.

12. J. Munro, H. Kobryn, D. Palmer, S. Bayley, and S. A. Moore, "Charting the coast: Spatial planning for tourism using public participation GIS," Curr. Issues Tour., vol. 22, no. 4, pp. 486–504, 2019.

13. N. Hanshaw and A. Osterwalder, "The Business Model Canvas," 2016. https://doi.org/10. 1017/CBO9781107415324.004.

14. M. Baralt, "Coding Qualitative Data," in Research Methods in Second Language Acquisition: A Practical Guide, 2012, pp. 222–244.

15. J. Saldaña, "The Coding Manual for Qualitative Researchers (No. 14)," Sage, 2016.

16. M. A. Hamdani and S. Utomo, "Sistem Informasi Geografis (SIG) Pariwisata Kota Bandung Menggunakan Google Maps Api Dan PHP," J. Teknol. Inf. dan Komun., vol. 11, no. 1, 2021.

17. J. Mango, E. Çolak, and X. Li, "Web-based GIS for managing and promoting tourism in sub-Saharan Africa," Curr. Issues Tour., vol. 24, no. 2, pp. 211–227, 2021.

18. J. Setiawan, M. S. Budiastuti, E. Gravitiani, and P. Setyono, "Business model canvas (BMC) approach for tourism management strategy of the top selfie kragilan, Mt. Merbabu National Park," Geo J. Tour. Geosites, vol. 35, no. 2, pp. 297–303, 2021.

19. R. Strulak-Wójcikiewicz, N. Wagner, A. Łapko, and E. Hącia, "Applying the business model canvas to design the E-platform for sailing tourism," Procedia Comput. Sci., vol. 176, pp. 1643–1651, 2020.

20. B. Devkota, H. Miyazaki, A. Witayangkurn, and S. M. Kim, "Using volunteered geographic information and nighttime light remote sensing data to identify tourism areas of interest," Sustainability, vol. 11, no. 17, p. 4718, 2019.

21. Z. Zhang and R. J. C. Chen, "Assessing Airbnb logistics in cities: Geographic information system and convenience theory," Sustainability, vol. 11, no. 9, p. 2462, 2019.

Comparison of the Application of Just In Time (JIT) Business Principles and Traditional Philosophy in the Development of Integrated Digital Flour Mill Technology

Jovan Febriantoko[1](✉), Ahmad Zamheri[2], Hendradinata[2], and Rian Rahmanda Putra[3]

[1] Department of Accounting, Politeknik Negeri Sriwijaya, Palembang, Indonesia
`Jovan.febriantoko@polsri.ac.id`
[2] Department of Mechanical Engineering, Politeknik Negeri Sriwijaya, Palembang, Indonesia
[3] Departement of Computer Engineering, Politeknik Negeri Sriwijaya, Palembang, Indonesia

Abstract. Coffee is main commodity that must be developed from the upstream. The development is closely related to the production process that prioritizes the implementation of good business principles and the application of appropriate technology. This study aimed to compare the application of business principles to the use of Integrated Digital Flour Mill technology, the potential, and the causes of inefficiency of Flour Mill technology. The study aimed to compare the application of Just in Time (JIT) and traditional philosophy and to find out the potential and causes of inefficiency through applied research using observational data collection techniques and literature study. Triangulation and member checks were carried out to check the validity of the data. JIT analysis used 17 JIT principles and was developed with the systems development analysis. The results and discussion in this applied research showed that the application of the business principles of the JIT production system to the Integrated digital flour mill technology had a good impact on efforts to optimize production costs. Based on the analysis of 17 JIT principles and analysis of system development, it was found the potential and causes of inefficiency that can be handled through the application of digital flour mill technology was integrated with impulse sealer, conveyor and a solar-powered.

Keywords: Flour Mill · JIT · digital · solar panel

1 Introduction

South Sumatra (Sumatera Selatan) is the largest producer of coffee in Indonesia and the second in the world. This follows the coffee cultivation area in South Sumatra reaching over 280 hectares. According to data from the Ministry of Agriculture in 2020, coffee production in South Sumatra reached 199,324 tons. South Sumatra's coffee production is more than a quarter of the country's coffee production, which is 773,410 tons [1].

The head of the South Sumatra Trade Office stated that the coffee trade as the largest supporting commodity in South Sumatra is experiencing a decline in downstream. This is

R. Martini et al. (Eds.): FIRST 2022, ASSEHR 733, pp. 137–150, 2023.
https://doi.org/10.2991/978-2-38476-026-8_16

due to the inefficiency of activities, especially exports because they have to go through Lampung. This is because Lampung coffee farmers better understand modern coffee packaging and selling techniques, so that coffee can be traded in various variants up to the export level. Expertise in processing coffee causes coffee connoisseurs in Indonesia and even abroad to be more familiar with Lampung coffee even though it comes from South Sumatra coffee farmers. This shows that South Sumatra coffee farming must be stimulated. Another problem faced by coffee farmers is the coffee grinding process, coffee packaging is not on time due to the far distance of the farm from the packaging site and the absence of electricity in the plantation area.

One of the farming groups in South Sumatra is the Besemah Jaya Farmer Group that grows coffee in Kota Pagaralam. This group used to market wrap coffee, but that activity was stopped due to poor management. Based on initial observations, other problems experienced by the partners are that they cannot optimize profits, cannot maintain the quality of the coffee grinder, cannot maintain the aroma and taste of the coffee, have not been able to carry out timely packaging in the farm area and the absence of electricity in the farm area. The partners have a strong desire to process ground coffee with better technology. Based on observational data, a more in-depth study is required with data collection and analysis. A summary of the problems raised in this study: (1) How does the application of business principles compare to the utilization of Integrated Digital Flour Mill technology?; (2) What is the potential and cause of technological inefficiency of the Flour Mill?

The specific objectives of the research are (1) to find out the comparison of the use of JIT production system business principles and traditional philosophy in an Integrated Digital Flour Mill; (2) knowing the potential and causes of inefficiency as a basis for producing Appropriate Technology (TTG) in the production of ground coffee with solar-powered coffee milling and packaging equipment.

The TTG used is expected to optimize profits, maintain the quality of ground coffee, lock the aroma and original taste of coffee with a good level of packing density, equipped with temperature inductors, solar-powered device mechanics, which allows timely. grinding and packing in the farm area. The reduction in electricity consumption is expected to reduce operating costs. Urgent research is the need for solar-powered coffee milling and packaging equipment. The technology is able to optimize yield, maintain coffee grind quality, timely packaging for aroma lock, and reduce operating costs.

2   Literature Research

2.1   Just in Time (JIT)

Just in Time is one of the most widely practiced management philosophies, techniques or methods with the aim of purchasing raw materials and producing goods only when they are needed and at the right time for use at each stage [2]. There are many problems faced by the industry especially the inefficiency in the purchasing and production system. Through the implementation of JIT, these problems can be overcome and eventually there will be savings that will increase the company's profits [3].

2.2 Arduino Uno Controller

Arduino is an open-source single-board microcontroller that has high flexibility in both software and hardware to facilitate electronic design in a variety of fields [4]. Arduino uses the ATMega IC as a program IC and the software has a processing language programming language. This language is very similar to C language, but the writing is close to human language. Arduino has many advantages compared to other microcontrollers which are cheap, simple, Open Source Software, Open Source Hardware.

2.3 Solar Panels

Solar panels are a collection of solar cells designed in such a way as to be more effective at absorbing sunlight. Solar cells are composed of several photovoltaic components or components that can convert light (photos) into electricity (voltaic) [5]. Basically, solar cells are composed of layers of silicon which are semiconductors, metal, an anti-reflective layers, and metal conductor strip. This layer plays an important role in generating electricity so that it can be used for all needs. The number of solar cells that are arranged into solar panels will be directly proportional to the energy obtained. The more solar cells used, the more solar energy is converted into electrical energy [6].

2.4 Digital Flour Mill Mechanics

According to [7] Pully is the drive system in coffee bean grinders and grinders. This system consists of several types depending on the time required in each flour session. The fastest pull was with a diameter of 6 inches with a time of 2.51 min and the slowest pull was a 3 inch with a time of 4.10 min. Pull with the fastest coffee bean flour shaft rotation is the 6 inch pulley reaching 5017 rpm and the slowest shaft rotation on the 3 inch pulley reaching 2460 rpm. The pull that produces the highest torque for coffee bean flour is with a diameter of 3 inches reaching 920 rpm, while the latter is a diameter of 6 inches 12.89N. The use of the pully system is believed to be able to maximize the coffee grind with a high degree of fineness so that the quality of the coffee powder is ideal.

A type of electric motor known as a dc motor is most commonly utilized in industry to aid in production [8]. DC motors are more often used for activities that require speed regulation than ac motors. In addition to controlling the speed of rotation, the dc motor control system also controls the direction of rotation of the rotor, clockwise or counterclockwise. One of the DC motor control systems is to use Width ModulationPulse (PWM) as a trigger on control drivers such as H-Bridge transistors.

3 Research Method

3.1 Types of Research

This type of research is a type of applied research. This research is a research that is used to solve a specific problem on a specific research object [9]. The subjects of the study are all reliable informants and have a direct relationship with the object of the study. The object of his study is a solar-powered coffee milling and packaging device.

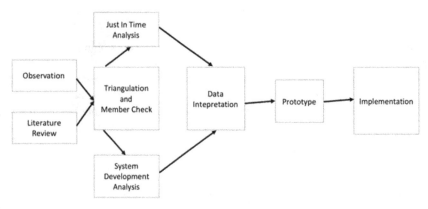

Fig. 1. Flow of Applied Research conducted

This technology is equipped with a temperature indicator to maintain the quality of the coffee grinding process.

This research is located in Besemah Jaya Farmer Group located in PagarAlam Village, Utara Pagaralam District, Pagaralam City, South Sumatra.

3.2 Data Collection Techniques

The Data collection procedure used is as follows [10]: (1) Observation, observing people doing certain activities being observed [11]; (2) Literature Review, data collection technique by examining theories relevant to the research problem.

3.3 Data Analysis

Before analyzing the data, the following methods are used to test the credibility of data through the following techniques [12]: (1) Triangulation is a strategy that uses multiple methods to collect and analyze data. The triangulation that is used is a triangulation of resources, methods, and time [13]; (2) Member Check is a method for determining whether the interpretation of observational data processing is appropriate for research partners [14].

The quality of solar-powered coffee grinding and packaging equipment, as well as the temperature indicators and gain projections embedded in the mechanism, are also the goals of the data collection and analysis methods (Fig. 1).

3.4 Method of System Development

There are two types of system development: software and hardware. The term "software development stage" refers to the system development life cycle (SDLC), which consists of the following steps: (1) System Analysis, in which problems and objects of study are investigated and a Proposed System workflow diagram is created;(2) System Design using Arduino based Firmware for temperature detector and yield optimization system; (3) Coding Process, microcontroller with C language; (4) System Testing Black Box Testing by providing test scenarios to the system.

4   Results and Discussions

4.1   Decision

Just In Time (JIT) Analysis

JIT analysis in research using 17 JIT principles [15]. Comparison of the effects of JIT implementation and Traditional Philosophy on Integrated Digital Flour Mill Technology can be detailed as in Table 1 (Tables 2, 3, 4, 5, 6, 7 and 8).

Table 1 shows a comparison of 17 JIT principles, namely Quality, Expertise, Errors, Inventory, Lot Size, Queue, Automation Value, Sources of Cost Reduction, Material Flow, Flexibility, Overhead Role, Labor Cost, Machine Speed, Purchase, Accelerate, Cleanliness, Horizon. The comparison is the result of observing the implementation of integrated digital flour mill technology from a business perspective. Through this assessment, a scientific study can be carried out that can be used as a flour mill development.

Table 1. Comparison of the Effects of JIT Implementation and Traditional Philosophy on the Group of Coffee Producer. Farmers Groups with Quality Criteria and Skills Criteria

Criteria	Impact of JIT Implementation	Effects of Traditional Philosophy Application
Quality	Fulfillment of quality without incurring additional costs in the ground coffee grinding and packaging process, where the coffee grinding process can be carried out in the field directly because the mechanical technology of this coffee grinder uses solar energy. Thus, reducing electricity costs. In addition, the process of packing ground coffee can also be carried out directly in the farm area to ensure that the aroma and taste of the coffee is better preserved. This can reduce transportation costs.	It requires payment to produce a quality product which is the cost of grinding coffee at a grinding equipment rental place. In addition, the packaging process must be carried out in different places that require coffee transport services so that the cost is higher. The process of transporting coffee for packaging can result in the loss or reduction of the coffee's original aroma and taste during the journey. Because the coffee powder is exposed to air before being packaged.
Skills	Farmer Group members are experts. The chairman of the Farmer Group and the University have the role of providing services to farmer group members to operate digital flour mill technology as an effort to improve the expertise of the farmer group which leads to increased knowledge related to the science and application of modern coffee milling and packaging technology.	Leaders of Farmers' Groups and Universities act as experts. Members of the Farmer Group act as servers according to the rules set by the experts. This causes members of the group to not have sufficient expertise and abilities in the use of coffee milling and packaging technology. This has the effect of not improving the ability and expertise of farmer group members over time.

Table 2. Comparison of the Effects of JIT Implementation and Traditional Philosophy on the Group of Coffee Producer. Farmers Groups with Error Criteria and Availability Criteria

Criteria	Impact of JIT Implementation	Effects of Traditional Philosophy Application
Error	Zero defects in implementation of technology is standard that must be met. Errors at the technology implementation stage are used as a reference in making improvements in the future. In addition, each recommendation note from the final evaluation results will be used as a future reference to update the digital flour mill technology in the future.	Errors must be studied without any reduction to avoid these errors so that the quality of the resulting ground coffee production is not optimal. Additionally, procedural errors caused by the absence of temperature control detectors caused previous coffee milling and packaging machines to suddenly overheat. This will affect the quality of the coffee grinder and tend to make maintenance of traditional coffee milling and packaging machines difficult.
Availability	the coffee supply becomes a burden which is the real problem. In this regard, the digital flour mmill provides a more practical integration feature, which is believed to be able to overcome the problem of coffee availability in the market. The milling and packaging process carried out in the same place can improve the timeliness in the kopo powder production process. This of course can ensure the availability of ground coffee in the market moretimely.	Coffee preparation has the benefit of ensuring smooth production, but with previous coffee grinder technology, there was still a long series of activities that took a long time starting from the coffee panne process, drying to milling and packaging. This is due to the fact that previous technology did not have integration features that allowed all processes to be carried out at one time and one place so it took a long time to produce ground coffee. This often results in late and often untimely availability of ground coffee in the market.

System Development Analysis

The designed coffee packaging control system consists of 5 (five) main parts which are: (1) Microcontroller Module, (2) Display System, (3) Push Button, (4) Power Supply and (5) DS18B250 Temperature Sensor. The microcontroller module functions as a control center that processes input data from temperature sensors or variable values entered through push buttons. Temperature values from temperature sensors and input variables will be processed and displayed on the system display to provide information to the user in the form of optimization parameters for the income obtained. So that users can carry out the correct process in the coffee bean processing production cycle.

Table 3. Comparison of the Effects of JIT Implementation and Traditional Philosophy on the Group of Coffee Producer. Farmers Groups with Lot Size Criteria and Line Up Criteria

Criteria	Impact of JIT Implementation	Effects of Traditional Philosophy Application
Lot Size	Must have a small Lot Size, where the digital flour mill has a coffee grinding capacity that is not too large so that the ordering capacity to grind and pack the ground coffee must match the capacity offer end by the digital flour mill.	Must have an economical Lot Size using the EOQ principle. In the use of traditional ground coffee grinding and packaging technology, the lot size or capacity of ordering ground coffee is still very necessary, which is calculated according to the need. This is due to and related to the cost of renting grinding equipment which tends to be high and if the farmers have traditional technology coffee grinding equipment, they also need to take into account the electricity costs that may arise. This results in the need to calculate the amount of coffee orders and other additional costs as well as calculation the price offered for each packet of ground coffee either according to the ability and purchasing power of the community. So, for this case, EOQ-based calculations are still very necessary if using traditional manufacturing technology that tends to be more complex and risks lowering profits.
Line Up	Avoiding long queues in the production and packaging process is the main thing in implementing a digital flour mill. The digital flour mill application is believed to be able to save time because all activities from harvesting coffee, grinding, and packing coffee powder can be carried out in the same location, which is in the garden of the farmer group without the help of electricity. This certainly increases the efficiency of the activity process and saves time in the coffee grinding and packaging process. The complexity and integration offered is expected to ensure the availability of ground coffee commodities in the market.	In practice, the use of traditional coffee grinding and packaging technology often results in lengthy processes as they must be carried out in different places. This often results in inefficiency in the process of preparing ground coffee in the market. In addition, there are several ground coffee factories that queque up so much that groups of farmers have to wait for a long time or even days to produce ground coffee which results in the income they will receive being late.

Table 4. Comparison of the Effects of JIT Implementation and Traditional Philosophy on the Group of Coffee Producer. Farmers Groups with Value Automation Criteria and Sources of cost reduction Criteria

Criteria	Impact of JIT Implementation	Effects of Traditional Philosophy Application
Value Automation	Automation is invaluable. Therefore, there is integration between technological blocks to ensure consistency of quality and taste of ground coffee. This automation is expected to speed up the process of grinding ground coffee, speed up the packaging process, and speed up the preparation of ground coffee in the market.	Automation is only carried out in the milling process, but traditional coffee milling machine technology does not yet have automation in terms of packaging, machine temperature control, and automation of solar energy use.
Sources of cost reduction	Reducing acquisition costs and speeding up product flow at production time are the main goals of implementing a digital flour mill. Due to the implementation of the technology, all process activities can be carried out at the same time and in the same place, in addition to reducing the cost of electricity consumption and packaging at the same time.	Cost reduction is done through labor reduction and increased machine utility. This causes the grinding machine to work harder which causes the machine to be more easily damaged and the cost of electricity will be high because the number of working hours of the machine is longer.

Table 5. Comparison of the Effects of JIT Implementation and Traditional Philosophy on the Group of Coffee Producer. Farmers Groups with Material Flow Criteria and Flexibility Criteria

Criteria	Impact of JIT Implementation	Effects of Traditional Philosophy Application
Material Flow	Coffee is close to the production process (pull system) so that the digital flour mill can ensure a better quality of ground coffee taste.	Coffee is placed separately outside the production area (push system). In this regard, the process of producing ground coffee and its packaging that is far apart often results in the aroma of ground coffee being contaminated with air which often causes less consumer statisfaction with the ground coffee products offered.
Flexibility	Flexibility is achieved through the compression of process lead times. The low lead time level offered by the digital flour mill application will lead to time efficiency. This is believed to ensure the availability of ground coffee products moretimely than before.	Any flexibility will incur the cost of excess machine capacity. Excessive engine capacity will of course cause high electricity and labor costs.

Table 6. Comparison of the Effects of JIT Implementation and Traditional Philosophy on the Group of Coffee Producer. Farmers Groups with Role of Overhead Criteria and Labor Cost Criteria

Criteria	Impact of JIT Implementation	Effects of Traditional Philosophy Application
Role of Overhead	Group members who manage those who do not add value are assumed to waste so much that with the digital flour mill application they can optimize the minimum number of workers but achieve high production capacity.	The overhead function is assumed to be the coordinating aspect of the coffee grinding process. It is assumed that the use of traditional coffee grinders will increase factory overhead costs. That is, by maximizing machine hours to catch up with ground coffee production capacity, it will inevitably increase the total cost of labor, machine maintenance and electricity costs.
Labor Cost	The cost for labor is classified as a fixed cost because the digital flour mill application does not require a lot of labor force with a high working capacity of the machine because the features provided by the digital flour mill are able to reduce labor costs.	Labor costs are classified as variable costs because in the use of traditional coffee grinders the number of hours used will be very influential and the wages given to workers. The higher the order of the coffee grinder, the higher the labor cost will be.

Table 7. Comparison of the Effects of JIT Implementation and Traditional Philosophy on the Group of Coffee Producer. Farmers Groups with Machine Speed Criteria and Purchase Criteria

Criteria	Impact of JIT Implementation	Effects of Traditional Philosophy Application
Machine Speed	The flour mill is assumed to be like a marathon, not too fast but able to run for a long time without stopping. The heat detection feature on the digital flour mill is also able to optimize the quality of machine work without increasing machine maintenance costs, because users can know when the machine needs to rest for a while.	The machine is likened to a sprinter but the duration is not too long because traditional coffee grinders tend to heat up easily. This is due to the absence of a heat sensor detector mounted on the engine body. This can also affect the machine's durability and high maintenance costs.
Purchase	The source of coffee raw materials comes from the farm itself or a certain party that consistently provides coffee beans for grinding ad packaging.	Receive a variety of coffees from many suppliers. This caused many queues which created uncertainty about the availability of ground coffee in the market.

Table 8. Comparison of the Effects of JIT Implementation and Traditional Philosophy on the Group of Coffee Producer. Farmers Groups with Expediting Criteria, Cleanliness Criteria and Horison Criteria

Criteria	Impact of JIT Implementation	Effects of Traditional Philosophy Application
Expediting	No speeding and working around the use of digital flour mill is allowed.	Work around and speed up part of the business system used for the use of traditional coffee milling machines.
Cleanliness	Cleanliness in line with the activity of producing ground coffee needs to be applied, this is in line with the principle of implementing solar energy as the main energy source of this technology.	Working and doing production that results in dirty is a consequence of business activities against the implementation of traditional coffee grinders.
Horison	Patience and patience will affect the entire business process towards the standard of zero defects.	The effects of the production process are expected in a short time when implementing a traditional coffee grinder.

Data: Observational Data, 2022

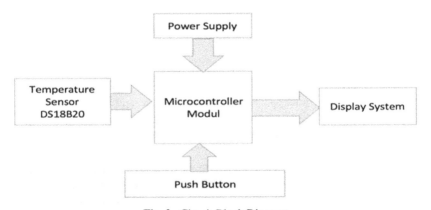

Fig. 2. Circuit Block Diagram

Figure 2 describes the development of the working system of the tool. In Fig. 2, the development of the tool work system has referred to the Just in Time business principle. Based on the circuit block diagram in Fig. 2, an integrated digital flour mill prototype can be made according to Fig. 3.

The prototype design in Fig. 3 describes the components in more detail related to the integrated digital flour mill technology that uses the JIT principle. The above design part can be explained as follows:

1. Solar Cells
2. Control Panel

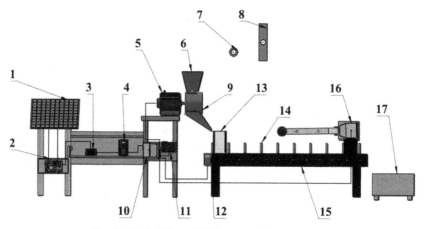

Fig. 3. Digital Flour Mill Prototype integrated with

3. Battery
4. Inverter
5. Motor Grinder
6. Hopper
7. Clamp Adapter Arbor
8. Grinder Blade
9. Smoothing Tube
10. Relay
11. LCD
12. Rope Control
13. Plastic/Packaging
14. Barriers
15. Belt Conveyor Machine
16. Impulse
17. Shelter

The instrument interface consists of an LCD and a 3 × 4 matrix keyboard. The LCD will display the temperature data reading from the DS18B20 sensor, and there is also a display to predict the result.

4.2 Discussion

Based on the results of previous data analysis, this applied research was carried out by developing and implementing TTG solar-powered coffee brewing and packaging with a temperature indicator as a measure of device performance effectiveness. This situation is due to coffee grinding and packaging equipment previously only being able to grind and pack coffee with electricity, unable to optimize results by applying JIT methods, unable to grind temperature-controlled coffee to maintain quality, unable to maintain the aroma & taste of coffee with the packaging density that is ideal, unable to carry out packaging on time in the farm area, due to the distance from the factory and packaging is very far, not yet able to use solar energy instead of electricity. to be used in the middle of the park where it is difficult to get electricity and can reduce operating costs.

Research of [16] states that the development of automatic coffee grinders can increase the production of ground coffee. The production yield is greater, which is originally 20 packages in one process to 40 packages. Besides [7] said the application of the Pulley system in coffee grinders and grinders has the highest speed so it is very efficient in terms of time and coffee fineness. In addition, the coffee bag packaging process is also more effective with the help of TTG packaging mechanics, this TTG is believed to speed up packaging time, increase density, and fill SNI coffee bags [17]. The ground coffee production process will be more effective because the Decision Support System (SPK) is built based on compliance with product criteria with management accounting based on Just In Time (JIT) which meets the objective of helping in checking aspects of inventory cost efficiency. and non-financial performance (production effectiveness, timeliness), delivery, and product quality [2]. In addition, research from [18] stating that the use of the Arduino microcontroller will provide effective work in controlling the temperature. It aims to make the equipment work more efficiently if it is used continuously. This past research will be integrated into new knowledge to solve problems in this applied research.

5   Conclusion and Suggestion

The results and discussion in this applied research show that the application of JIT production system business principles to Integrated digital flour mill technology has a positive effect on efforts to optimize production costs. Based on the analysis of 17 JIT principles and system development analysis, it was found the potential and causes of inefficiency that can be controlled through the application of digital flour mill technology integrated with solar-powered impulse sealing conveyors.

Future research is expected to provide updates on the technology currently in use through integration with operating systems on gadgets. The implications of this study are expected to solve problems in coffee plantations.

Acknowledgments. This research is the result of Sriwijaya State Polytechnic Superior Applied Research. This activity can be carried out with funding from POLSRI PNBP and the involvement of research partners. All research materials are the responsibility of the researcher.

References

1. G. E. Tresia, W. Puastuti, and I. Inounu, "Carrying Capacity for Ruminant Based on Plantation Byproducts and Potency of Enteric Methane Emission," *War. Indones. Bull. Anim. Vet. Sci.*, vol. 31, no. 1, pp. 23–36, 2021.
2. A. Aznedra and E. Safitri, "Analisis Pengendalian Internal Persediaan Dan Penerapan Metode Just In Time Terhadap Efisiensi Biaya Persediaan Bahan Baku Studi Kasus PT. SIIX Electronics Indonesia," *Meas. J. Account. Study Progr.*, vol. 12, no. 2, pp. 120–132, 2018.

3. Z. Li, Q. Ying, W. Yan, and C. Fan, "Does just-in-time adoption have an impact on corporate innovation: evidence from China," *Account. Financ.*, 2021.

4. L. Louis, "Working Principle of Arduino and Using it as a Tool for Study and Research," *Int. J. Control. Autom. Commun. Syst.*, 2016, doi: https://doi.org/10.5121/ijcacs.2016.1203.

5. Z. Iqtimal, I. D. Sara, and S. Syahrizal, "Aplikasi sistem tenaga surya sebagai sumber tenaga listrik pompa air," *J. Komputer, Inf. Teknol. dan Elektro*, vol. 3, no. 1, 2018.

6. M. Rajvikram and S. Leoponraj, "A method to attain power optimality and efficiency in solar panel," *Beni-Suef Univ. J. basic Appl. Sci.*, vol. 7, no. 4, pp. 705–708, 2018.

7. M. Azmy Tsaqib, "VARIASI DIAMETER PULLY SISTEM PENGGERAK PADA MESIN PENGGILING DAN PENEPUNG BIJI KOPI." DIII Teknik mesin Politeknik Harapan Bersama, 2021.

8. M. I. Esario and M. Yuhendri, "Kendali Kecepatan Motor DC Menggunakan DC Chopper Satu Kuadran Berbasis Kontroller PI," *JTEV (Jurnal Tek. Elektro dan Vokasional)*, vol. 6, no. 1, pp. 296–305, 2020.

9. M. Baimyrzaeva, "Beginners' Guide for Applied Research Process: What Is It, and Why and How to Do It," *Univ. Cent. Asia*, vol. 4, no. 8, 2018.

10. P. D. Sugiyono, "Metode Penelitian Bisnis: Pendekatan Kuantitatif, Kualitatif, Kombinasi, dan R&D," *Penerbit CV. Alf. Bandung*, 2017.

11. W. Olsen, "Observation Methods," *Data Collect. Key Debates Methods Soc. Res.*, 2012, doi: https://doi.org/10.4135/9781473914230.n20.

12. L. Birt, S. Scott, D. Cavers, C. Campbell, and F. Walter, "Member checking," *Qual. Health Res.*, vol. 26, no. 13, pp. 1802–1811, 2016, doi: https://doi.org/10.1177/1049732316654870.

13. N. Carter, D. Bryant-Lukosius, A. DiCenso, J. Blythe, and A. J. Neville, "The Use of Triangulation in Qualitative Research," *Oncol. Nurs. Forum*, 2014, doi: https://doi.org/10.1188/14.onf.545-547.

14. L. Gelling, "Qualitative Research," *Qual. Res.*, 2015.

15. A. Diana and F. Tjiptono, "Total Quality Management (TQM)," *Andi, Yogyakarta*, 2001.

16. J. A. Wabang, F. E. Laumal, R. B. Suharto, N. Lapinangga, and J. I. B. Hutubessy, "Optimizing Coffee Management in Wawowae Village through Increasing Human Resources and Machine Development [Optimalisasi Pengelolaan Kopi di Desa Wawowae melalui Peningkatan Sumber Daya Manusia dan Pengembangan Mesin]," *Proceeding Community Dev.*, vol. 2, pp. 502–509, 2019.

17. S. Mahdalena, "MANAJEMEN PENGEMASAN BUBUK KOPI ARABICA KORINTJI PADA PT. ALKO SUMATRA KOPI KABUPATEN KERINCI." Agrobisnis, 2021.

18. S. Herawati, "Rancang Bangun Sistem Monitoring Suhu Ruangan Bagian Pembukuan Berbasis Web Meggunakan Mikrokontroler Arduino Uno R3," *J. Teknol. Inf. dan Komun.*, vol. 13, no. 1, pp. 18–33, 2018.

Village Income and Economic Growth for Poverty Reduction on South Sumatra Province

Zulkifli, Ibnu Maja, Rita Martini$^{(\boxtimes)}$, Sukmini Hartati, and Mardhiah Mardhiah

Politeknik Negeri Sriwijaya, Palembang 30139, Indonesia
ritamartini@polsri.ac.id

Abstract. Village community welfare research is urgently needed, particularly in the areas of village funds (VF), village fund allocations (VFA), village original income (VOI), and economic growth (EG). Samples taken from fourteen districts and cities in South Sumatra for five years (in 2016–2020). It was found that the poverty rate is influenced by VF, VFA, and VOI. Economic growth partially does not affect poverty. Subsequent findings, simultaneously all independent variables can affect poverty. It is recommended for future researchers to increase the quantity of data, increase the observation period, and further explore the variables to be studied. Regency and city government of South Sumatra should continue to increase the rate of economic growth in order to promote people's prosperity by using village spending.

Keywords: Village Fund · Village Original Income · Economic Growth · Poverty

1 Introduction

The Central Statistics Agency, Republic of Indonesia (CSA) revealed that in 2021 in South Sumatra there will be an increase in the poverty rate of 12.84%. This condition places this province in tenth place in Indonesia, and for the island of Sumatra it is in third position. CSA also released that the poor population is more dominant in villages. The Government of Indonesia has implemented various policies to address these societal problems, including by launching a village fund program and village fund allocations. The increase in VF and VFA is expected to reduce the poverty rate.

One of the village developments carried out is in the form of efforts to improve people's welfare. Rural poverty is expected to decrease with an increase in VOI. VOI aims to generate income for village prosperity. Findings [1–3] result that poverty is influenced by VF and VFA significantly. On the other hand [4, 5] proves that VFA does not affect poverty. VOI has a significant effect on poverty. Other findings partially [1, 6] reveal that the poverty rate is affected by VFA. Economic growth can affect poverty variables [7]. In this study, the independent variable was added, namely economic growth.

VF [8] is intended to organize government, village development, coaching, and community empowerment. The State Revenue and Expenditure Budget determines these

R. Martini et al. (Eds.): FIRST 2022, ASSEHR 733, pp. 151–155, 2023.
https://doi.org/10.2991/978-2-38476-026-8_17

funds, which are then allocated to the district or city Regional Revenue and Expenditure Budget. The village fund allocation is worth ten percent of the balanced fund after special funds have been allocated [9]. Furthermore, VOI [9] is obtained from various village government efforts to collect the funding needed to finance routine activities or development activities. Economic growth [10] is the development of various economic activities that can increase the goods and services produced by society which ultimately lead to an increase in their welfare. Poverty indicates the condition of individuals or communities who are unable to experience various alternatives and opportunities to fulfill their primary needs. These needs include health, eligibility, freedom, and self-confidence [11].

In this research, four hypotheses will be tested. Hypothesis testing will be carried out on the four research variables, either partially or simultaneously. Test symbols are denoted as: VF affects poverty (H_1); VFA has an effect on poverty (H_2); VOI affects poverty (H_3); Economic growth affects poverty (H_4); and Poverty rate can be influenced by VF, VFA, VOI, and economic growth together (H_5).

2 Research Methodology

For this study, data from reports published by the local government were used. The village revenue and expense budget's budget realization report is where the information is found. The research study covers all seventeen regencies and cities in the province of South Sumatra. Based on certain considerations, data samples were taken from fourteen districts and cities.

Poverty (Pv), village funds (VF), village fund allocation (VFA), village original income (VOI), and economic growth were the four variables examined (EG). Several linear analysis equation are used to test hypotheses.

When the variables studied are examined separately or together, the coefficient of determination serves as a measure of how well the variable can influence or cause change for the factor being measured. The decision to test F is based on the significance point that is bigger than 0.05. Furthermore, if the calculated F_{count} exceeds F_{table}, the decision H_0 is not accepted and H_1 is accepted.

The t test was conducted to obtain the magnitude of the relationship between each explanatory factor in describing its various influence values. The decision making is seen from the value of t_{count} which is smaller than t_{table}, so it is decided that H_0 will be accepted and H_1 will be rejected.

3 Result and Discussion

3.1 Result

Hypothesis testing is carried out to produce an overview of the relationships and influences shown in this equation:

$$Pv = 9.693 + 0.00000015VF + 0.00000019VFA + 0.00000356VOI + 0.802EG + e \quad (1)$$

The regression model illustrates that VF, VFA, VOI, and EG are positively related to poverty. It was found that VF had a $t_{count} > t_{table}$ (4.223 > 1.997) and a sig value < 0.05, which partially affected poverty. The VFA variable has a $t_{count} > t_{table}$ (4.151 > 1.997) and is significant, and it is concluded that it is partially influential. VOI shows $t_{count} > t_{table}$ (5.263 > 1.997) and is significant, the conclusion is also influential. The EG variable has a $t_{count} < t_{table}$ (0.867 < 1.997) with a significant value of more than 0.05 (0.389 > 0.05). The conclusion obtained partially that economic growth has no effect.

Based on the F test, the calculated F results are 44.984. The results obtained for Ftable are 2.51. Because $F_{count} > F_{table}$, then H5 can be accepted. This significance shows a value of 0.000 and a calculated F value of 44.984 > 2.51. So, VF, VFA, VOI, and economic growth will affect poverty.

Adjusted R Square, which is the outcome determination value, is 0.718. This implies that these independent variables have an influence contribution of 71.8% for the dependent variable.

3.2 Discussion

Synergized results were obtained for the function of rural funds, namely increasing village prosperity and increasing the standard of living of village communities and reducing village poverty. There is a positive and significant relationship where it is expected that village funds will affect the reduction of district and city poverty rates in this province. This finding also supports [2, 5, 12] which states that the condition of prosperity or poverty alleviation in districts or cities is highly dependent on the availability of village funding. Village funds can explain rural poverty [3]. This means that village funds that are increasingly optimal will affect the level of welfare of the community.

Villages are funded from appropriations and transferred by the central government is aimed at alleviating poverty and inequality as well as for the prosperity of rural communities. In reality, the purpose of allocating village funds has been achieved by the district and city governments in the autonomous region of South Sumatra province. In conclusion, determination of funds for villages contributes to poverty reduction. If the allocation of village funds increases, it will affect the district and city poverty rates in this province. The results of research [1] are also evidence that village fund allocations have a strong effect in a positive direction to reduce poverty. Village funds allocated optimally function to increase village prosperity. Likewise [2] revealed that the allocation of funds in a village will affect the district or city poverty rate. Research findings [4] differ in that the position of poverty is not affected by village fund allocations. The probability that the results of an observation will occur differs from the amount of data and the time of observation.

Village original income, namely as a source of strengthening village finances to build and manage, among other things, related to its welfare. There is a reciprocal relationship between the original income sourced from the village and poverty alleviation. These conditions support [6] which proves that income originating from a village has a strong influence in a positive direction. The implication is that the more optimal the village income, the more optimal the welfare of the community.

This study's findings demonstrate that economic expansion has little impact on poverty levels. Economic growth should be able to greatly contribute to reducing the poverty rate in regencies/cities, namely if economic growth in previous years was high and the growth rate of Gross Domestic Product was higher, the poverty rate would fall faster. Practically speaking the economic growth of the South Sumatra regional government has not been able to contribute to poverty alleviation. Theoretically it should be stated that [7, 14–16] economic growth will affect the position of district/city poverty levels.

4   Conclusion

The research findings indicate that poverty is positively and significantly influenced by VF, VFA, and VOI. However, economic growth partially has no effect on poverty. Period. If taken simultaneously, the VF, VFA, VOI, and economic growth show a strong influence on alleviating poverty in district and city governments within the province of South Sumatra.

To get more comprehensive evidence related to this phenomenon. Future research can extend the observation time period. The findings in this study are only limited from observations during 2016–2020.

References

1. Dewi, R. S., & Irama, O. N.: Pengaruh Pendapata Desa dan Alokasi Dana Desa terhadap Belanja Desa dan Kemiskinan. Jurnal Riset Akuntansi Multiparadigma (2018).
2. Widiawati, D., Yuliani, N. L., Purwantini, A. H.: Analysis of Determinants on Village Fund Management Accountability. Urecol Journal. Part B: Economics and Business. 2(1) 9–19 (2022)
3. Martini, R., Chalifah, S., Pisey, K. K., Sari, K. R., Wardhani, S. W., Aryani, Y. A., Zulkifli, Choiruddin.: The Local Government Performance in Indonesia. In: Proceedings of the 2nd Forum in Research, Science, and Technology. Atlantis Press. https://doi.org/10.5220/000915 1700002500 (2022).
4. Lalira, D., Nakoko, A. T., & Rorong, I. P.: Pengaruh Dana Desa dan Alokasi Dana Desa terhadap Tingkat Kemiskinan di Kecamatan Gemeh Kabupaten Kepulauan Talaud. Jurnal Berkala Ilmiah Efisiensi (2018).
5. Martini, R., Widyastuti, E., Hartati, S., Zulkifli, Mardhiah.: Poverty Reduction in South Sumatera with Optimization of Village Funds, Allocation of Village Funds, and Village Original Income. In: Proceedings of the 5th FIRST T3 2021 International Conference. Atlantis Press. https://doi.org/10.2991/assehr.k.220202.020 (2022).
6. Kawulur, S., Koleangan, R. A., & Wauran, P. C.: Analisa Pengaruh Pendapatan Asli Desa dan Dana Desa dalam Menurunkan Tingkat Kemiskinan di 11 Kabupaten Privinsi Sulawesi Utara. Jurnal Berkala Ilmiah Efisiensi (2019).
7. Safitri, N. A. (2020). The Influence of Economic Growth, Education, Open Unemployment Rate, Government Spending on District/City Poverty Rates in West Kalimantan Province. Development and Equity Journal. 9(2).
8. Peraturan Menteri Dalam Negeri Republik Indonesia Nomor 113 Tahun 2014 tentang Pengelolaan Keuangan Desa.
9. Undang-Undang Nomor 6 Tahun 2014 tentang Desa.

10. Yulihartini, D. T., Sukarno, H., & Wardayati, S. M.: Pengaruh Belanja Modal dan Alokasi Dana Desa terhadap Kemandirian dan Kinerja Keuangan Desa di Kabupaten Jember. Jurnal Bisnis dan Management. 12(1). 37-50 (2018).

11. Martini, R., Zulkifli, Z., Hartati, S., & Widyastuti, E.: Peran Pendapatan Desa untuk Belanja Desa di Kabupaten Lahat. Ekonomi & Bisnis, 19(2), 181-187 (2020).

12. Martini, R., Widyastuti, E., Hartati, S., Zulkifli, Mayasari, R., Mardhiah.: Poverty in South Sumatra Province Is Viewed from Village Fund and Village Fund Allocation. In: Proceedings of the 4th Forum in Research, Science, and Technology (FIRST-T3–20). Atlantis Press. https://doi.org/10.2991/ahsseh.k.210122.018 (2021).

13. Sujarweni, V.: Village Accounting: Guidelines for Village Financial Management. Fokus Media, Bandung (2015).

14. Somadi, T, Martini, R., Firmansyah, Pangaribuan, L. V. R., Sari, K. R., & Wardhani, R. S.: Determinant of Regional Financial Independence: Regency/City Government at South Sumatra Province. In: International Conference on Industrial Revolution for Polytechnic Education. 1(1) (2019).

15. Romi, S., & Umiyati, E.: The Influence of Economic Growth and Minimum Wage in Jambi City. e-Journal of Economic Perspectives and Regional Development. 7(1) (2018).

16. Martini, R., Zulkifli, Z., Hartati, S., & Widyastuti, E.: Dimension of Village Expenditure in Development Sector. In: 3rd Forum in Research, Science, and Technology (FIRST 2019), pp. 6–9. Atlantis Press (2020).

A Financial Record Practice for Small and Medium Enterprises: A Comparative Study of Malaysia and Indonesia

Yuli Antina Aryani[1], Hadi Jauhari[2(✉)], Rosmaria Binti Ismail[3],
Nurul Safwanah Binti Muhammad Saleh[3], and Yuliana Sari[1]

[1] Accounting Department, Politeknik Negeri Sriwijaya, Palembang, Indonesia
[2] Department of Business Administration, Politeknik Negeri Sriwijaya, Palembang, Indonesia
ha.di@polsri.ac.id
[3] Department of Commerce Polytechnic of Melaka, Malacca, Malaysia

Abstract. This study identifies bookkeeping practices among SMEs in the city. Palembang, Indonesia and Terengganu State, Malaysia, and for comparing levels of knowledge, skills, recording methods and attitudes towards record keeping in record-keeping practices in Indonesia and Malaysia. The population of this study includes all songket weaving and batik SMEs located in Palembang City, Indonesia and Terengganu State, Malaysia. Based on data recorded at the Palembang City Industry Office, there are 29 SMEs in songket weaving in Palembang, Indonesia and 30 SMEs for typical Malaysian batik cloth in Terengganu, Malaysia. The research time is 8 months in 2022 used a non parametric statistical sampling method, namely the Wilcoxon Signed Rank Test. The results showed that there are significant differences in the practice of financial recording in the city of Palembang, Indonesia and the state of Terengganu, Malaysia, especially in accounting knowledge and recording methods. However, when viewed from the Skills and Attitudes towards Recording, no significant difference in the practice of financial recording.

Keywords: SMEs · Accounting Knowledge · Skill · Financial Recording · Recording Method

1 Introduction

In 2021, the number of SMEs will be 64.2 million and contribute 61.07 percent to the Gross Domestic Product [1]. This condition proves that the SMEs sector continue to operate in the midst of Covid 19 conditions that have occurred since 2021, of course this is the main reason for the government to give great attention to SMEs as contributors to the national economy.

Besides Indonesia, Malaysia is also very concerned about developing SMEs, because SMEs are important contributors to stimulating economic growth, increasing Gross Domestic Product (GDP) and employment. In Malaysia, all SMEs registered with the Companies Commission of Malaysia, there are as many as 907,065 SMEs registered

R. Martini et al. (Eds.): FIRST 2022, ASSEHR 733, pp. 156–162, 2023.
https://doi.org/10.2991/978-2-38476-026-8_18

in Malaysia, of which more than 76% are represented by micro enterprises [14]. In Malaysia, SMESs are the cornerstone of the country's economy. This represents 97.2% of all commercial establishments in 2020.

Data from the Malaysia Statistical Business Register, in 2020, in Malaysia is 97.2% of the total commercial businesses. In terms of commercial size, micro-enterprises account for 78.4% (903.174), the largest share for SMEs. According to [2], the main focus of SMEs is to create companies that are innovative and competitive and have high resilience to compete in the global rankings. Therefore, it is important for SMEs to try to improve the performance of the companies they run.

To remain able to survive and thrive, SMEs must be responsive and able to overcome challenges, including one related to poor financial records. Accounting records are very important for decision making and knowing business performance [3]; [4], Bookkeeping will help SMEs to grow [5]. In practice, bookkeeping is a difficult thing for SMEs entrepreneurs because of limited knowledge of accounting [6], and the assumption that financial statements are not important for SMEs owners [7]. Business owners do not have proper records and do not have the separation of business and personal transactions [5, 8]. Some SMEs owners rely on their memory rather than recording transactions accurately [9]. As revealed by [10], keeping accounting records is expensive, and difficulties in maintaining an accounting system. In contrast, according to [11], manual recording to electronic records has simplified most of the bookkeeping expenses and is more reliable and accurate.

There are not many studies that compare the practice of financial records used to measure the achievement of SMEs performance in Indonesia and Malaysia. Therefore, this study analyzes SMEs in the two countries. The formulation of the problem being tested is the financial recording practice of SMEs seen from accounting knowledge, skills, recording methods and attitudes towards recording. How does the practices of Islamic boarding schools in Indonesia and Malaysia need to be compared? The research is intended to find out the factors that influence the practice of financial recording on SMEs in Indonesia and Malaysia and to compare the level of knowledge, skills, recording methods and attitudes towards recording in financial recording practices in Indonesia and Malaysia. The contribution of this research is to provide important indicators of SMEs financial recording practices and add to the literature on SMEs accounting practices.

2 Literature Review and Research Hypotheses

Based on Government Regulation no. 7/2021 Article 35 paragraph concerning SMEs business capital, (1) Micro Enterprises: the meaning of SMEs in the micro business category is a business that has a maximum business capital of 1 billion and does not include land and buildings for business. (2) Small Business: then, those classified as SMEs in the small business category are those that have a business capital of more than 1–5 billion (3) Medium Enterprises: SMEs are categorized as medium businesses, namely business capital of more than 5–10 billion and does not include land and building places for business.

The decision to do good record keeping allows business to plan properly and reduce the misuse of resources [12]. The recording method follows generally accepted financial accounting standards, especially for SMEs used SAK ETAP, this standard is the standard used to regulate non-profit institutions. Where not regulated in IFRS. There are many non-profit organizations that require standards that regulate their activities causing Indonesia to apply this standard, as well as in Malaysia. Based on this framework, the hypotheses can be proposed:

H1:   There is a difference in the average knowledge of bookkeeping in the practice of financial recording in Palembang City, Indonesia and Terengganu State, Malaysia.
H2:   There is a difference in average skills in the practice of financial records in Palembang City, Indonesia and Terengganu State, Malaysia.
H3:   There is a difference in the average recording method in the practice of financial recording in Palembang City, Indonesia and Terengganu State, Malaysia.
H4:   There is a difference in the average attitude towards recording on financial recording practices in Palembang City, Indonesia and Terengganu State, Malaysia.

3   Research Methodology

Type of research is a qualitative research on the perception of financial records in songket weaving and batik painting SMEs. Songket Weaving SMEs were chosen as the research sample from many types of SMEs in Indonesia. The famous songket woven fabric is in Palembang, because songket woven fabric is a typical handicraft of the city. While in Malaysia, Terengganu State is indeed famous for its batik painting and songket weaving companies. As a heritage product, batik is able to support cultural tourism activities and the country's fashion industry. The achievements of most batik firms are still dominated by small and simple business enterprises. In fact, a number of batik companies are micro. The population of this study includes all songket weaving and batik painting SMEs located in the city of Palembang, Indonesia and the State of Trengganu, Malaysia. Based on data from the Industry Office of Palembang City, there are 29 SMEs of songket weaving in Palembang, Indonesia and 30 SMEs of typical Malaysian batik cloth in Terengganu, Malaysia. Research instruments are developed by referring to and comparing with previous studies. For indicators of Knowledge of Bookkeeping and Skills, refer to [13], while for indicators of Recording Methods and Attitudes to Bookkeeping, it is adopted from [4, 5]. The following questions were asked to respondents:
Knowledge of Bookkeeping.

1.   I know bookkeeping is important
2.   I can explain the concept of bookkeeping.
3.   I can explain how bookkeeping practices and rules.
4.   I can identify the benefits a small business derives from proper bookkeeping.
5.   I can explain the basics of bookkeeping for a small business.
6.   I have the appropriate level of education to do bookkeeping.
7.   I have taken a bookkeeping course
8.   I am good at teaching people to keep books
9.   I have learned bookkeeping in a week
10. I can record financial transactions

Skills

1. I can distinguish between transactions for expenses and purchases
2. I can calculate gross profit or loss on a daily basis
3. I can fill out source documents for business transactions. Etc: invoices, receipts
4. I can check transactions over time using bookkeeping
5. I can handle record keeping systematically
6. I can identify transactions for expenses and income
7. I have cash withdrawal records and good for personal use.
8. I have records of business assets, liabilities and equity
9. I can easily find and record business transactions
10. I can record and manage outbound business inventory

Recording Methods

1. I keep bookkeeping records manually.
2. I keep bookkeeping records using Microsoft excel.
3. I keep bookkeeping records using accounting software

Attitude to Recording

1. I can afford the cost and time for record keeping.
2. Record keeping is key to business success
3. Record keeping is a tedious activity
4. Some businesses such as micro and small businesses do not require record keeping
5. Very good for recording all transactions business.
6. Keep records of transactions business.
7. How to hire an accountant to assist in the accounting records.
8. My business is very successful even though I don't use note
9. I would really appreciate being given the opportunity to learn more about note-taking.
10. My business is not big enough to keep the books.

The stages in testing the hypothesis used in this study are seen from the results of the normality test if the average data is normally distributed, then the statistical test technique used is parametric statistics, namely paired sample t test with α 0.05. If the average *abnormal return* not normally distributed, then the statistical test technique used is non-parametric statistics, namely the Wilcoxon Signed Rank Test with a significance level (α) 0.05. The criteria used for drawing conclusions are if the (α) > 0.05, then H_0 accepted, and level (α) < 0.05, then H_0 rejected.

4 Result and Discussion

From the total of 59 questionnaires distributed to each of 29 SMEs in Palembang City, Indonesia and 30 SMEs in Terengganu State, Malaysia, it is known that 55 questionnaires were returned and used. The rate of return of the questionnaire (response rate) and can be used (response use) of 81.25% with details as many as 30 respondents from the city of Palembang, Indonesia and as many as 22 respondents from the state of Terengganu, Malaysia. The statistical test tool that can be used to determine the difference with the non-parametric test is the Wilcoxon Signed Rank Test.

Value of sig. (signification) is below the level of 0.05, then H0 is rejected and H1 and H3 are accepted meaning that there are differences in the average knowledge of accounting and recording methods on financial recording practices in Palembang City, Indonesia and Terengganu State, Malaysia. While H2 and H4 are rejected, it means that skills and attitudes towards recording practices financial recording Palembang City, Indonesia and Terengganu State, Malaysia there is no difference in the average shown by the sig level. (signification) is above the level of 0.05.

The results of H1 is accepted, or there is a difference in accounting knowledge in the practice of financial records in the City of Palembang, Indonesia and the State of Terengganu, Malaysia. Due to the low knowledge of UKM treasurers of less disciplined accounting records, either in the form of daily, weekly, monthly, and so on.

The results of H2 is rejected with a significance level of 0.986 > 0.05, which means there is no difference. Skills in the practice of recording SMEs finances in Palembang City, Indonesia and Terengganu State, Malaysia. This finding proves that employees or administrative staff at SMESs in these two countries are already qualified and already have technical skills in the field of accounting.

The results Wilcoxon Signed Rank Test showed a sig. (tailed) value which is smaller than 0.05 (0.007 < 0.05), which means H0 rejected and H3 accepted, meaning that there are differences in recording methods in financial recording practices in city of Palembang, Indonesia and the state of Terengganu, Malaysia. Of course this finding is appropriate considering that each country has different accounting standards and treatment, because usually the State intervenes to authorize the accounting profession and that is why accounting standards vary around the world. This difference in recording methods can also be caused by several factors such as the political, economic, and social conditions of each country, as revealed [15] that in Indonesia, SMEs standards require additional standards.

Significance level of 0.265 which is above 0.05, this means that there is no difference in attitudes towards recording the practice of financial recording of SMEs in Palembang City, Indonesia and Terengganu State, Malaysia. This is because there is an average attitude that is supported by the same culture both in Indonesia and Malaysia so that it tends not to make the results of financial reporting different. The implementation of records to provide informative financial reports is something that is still considered difficult for SMEs actors both in Palembang City, Indonesia and Terengganu State, Malaysia. The absence of differences in financial recording practices is basically determined by the attitude of the accounting information of business actors who act as decision makers.

5   Conclusion

Based on the results, can be concluded that there are significant differences in the practice of financial recording in Palembang City, Indonesia and Terengganu State, Malaysia, especially in Accounting Knowledge and Recording Methods. However, when viewed from the Skills and Attitudes towards Recording, and no difference in the practice of financial recording. An important implication of this finding is that there are 2 challenges practices financial recording, namely First, SMEs managers must have human resources who have accounting knowledge and maximize recording methods according to financial standards generally applicable in each country.

This study has limitations, including this research only examines descriptively about the practice of financial records viewed from 4 internal aspects. In future research, it is suggested to examine the external aspect. This study also only uses samples from 2 cities in each country. If possible, investigations can be carried out on a wider sample and from a similar cluster of countries.

References

1. https://www.ekon.go.id/publikasi/detail/3331/government-support-capital-for-UMKM-as-a-strategy-support-national-economy
2. Yahya, NAI, Abu Bakar, NR, Shaharuddin, NS, & Bakar, NS (2021). Practice of Management Accounts among Small and Simple Companies (SMESs) in Kuala Lumpur and Selangor. *Journal of Management & Muamalah, Vol. 11, No. 1,* 44 – 59.
3. Abdul Rahamon, OA, Adejare, AT (2014). The Analysis of The Impact Of Accounting Records Keeping on The Performance of The Small Scale Enterprises. *International Journal of Academic Research in Business and Social Sciences, 4*(1), 1 -17.
4. Aladejebi, O., Oladimeji, JA (2019). The Impact of Record Keeping on The Performance of Selected Small and Medium Enterprises in Lagos Metropolis. *Journal of Small Business and Entrepreneurship Development, 7* (1), 28 -40.
5. Adeyemi, MS, & Akanji, AA (2020). Role of Book Keeping on Sustainability of Small and Medium Enterprises in Nigeria. *Methods, 4* (9), 140-154.
6. Isabel, T., Fernandes, M. (2015). Financial Literacy Levels of Small Business Owners and it Correlation with Firms' Operating Performance. *Master in Finance Dissertation.*
7. Kwak, S., Jeon, H. Good, Sh (2013). Korea's Cooperation Schemes to Development of Small and Medium Enterprises in Ethiopia. *KIEP Research Paper. World Economics, 3*(54), 13-54.
8. Roslan, N., Pauzi, NFM, Ahmad, K., Shamsudin, A., Karim, MS, & Ibrahim, SNS (2018). Preliminary investigation: Accounting literacy among small business owners.*International Journal of Academic Research in Business and Social Sciences,8* (10), 32–47.
9. Musah, A., Ibrahim, M. (2014). Record Keeping and the Bottom Line: Exploring the Relationship between Record Keeping and Business Performance among Small and Medium Enterprises in the Tamale Metropolis of Ghana. *Research Journal of Finance and Accounting, 5*(2).
10. Ibrahim, M. (2015). Impact assessment of accounting system on the performance of small and medium enterprises (SMEs) in Bauchi metropolis, Nigeria. *Proceedings of 32nd the iier International Conference, Dubai, UAE,* 8th
11. Azman, NA, Mohamed, A., Jamil. (2021). Artificial Intelligence in Automated Bookkeeping: a Value added Function for Small and Medium Enterprises.*JOIV: International Journal on Informatics Visualization, 5* (3), 224 - 230.

12. Mwebesa, Kansiime, C., Asiimwe, B., Mugambe, P. Rwego. (2018). The Effect of Financial Record Keeping on Financial Performance Of Development Groups In Rural Areas Of Western Uganda. *International Journal of Economics and Finance*, 10(4), 136-145. doi:https://doi.org/10.5539/ijef.v10n4p136.

13. Masliza Idani binti Mahmood, Nurul Safwanah binti Muhammad Saleh. (2018). A Financial Record for Bookkeeping Practices among Wholesale Markets at Central Melaka. *8th National Conference in Education Technical & Vocational Education and Training (CiE-TVET)*

14. SME Corporation Malaysia. (2021). SME Statistics. Retrieved from https://www.smecorp.gov.my/index.php/en/policies/2020-02-11-08-01-24/sme-statistics.

15. Dewanti, DK, & Kiswara, E. (2015). *Comparative study of the level of compliance with the adoption of the International Financial Reporting Standard in 12 countries* (Doctoral dissertation, Faculty of Economics and Business).

Role of Preventive and Functional Control in Budget Control Effectiveness

Kartika Rachma Sari[1], Dwi Kurnia Oktora Putri[1], Rita Martini[1(✉)],
Kartini binti Che Ibrahim[2], Desri Yanto[1], and Yulianto Wasiran[1]

[1] Politeknik Negeri Sriwijaya, Palembang, Indonesia
ritamartini@polsri.ac.id
[2] Politeknik Mukah, Mukah, Sarawak, Malaysia
kartini@pmu.edu.my

Abstract. The goal is that the government can control wastage of expenditure. Budgeting in order to prevent budget irregularities, such as irresponsibility to the budget, inappropriate budgets and others. There is a need for research to determine the impact of preventive and functional control on the effectiveness of budget control. The population of this research are 32 of the regional organizations of the Palembang city government. The data collection technique used a saturated sample technique by distributing questionnaires. SPSS is used in this study to perform multiple linear regression analysis. The test results show that preventive and functional controls have a strong effect on budgets that are controlled effectively. In this study shows that preventive control and functional control together have an effect on the effectiveness of budget control. The budget function achieved as a control tool is the effectiveness of the budget.

Keywords: Budget · Preventive Control · Functional Control

1 Introduction

As a control tool, the budget provides a detailed plan for government revenues and expenditures so that expenditures are made accountable to the public [1, 2]. Each government agency has a budget for operational activities that support the work activities of the government agency. The budget is very important to achieve good performance and participate in the government's role to serve the community. Especially in the realization of expenditures [3] that cannot be accounted for by the Palembang city offices, found weaknesses in internal control and non-compliance with laws and regulations as quoted from the Report on the Inspection Results of the Financial Audit Agency on the Palembang City Government Financial Report 2020.

Local government was also asked by the Corruption Eradication Commission to strengthen regional inspectorates, as reported by Media Indonesia by [4].The regional inspectorate is a navigator for regional governments that must be empowered to oversee development programs. Inspectorates can also be used to assess the efficiency of local government management, allocated budgets, and local revenues. The deputy chairman

R. Martini et al. (Eds.): FIRST 2022, ASSEHR 733, pp. 163–168, 2023.
https://doi.org/10.2991/978-2-38476-026-8_19

of the Corruption Eradication Commission also warned that local governments must refrain from wasting budgets and so that regional officials do not abuse their positions. The role of the regional inspectorate is considered important to monitor the potential for budget waste, prevent irregularities, and oversee regional development programs.

This research is modification of [5] with an update on the adjustment of research variables, namely functional control and focusing on the Palembang city government. In order to obtain accurate results, sampling was carried out on all regional organizations of the Palembang city government, and saw the results of each variable which varied.

2   Literature Review and Research Hypotheses

Preventive control according to [6] is supervision carried out before the start of the implementation of an activity, or before the occurrence of state financial expenditures. Preventing irregularities in the implementation of activities is the main objective of preventive control. Evidence [5, 7–11] that preventive control has a positive and strong effect on effective controlled budgets. However, according to [12, 13] preventive controls do not have a strong effect on the effectiveness of budgetary controls.

Especially the regional organization, basically carries out preventive control in order to prevent deviations in budget execution. Local governments will be burdened and disadvantaged if significant deviations occur, but budget implementation must continue [2, 14]. This explanation shows how closely related preventive oversight and budget effectiveness are. There is no longer a budget that is not accounted for and can create a budget that is right on target according to the plan if the existing budget is monitored for its use according to its designation. The effectiveness of a budget is closely related to preventive oversight. The effectiveness of budget control will increase along with good preventive control.

Functional control [11] affects the effectiveness of budget control. However, functional control [12] is not strong enough to create effective control plans. Functional supervision [15] is supervision by an institution or section that has supervisory roles and duties through inspection, testing, investigation, and assessment. The responsibility to ensure that supervision is carried out properly rests with the institution/agency/core that carries out the supervision through inspection, testing, assessment, monitoring, and evaluation. This activity [16] is to ensure that the government of a region runs in line with the planning and statutory regulations stipulated in order to realize state employees who are protected from corruption, cooperation, and differences in treatment.

Research hypothesis:

H1 :   The effect of preventive control on effectiveness of budget control.
H2 :   The effect of functional control on effectiveness of budget control.
H3 :   The effect of preventive control and functional control on effectiveness of budget control.

3   Research Methodology

The data analyzed were the results of questionnaire answers to regional apparatus organizations in the city of Palembang, totaling 32 as listed in [17]. This study used a saturated sample with five respondents, including Budget User Authority, Expenditure Treasurer, Commitment Making Officials, Financial Administration Officials-Regional Work Units, and Technical Implementation Officers of Activities.

The analytical instrument used is a multiple linear regression program using SPSS type 26. With this analytical method [18] a measure of the magnitude of the influence of the observed variables will be obtained. The multiple linear regression equations in this study are:

$$EBC = a + \beta_1 PC + \beta_2 FC + e \tag{1}$$

Description:

EBC   : Effectiveness of budget control
a   : Constant
β_1, β_2 : Regression coefficient
PC   : Preventive control
FC   : Functional control
e   : error

The tests carried out include the classical assumption test (which consists of normality, multicollinearity, and heteroscedasticity tests) and hypothesis testing.

4   Result and Discussion

The results of the hypothesis test show that the preventive control variable has a sig value of 0.000 which is smaller than 0.05, meaning that the variable is significant and has a t-$_{count\ value}$ (4.490) > t-$_{table}$ (1.981). The test results show that the preventive control variable has a positive and partially significant effect on the effectiveness of budget control. Thus, it is concluded that H_0 is rejected or H_1 is accepted. Preventive control which has the dimensions of granting approval, authorization, asset security, and segregation of duties affects the effectiveness of budget control. The better the preventive control on regional organization in the Palembang city government, the better the level of effectiveness of budget control, and it will happen the other way around.

This evidence supports [5, 7–11, 19] it was found that preventive controls have a strong influence on effective financial planning controls. The existence of preventive control is needed because it can prevent problems from arising so as to help achieve control over budget execution. Preventive control [20] is supervision carried out on an activity before the activity is carried out so that it is expected to prevent irregularities. This interpretation is in line with [21] which states that preventive control is a form of prevention of irregularities that can burden or harm the state.

Furthermore, the hypothesis test produces a functional control variable that has a significance of 0.003 which is less than 0.05, meaning that the variable is significant and has a t-$_{count\ value}$ (3.083) > t-$_{table}$ (1.981). Evidence is obtained where functional control has a strong effect partially on the effectiveness of budget control. So, we will get the conclusion of rejecting H_0 or accepting H_1. Therefore, functional control with the dimensions of supervision, assessment, investigation, and assessment has an effect on the effectiveness of budget control. Increasing functional control, budget control will be more effective, and vice versa.

Functional control has an influence on the effectiveness of budget control [11]. Functional control [15] is the supervision carried out by the institution/agency/unit which has the duty and function of supervising through inspection, testing, investigation and assessment. Supervision carried out by the institution/agency/core which has the task of supervising through inspection, testing, assessment, monitoring, and evaluation. The following regression equation:

$$EBC = 7.495 + 0.251 \ PC + 0.228 \ FC + e \tag{2}$$

The regression equation obtained explained:

1. The value 7.495 indicates that the independent variable, namely preventive control and functional control, is 0, then the effectiveness of budget control is 7.495.
2. The preventive control variable has a value of $+ 0.251$, indicating that there is a unidirectional relationship between this variable and the effectiveness of budget control. If the value of this variable increases by one point, the effectiveness of budget control will also increase by 25.1%.
3. Value $+ 0.228$, indicating a unidirectional relationship between functional control variables and budget control effectiveness variables. If this value increases by one, then the value of the effectiveness of budget control will increase by 22.8%.

Furthermore, the hypothesis test result $t_{count} > t_{table}$ (4.490 > 1.981) and sig value < 0.05 are the values of the preventive control. This shows that preventive control does not have a very strong effect on the effectiveness of budget control. $T_{count} > t_{table}$ (3.083 > 1.981) and sig < 0.05 are the values of the functional control. This indicates that functional control has limited effect on the effectiveness of budget control.

The computed F of the F statistical test is 28.034, as seen in the results of the F statistical test. The F_{table} of 3.08 yielded the following results. H_1 is acceptable because $F_{count} > F_{table}$. H_3 is accepted based on the significant value in the F test being less than 0.05, which is 0.000, and the estimated F_{value} being 28.034 > 3.08 (F_{table}). As a result, preventive control and functional control all have an impact on poverty.

Preventive control and functional control together have a positive and significant effect on the effectiveness of budget control. This can be said to have a significant positive effect, it is obtained that the calculated $F_{value} > F_{table}$ (28.034 > 3.08). In addition, seen also from the level of significance obtained 0.000 which means less than 5%. Thus, it can be stated that overall the independent variables have a positive and significant influence on the effectiveness of budget control. This means that H_0 is rejected or H_1 is accepted. An increase in adequate performance-based budgeting as well as preventive control and maximum functional control will increase the effectiveness of budget control for the regional organization in the Palembang city government. This is also supported by the results of the coefficient of determination test that has been carried out. The Adjusted R Square value is 0.334, meaning that the magnitude of the influence given by the preventive control and functional control on the effectiveness of budget control variables in the regional organization in the Palembang city government is 33.40 percent.

Overcoming obstacles and deviations [19, 21] can be carried out efforts such as detecting and controlling deviations and their consequences. Detecting fraud needs to be done in order to prevent waste, leakage, and irregularities in the use of authority, energy, money, and state-owned equipment, so that an orderly, clean, authoritative, successful and efficient apparatus can be developed. The element of overcoming these obstacles and irregularities, especially on the obstacles of human resources in the preparation of the budget for the regional organization in the Palembang city government has gone well. This is because the dimensions of overcoming obstacles and deviations as indicators that have the highest value are found in human resource constraints in the preparation of the budget.

5 Conclusion

In the Palembang city government, it was found evidence that an effectively controlled budget is very dependent on preventive control and functional control partially or simultaneously. As well as for further research, researchers can use the regional organizations in a larger and wider environment such as the regional organizations in South Sumatra province, use a direct interview approach to collect data, add other variables in research, and specifically for the functional control variable it should be distributed only to those who are related, namely inspectorate.

References

1. Mardiasmo. (2018). *Public sector accounting.* Yogyakarta: CV Andi Offset.
2. Putri, VN, Pisey, KK, Mardhiah, & Martini, R. (2021). Determinants of Regional Budget Absorption in the Regional Apparatus Organization of Palembang City. Atlantis Highlights in Social Sciences, Education and Humanities, volume 1. *Proceedings of the 4th Forum in Research, Science, and Technology (FIRST-T3–20).* 162–166. https://doi.org/10.2991/ahsseh.k.210122.028
3. Audit Board of the Republic of Indonesia. (2021). *Audit Result Report on the 2020 Financial Statements.* Jakarta: Supreme Audit Agency.
4. Winata, D. K. (2021). KPK Asks Regional Inspectorate to Strengthen Budget Oversight. *Media Indonesia*: https://mediaindonesia.com/politik-dan-law/410319/kpk-minta-inspektorat-area-perkuat-pengawasan-anggaran
5. Novita, A. (2021). Effect of Performance-Based Budgeting, Preventive Monitoring, and Detective Control on the Effectiveness of Budget Control. *Journal of Science and Research,* 1–20.
6. Baswir, R. (2000). *Indonesian Government Accounting.* Yogyakarta: BPFE-Yogyakarta.
7. Saputra, G., & Sujana, E. (2021). The Effect of Performance-Based Budgeting, Preventive Supervision and Detective Supervision on the Effectiveness of Budget Control in OPD in Buleleng Regency. *Scientific Journal of Accounting Students,* 373–382.
8. Haryoto, A. (2020). The Influence of Performance-Based Budgeting, Preventive Monitoring and Detective Supervision on the Effectiveness of Budget Control. *Journal of Accounting Science and Research,* 1–18.
9. Fajri, A. (2018). The Effect of Preventive Control and Detective Oversight on the Effectiveness of Budget Control. *Tower of Science,* 1–9.

10. Amin, M. (2018). The Effect of Preventive Supervision and Detective Supervision on the Effectiveness of Budget Control at the Government Inspectorate of South Sulawesi Province. *Economics Bosowa Journal*, 88–101.
11. Arini, TD (2017). Effect of Inherent Control, Functional Supervision, Preventive Supervision, Detective Supervision and Performance-Based Budgeting on the Effectiveness of Budget Control. *JOM Fekon*, 236–250.
12. Dendi, V. (2017). Effect of Inherent Control, Functional Supervision, Preventive Supervision, Detective Supervision and Performance-Based Budgeting on the Effectiveness of Budget Control. *JOM Fekon*, 1741–1755.
13. Biantoro, SY (2019). Effect of Preventive Supervision, Detective Supervision and Performance-Based Budgeting on the Effectiveness of Surabaya OPD Budget Control. Journal of Accounting Science and Research, 1–17.
14. Martini, R., Agustin, R., & Sari, KR (2020). Accrual Discretion Policy on Excess/Less Budget Financing at the Provincial Level. *TEST Engineering & Management*, 82, 9925-9935.
15. Sumarsono, Sonny. (2010). *Government Financial Management*. Yogyakarta: Graha science.
16. Sururama, R., & Amalia, R. (2020). *Government Supervision*. Bandung: CV Cendekia Press.
17. Mayor of Palembang. (2020). *Palembang Mayor Regulation Number 12 of 2020 concerning Amendments to Palembang Mayor's Regulation Number 96 of 2018* concerning the Establishment of the Organization and Work Procedure of the Palembang City Regional Research Council. Indonesia.
18. Priyastama, R. (2020). *The Book of SPSS, Data Processing and Analysis*. Yogyakarta: Start Up.
19. Martini, R., Hartati, S., Zulkifli, Z., & Widyastuti, E. (2019). Sistem Pengendalian Intern Pemerintah atas Akuntabilitas Pengelolaan Keuangan Dana Desa di Kecamatan Sembawa. *Jurnal Akademi Akuntansi*, 2(1). https://doi.org/10.22219/jaa.v2i1.8364
20. Nafarin, M. (2017). *Budgeting*. South Tangerang: Open University.
21. Halim, A., & M. Iqbal. (2019). *Interest Series Regional Financial Management: Regional Financial Management*. Yogyakarta: UPP STIM YKPN.

South Sumatra Business Showcase; Development South Sumatera Traditional Products Information System

Desi Apriyanty[1](✉), Bainil Yulina[2], Sarikadarwati[2], and Pridson Mandiangan[3]

[1] Department of Informatics Management, Politeknik Negeri Sriwijaya, Palembang, Indonesia
aprilananda@yahoo.co.id
[2] Department of Accounting, Politeknik Negeri Sriwijaya, Palembang, Indonesia
[3] Department of Business Administration, Politeknik Negeri Sriwijaya, Palembang, Indonesia

Abstract. Entrepreneurs must figure out how to serve clients fast and give them the information they need without being constrained by space, time, or distance when they run a firm. Because variables like the company's location, operating hours, and lack of product information may lower sales and even force clients to switch to better alternatives. In order to promote sales of various batik and culinary specialties in the South Sumatra region, this study aims to design a web-based E-Commerce Application system called the South Sumatra Business Storefront. This system will contain product data list features, data input, and available product information. The waterfall technique, which includes stages for system design, development, integration, operation, and maintenance, is the research methodology employed. MySQL serves as the database and PHP programming language. Data collection techniques using observations, interviews, and literature study. The output of this study resulted in a Business Storefront that is embodied in the form a of storefront portal web which has an MSME account and a compathatn who supports the marketing of MSME products and monitoring the performance of using the storefront portal. Through the South Sumatra business storefront, Indonesian people can access transaction information on sales of Batik products and traditional South Sumatran culinary delights.

Keywords: Information System · Business Storefront · E-Commerce · MSME

1 Introduction

Especially since the crisis hit Indonesia, the role of SMEs in the Indonesian economy has increased significantly. The crisis has proven that the resilience of small businesses is stronger than that of most large companies. His one of the biggest problems facing his MSME Entrepreneur (Micro/UKM) in Indonesia is marketing. In fact, his inexperienced MSMEs do not yet have a large market reach and reliable marketing capabilities. These trusted marketing skills can be improved with the guidance of a scientist. Universities apply the principles of joint commerce or joint marketing, so they can help marketing for MSMEs. In collaborative commerce, MSMEs, academics are called coaches in this

R. Martini et al. (Eds.): FIRST 2022, ASSEHR 733, pp. 169–180, 2023.
https://doi.org/10.2991/978-2-38476-026-8_20

case, and customers work together to buy and sell. Collaboration is done by building a web portal or website that can be accessed by third parties. South Sumatra has 4 local governments and 13 district governments. Tie-dye is a region-specific product found in every city and region. Tie-dyeing is a product of local wisdom as each region and city has its own unique style, such as Jupuri B Palembang Batik, Duren Le Buklingau Batik, Gumbo Banyuasin Batik, Musi Banyuasin Sake Batik. This batik has various patterns and motifs. However, the presence of Kabu/City Batik in Sumatra is very important.

At that time, the people of Indonesia, especially those of South Sumatra, did not know much about the batik trade in the South Sumatra region. Out of this research effort, the South Sumatra Business Showcase is the development of an informational business application to showcase batik varieties from four regions of South Sumatra, three typical food types of the South include:, Regional Sumatra, Pempek, Kempran, Crackers, and many different types. The typical cake of Palembang. This his website is part of the MSME storefront web portal. UMKM web portal has two types of accounts for him: MSME account and coach or research team. In addition, MSME accounts have features that support MSME marketing. Coach accounts, on the other hand, have the ability to monitor MSME usage in the storefront portal. The Indonesian community can access transaction information through the South Sumatra Business storefront. Hence, the title of this article is Designing a Business Storefront Information System for Traditional Product Storefronts in South Sumatra.

2   Literature Study

Definition of Business Storefront
According to [1] buyers can quickly view an online store's homepage or feed, so that the online storefront can determine if a product works. Therefore, the appearance of online shops on social media should be made more attractive.

Information Technology Approach
In [2] said that business circles widely use the information technology approach to boost the sales business. In fact, [3] the importance of IT is increasingly being acknowledged and used, particularly in advancing marketing techniques, one of which is the website [4].

Definition of E-*Commerce*
According to [5] the findings of earlier studies conducted by [6], the results of a previous study conducted by the Informatics Research Program at the University of Surakarta were: "A solution to the problem from a PHP and MYSQL-based online shop application (E-commerce). published a journal titled Businesses already have websites but do not yet have online stores, resulting in poor marketing of their products. [8th place]. So are the programming language PHP and the MySQL database. This program was created using the waterfall process. This study investigated user application acceptance rates using experimental and quantitative methods.

It can be inferred that this application is functioning well based on the Unified Modeling Language (UML) tool is used as the modeling language in the system development technique [6, 7]. This study creates a website-based marketing platform with an online store for CV. Cakcuk Surabaya so that the available consumer communication channels are more effective. Interactive as an information medium for waste processing so that it has android-based economic value.

According to [8], Information Systems Study Program, Faculty of Engineering and Computer Science, Universitas Islam Indragiri, in Its publication, E-Commerce Sales of Clothing on Web-Based Mariati Stalls, examines sales reports and transactions, simplifying the transaction process for vendors and purchasers in addition to disseminating sales data in the form of reports both in the form of reports.

Consumers can browse products and product information, providing sellers and buyers with transaction convenience. E-commerce also means advertising, selling and providing the best support and service through his webshop 24 h a day for every customer, according to Garner [4, 9], is the process of purchasing and reselling goods and services via online consumer services on the Internet. The letter e, which is short for electronic, has gained popularity as a prefix for other terms related to electronic transactions. According to [3, 10], the concept of e-commerce in question is the buying and selling of goods and services through the Internet using online computer services.

Micro, Small, and Medium Enterprises (MSMEs)
The government has always prioritized the MSME business unit as it still causes problems. According to Law No. 20 of 2008 on MSMEs, MSMEs are defined as follows a micro business is a profitable business owned by individuals and small businesses that follows the legal definition of a micro business.

The law [11] states that the value of net worth, the value of assets excluding land and buildings for business premises, or annual sales revenues are the criterion used to define MSMEs. Using the following standards:

a. A business is considered a micro business if it meets the following requirements: a) Net assets not exceeding IDR 50,000,000.00 (50 million Rupiah) (excluding land and buildings used as a place of business)
b. Sales of up to IDR 300,000,000.00 each year (three hundred million rupiah).
c. The requirements for small businesses are as follows: Net assets of at least IDR 50,000,000.00 (50 million rupiah) and up to IDR 500,000,000.00 (500 million rupiah), excluding land and buildings used as a place of business; Generate annual sales. (2.5 billion rupiah).

Definition of Information
"Information is data managed and processed to produce meaning and support decision-making" write [12] explains that "Information is data that has been structured, has had applications, and has been beneficial." Given the two definitions given above, it is clear that information has the connotation of a managed set of data with applications and advantages in decision-making.

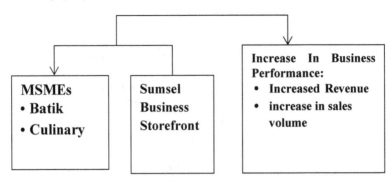

Fig. 1. Frame of mind

Definition of Information System's

"An information system is a system that is arranged methodically and consistently From a network of connected information flow each aspect a system that facilitates communication between functional sections or units," state Agus Irwan et al. (2016:8). According to [9, 12], information systems are structured methods of gathering, entering, processing, and storing data as well as storing, managing, and regulating information in order to help an organization achieve its objectives. An information system is a system that is systematically assembled from a network within an organization that connects each part. This organization supports the operation function in data collection, entry, processing, and storage by delivering information reports so that there is communication between functional parts or units and can accomplish the goals that have been set.

Data Flow Diagram (DFD)

DFD, according to [10, 13], is a logical model that describes what happens throughout data processing, from the origin and use of the data, to the location of the data and the processes that created it, to the interactions and processes that take place within the data.

The frame of mind

The frame of mind in this study is shown in Fig. 1.

3   Research Methodology

3.1   Analysis Method

The descriptive analysis technique of research was used in this study to gather data, analyze it, and investigate potential issues in order to gain fresh understandings that may be used to guide policy.

Tools and Materials Needed in making a website

- Laptop/Computer: used to make coding and publish a website.
  Laptop/Computer: Internet network: used so that a laptop or computer can access online search engines because in publishing a website, an internet network is needed to make coding and publish a website.

- Domain: the function of the domain is to provide an identity to a website so that there is no duplication and its nature is unique. Therefore, the purpose of using hosting is to store information and data belonging to the website.
- Hosting: The main function of hosting is indeed to store data. The data you want to display to visitors must be uploaded and stored in the hosting so it can be displayed. Because hosting serves as storage space
- Search Engine: a search engine application such as Chrome, Mozilla, Microsoft Edge, and so on that is used to access pre-hosted websites.
- Other supporters:
- Xampp: Using the Apache HTTP Server software as a stand-alone server (localhost), or, to put it another way, one that is reachable even when offline. PHP is a programming language used to create the MySQL database and the translation language.
- Visual Studio Code: used to research code (Coding) in website creation, be it creating an interface page or creating code in each action on each button so that it can be saved into the database
- PHP: programming language used in website creation

3.2 Object of Data Collection

According to the title chosen, the partners were the proprietors of MSME of South Sumatra batik fabrics and traditional gastronomy in South Sumatra, who were employed as the object of data collection, which became the topic of research., consisting of Mr. Potato (Palembang), Wong Kito Gallery (Musi Banyuasin), Linggau Batik Studies (Lubuklinggau), Dipa batik juju (Muara Enim), Kemplang Crackers 519 Mackerel Cap, Dapur Ita Business, and pempek Rayhan.

3.3 Design of Data Collection

The waterfall model framework of the SDLC (Software Development Life Cycle) was employed in the study's design. This approach is frequently referred to as the lifeline classic or the linear sequential model (Sequential Liniear) (Classic Life Cycle). The System Development Life Cycle (SDLC), as defined by [11, 18], is the process of creating or updating a software system employing models and methodologies that have previously been used to create software systems (based on best practices or well-tested methods). The waterfall model offers a sequential or sequential approach to the steps of analysis, design, coding, testing, and support in the software life cycle.

4 Results and Discussion

Research Implementation

1. Identify problems, opportunities, and research objectives.
   At this stage researcher tries to examine the problems that exist in the community and tries to solve these problems which will later become the research objectives. The problem that will be solved by the researchers is the lack of marketing media

for MSME of South Sumatera's batik and culinary products which affect to limited scope of marketing from the MSME products with good quality. So in this study the researchers try to solve these problems by offering solutions in the form of making e-commerce named as South Sumatera Business Showcase to increase the income of the MSME subjects.

2. Conducting a literature study, while based on the problems found previously, several theoretical basis were obtained.

3. Analyzing functional requirements.
   At this stage the researcher tries to make e-commerce specifications. The functional requirements for e-commerce applications are as follows:

   a. Accounts, in general accounts in the application are divided into 3 types of users related to system access rights, namely: buyers who are the consumers of products, sellers who are the MSME in the Malang Regency of Economic Enterprise and Micro Business, and system administrators who are the member of Malang Regency of Economic Enterprise which functions to verify the buyer and seller accounts in order to make sure that the whole sellers are the MSME subjects located in Malang Regency.

   b. Home page, serves to display information related to user accounts that contain user identities such as names, contact number, address, email address, and bank account number.

   c. Dashboard, is a feature that serves to display information about the summary of user account. For buyer and seller accounts it contains a list of transaction and balances, which consist of active balance and withdrawal balance, while for the system administrator accounts contains a summary of all transaction that occur in self-trading, number of buyers, number of sellers.

   d. Transaction, is a feature that serves to display information about transactions that occur. In this transaction feature, the buyer can monitor whether the request for goods or services is received by the seller, and from the seller's point of view, the seller can approve the request for the transaction for goods or services.

   e. List of Goods, this feature mainly owned by the seller, it serves to display a list of goods or services being sold, provide prices, has the ability to input the number of the goods and add information of the goods or services by the form of photos, specification, and additional descriptions.

   f. Feedback is a feature that allows users to rate the effectiveness of transactions involving goods or services sold by MSME subjects. With this feature, it is believed that the quality of goods and services would increase and that it will be simpler for customers to decide which items and services to buy.

   g. Settings, this feature serves to further manage the account to be detailed, such as changing email addresses, mobile phone numbers, or changing profile pictures.

4. Designing the system that would be recommended, as shown in Fig. 2.
   The Business Showcase application is an integrated system of digital sales media and MSME partners which is described in Figs. 3 and 4.

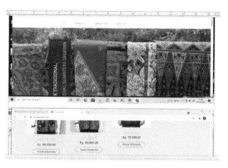

Fig. 2. South Sumatera Business Showcase

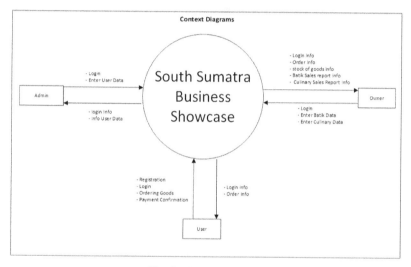

Fig. 3. Context diagram

The system designed in the application consist of users which detailed as follows:

1. Use Case Diagram

   In general, there are three actors in usage diagram design, namely system administrators, sellers from MSME, and buyers.

   In the system administrator use case diagram, system administrator users can verify seller and buyer accounts, they can also view buyers and sellers data, and view dashboards by logging in first (Fig. 5).

   In the seller's use case diagram, the seller user can perform several activities such as registering requirements in order to be able to login into the system and access the system, updating product data, updating transaction, updating seller's info, and viewing dashboard (Fig. 6).

   In the buyer use case diagram, the buyer can perform several activities such as registering requirements in order to be able to login into the system and access the

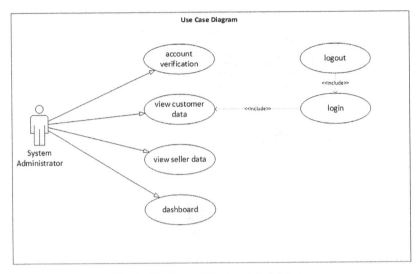

Fig. 4. Use Case of System Administrator

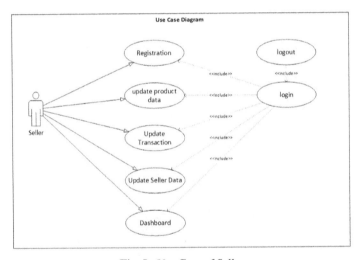

Fig. 5. Use Case of Seller

system, viewing product, updating transaction, updating buyer's info, and viewing dashboard (Fig. 7).

User Interface Design
The result of the Business Showcase information system design shows the appearance of the application created is shown in Figs. 8, 9, 10 and 11.

A web-based marketing medium with an e-commerce system called South Sumatra Business Showcase is the result of the study as a more effective way of communicating with customers. The advent of electronic commerce, also known as e-commerce, has

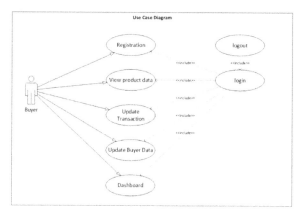

Fig. 6. Use Case of Buyer

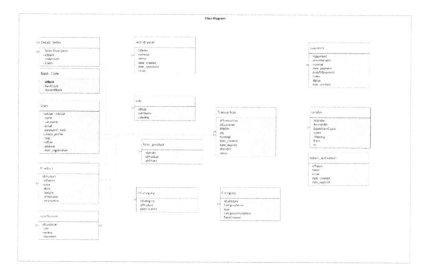

Fig. 7. Class Diagram

forced his MSME tie-dye and cookware manufacturer in South Sumatra to make great efforts to improve performance and expand existing applications.

This is consistent with and lends support to research by [6, 7], which discusses the need for more effective and efficient information systems in order to expand and speed up the promotion and marketing process.

E-commerce, as defined by [14], is the exchange of goods, services, and information over computer networks, most of which are the Internet.

With the use of this website, vendors may effortlessly advertise their goods to a larger audience. In addition, it should be mentioned that, in accordance with the findings of [6, 7]. This information system requires strong system security and development in a more professional direction in order to provide high quality information. Regular data

Fig. 8. Login Page

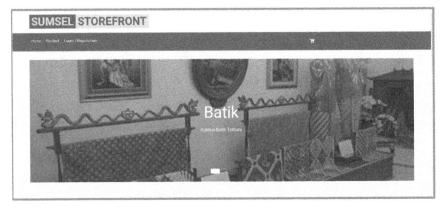

Fig. 9. Dashboard

Fig. 10. Shopping Feature

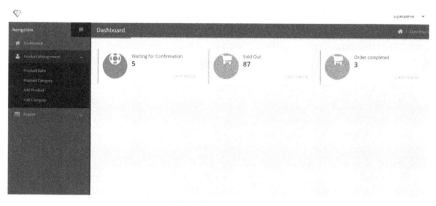

Fig. 11. Showcase

backups are also necessary in the event that the Web server crashes or is lost. On the web safety page, it is advised to perform routine monitoring to prevent unpleasant things from happening. To optimize the interface, the web page's appearance needs to be upgraded. Regular maintenance must be performed on both the hardware and the software.

5 Conclusion

Researchers can make several conclusions based on the information provided previously, that the existence of a website can improve the service and quality offered by technological advances. Product marketing on the Sumbatiksel website makes it easier for customers to shop, find out what items they want to buy, save time when making reports so it doesn't take long.

References

1. F. Keikha and E. Sargolzaei, "Designing two-dimensional electronic business-to-consumer models' map by fuzzy delphi panel," *J. Theor. Appl. Electron. Commer. Res.*, vol. 12, no. 2, pp. 21–36, 2017, doi: https://doi.org/10.4067/S0718-18762017000200003.
2. H. Sorensen, "The Successful Entrepreneur: The Role of Market-Oriented Business Development," *SSRN Electron. J.*, 2012, doi: https://doi.org/10.2139/ssrn.2128550.
3. M. B. Prescott and S. A. Conger, "Information technology Innovations: A classification by IT Locus of impact and research approach," *ACM SIGMIS Database*, vol. 26, no. 2–3, pp. 20–41, 1995, doi: https://doi.org/10.1145/217278.217284.
4. D. Gelrandy, O. D. Nurhayati, and E. D. Widianto, "Pembuatan Aplikasi 'Warung Keluarga' Sebagai Aplikasi E-Commerce Berbasis Web dan Mobile," *J. Teknol. dan Sist. Komput.*, vol. 4, no. 2, p. 432, Apr. 2016, doi: https://doi.org/10.14710/jtsiskom.4.2.2016.432-441.
5. J. M. Joshi and G. M. Dumbre, "Basic concept of e-commerce," *Int. Res. J. Multidiscip. Stud.*, vol. 3, no. 3, pp. 1–5, 2017.
6. R. Imam, "Aplikasi Toko Online (E-Commerce) Berbasis PHP dan MYSQL," *Univ. Surakarta*, 2016.

7. A. Y. Effendy and Y. S. Kunto, "Pengaruh Customer Value Proposition Terhadap Minat Beli Konsumen Pada Produk Consumer Pack Premium Baru Bogasari," *J. Manaj. Pemasar. PETRA*, vol. 1, no. 2, pp. 1–8, 2013.

8. Masitah, "E-Commerce Penjualan Pakaian Pada Lapak Mariati Berbasis Web," *J. Intra-Tech*, vol. 2, no. 2, pp. 1–11, 2018.

9. G. Bryan A, H. Abdul, and Barakatullah, "Konsep belanja E-Commerce," 2005.

10. A. Halim and T. Prasetyo, *Bisnis E-Commerce : studi sistem keamanan dan hukum di Indonesia/Abdul Halim Barkatullah, Teguh Prasetyo*. Yogyakarta: Pustaka Belajar, 2005.

11. Utami and Khasanah, "Sistem informasi Penjualan Kerajinan Tempurung Kelapa Berbasis Web pada Butik 'Wood & Coconut,'" *J. dan Penelit. Tek. Inform.*, 2018.

12. Krismiaji, *Sistem Informasi Akuntansi*. Yogyakarta: UPP STIM YKPN, 2015.

13. A. Kristanto, *Perancangan Sistem Informasi dan Aplikasi*, Edisi revi. Yogyakarta: Gaya Media, 2018.

14. Widani, "Menguji Ketajaman Implementasi E-Commerce Dalam Penjualan Kamar Hotel di Bali," *Manaj. dan Bisnis*, vol. 16 (2), 2019, doi: https://doi.org/10.38043/jmb.v16i2.2042.

Introduction to Islamic Economic Methodology

Ugi Suharto[(✉)]

University of Buraimi, Al-Buraimi, Oman
usuharto@ahlia.edu.bh

Abstract. This paper suggests that in the process of Islamization of economics, three methods namely 'negation', 'integration', and 'value addition' can be applied simultaneously to the existing body of conventional economics. What is inherently in conflict with Islamic worldview must be rejected and negated. Likewise, what is in line with it must be accepted and integrated into Islamic economics. Moreover, Islamic economics must also give new contributions to this conventional science by adding more universal Islamic values acceptable to humanity. Then what to negate, integrate, and value add, is to be guided by the Islamic worldview, which is a prerequisite for Islamization of knowledge.

Keywords: Islamic Economic · Conflict

1 Introduction

A prominent Islamic economics scholar, Dr. Umer Chapra, revealed that Islamic economics is "economics with an Islamic perspective" [1]. Of course, what he meant by 'economics' here was none other than conventional economics discipline. The "Islamic perspective" he told is the worldview of Islam because he also connects the term 'perspective' with other words such as 'vision,' and 'worldview.' So, in short, Islamic economics is conventional economics that is in line with the Islamic worldview.

Islam's worldview needs special attention from the Islamic economics discipline. The adjective "Islamic," associated with "Economics," is not just a patch without a meaning. But it has a profound purpose which includes not only the "religious" aspect that is often understood in a narrow sense but also a broad aspect of "civilization." Therefore Islamic economics is also economics born out of Islamic civilization or the 'tamaddun' of Islam, not just economics of the "religion" of Islam. What is interesting is the origin of the word "tamaddun" which means "civilization," and comes from the word "din," meaning "religion". A contemporary Muslim thinker, Syed Muhammad Naquib al-Attas, said that the words "din," "Madinah," and "tamaddun" are derived from the same Arabic root word [2]. So Islamic civilization is the civilization that grew up from the Din of Islam itself. Thus Islamic economics is no exception too; it is an economics based on the Islamic Din, developed in Islamic civilization and its 'tamaddun.' Because of that broader sense, Islamic economics is more "civilizational" rather than "religious," even though in Islam, the basis of that "civilization" is also "religion." As for the Islamic worldview, it is a set of permanent principles (tsawabit) and never change, usuli, qat'i, ijma', muhkamat,

R. Martini et al. (Eds.): FIRST 2022, ASSEHR 733, pp. 181–195, 2023.
https://doi.org/10.2991/978-2-38476-026-8_21

ma'lum min al-din and wahdah. This is What constitutes "the hardcore" of Islam? Other than this is termed mutaghayyirat, far'i, zanni, khilaf, mutasyabihat, and kathrah, which are "the protective belt" using the terminology of Imre Lakatos [3]. The Muslim scholar who greatly talks about the notion of "Islamic worldview" nowadays is Syed Muhammad Naquib al-Attas in his book Prolegomena to the Metaphysics of Islam.

Indeed, before we talk about Islamic economics, comprehending the notion of "Islamic worldview" is a must because we have stated above that Islamic economics is conventional economics which is in line with the "Islamic worldview." But for the sake of not raising an issue in the mind of the reader, especially for those who consider the worldview less relevant, I will postpone touching the point of the Islamic worldview later in the other part of the paper. Islamic economics cannot be separated from conventional economics. The paradigm of traditional economics will remain functional in constructing the core of Islamic economics and its practice. The traditional economics theory will remain significant in Islamic economics discourse, whether micro or macro.

The book Readings in Microeconomics – An Islamic Perspective [4] is an example of the discourse in Islamic economics that uses conventional microeconomics analysis. According to Islamic perspectives, topics like 'consumer behavior,' 'producer behavior', 'market structure', 'resource allocation', 'distribution,' and others were discussed in that book. Besides that, the Islamic economics discipline also reflects the paradigm of positive economics and normative economics. What is said as 'law of demand', 'law of supply', 'law of diminishing marginal utility', and 'law of diminishing return' in the positive economics paradigm will also apply in Islamic economics. Even some normative economic aspects, be it from capitalism or socialism, remain functional in the practice of the Islamic economic system.

The issue is how far the influence of conventional economics paradigm in formulating Islamic economics as a discipline in the future. What is the Islamization of Economics all about as being actively discussed nowadays? To answer this, one needs to have a master's in conventional economics as well as Islam at the same time. It is true that the fiqh muamalat has a close connection with the discipline of economics. Still, the dimensions of economics are much bigger than just the legal and ethical aspects of fiqh muamalat. The discipline of economics covers science and its scientific methodology, which are not covered by fiqh muamalat. Despite it, Islamic economics certainly will apply the fiqh muamalat as one of its normative economics aspects.

Deriving some lessons from our past scholars in dealing with the disciplines originally out of Islamic civilization and later integrated into it, we can make an analogy for the case of conventional economics and the Islamic one. For example, in the case of the discipline of philosophy, which has been integrated into the Islamic civilization, there are three different positions of the scholars:

1. Ibnu Sina and other Muslim peripatetic philosophers generally accepted philosophy without looking at its negative aspects.
2. Al Ghazali accepted some and refused some other aspects.
3. Ibnu Taymiyyah viewed philosophy negatively.

Indeed, there are differences in the dimensions between the discipline of philosophy and economics. Philosophy has more intellectual and theoretical dimensions whereas economics is not fully theoretical since its practical aspect is also bigger. As for other discipline like medicine has a more practical dimension to it. We do not hear that Ibnu Sina, Al Ghazali, and Ibnu Taymiyyah had different views in accepting this Greek medical science legacy. This does not mean that all conventional practices are welcome in Islamic economics because applying the discipline of economics differs from the ones in medical practices.

Economics has its reasoning as well as practicing dimensions. In other words, the knowledge (al-'ilm) and the practice (al-'amal) side of economics are peculiar to its discipline. Methodologically, conventional economics must be compared with the standard of Islamic knowledge. An example is the concept of 'want' in traditional economics must be compared with the concept of 'daruriah.' 'hajjiah', and 'kamaliyah' in usul fiqh. 'Unlimited wants' as what is being claimed by conventional economics can furthermore be questioned in Islamic economics because of the concept 'tama" (greed) and 'qana'ah' (self-satisfaction) in Islamic ethics and tasawwuf.

As for the above aspect, then the epistemology of Islam is needed. Then the knowledge of theology (Kalam) plays its role when it comes to the dialog with the foundations of conventional economic thought. Whether the economic assumptions and theories have attained the degree of certain knowledge (qat'i) or are still at the level of doubt (zanni); that matter should be debated first. For instance, the concepts of 'wants,' 'scarcity,' 'rationality', 'maximization', 'self-interest', 'ceteris paribus', in conventional economics, which are focused on the aspect of human profit-loss calculation, for sure cannot be taken for granted as 'certain knowledge' in Islamic economics.

On the practical side, the application of conventional economics should also be compared with the standard of Islamic practices. For instance the application of usury (riba) in conventional economics eventhough supported by various theories of interest, will remain questionable and cannot be considered for its compatibility with practical Islamic standards. With that notion of ribawi-interest, the idea of factors of production which claims that the capital factor will generate interest return, cannot be used in the theory of Islamic economic production.

As a response to the above theory, some scholars of Islamic economics have tried to come up with some Islamic economics production theory alternative. Fahim Khan, for example, has divided the Islamic economic production factors, instead of four factors, into only two factors, namely "hired factors of production" (HFP) dan "entrepreneurial factors of production" (EFP) [5]. This is in line with the concept of "ujrah" and "ribh" in fiqh al-muamalat. The parts of conventional economic production factors like land and labor are included in HFP and get ujrah (fixed compensation) for the use of the usufruct. In contrast, the capital and entrepreneur are included in EFP and get ribh (floating profit).

Consequently, there are many topics and practices of conventional economics that can be responded to from the Islamic economics perspective. The publication of various literature concerning Islamic economic thought has demonstrated vibrant research in Islamic economic studies within the conventional economic discipline. Muhammad Nejatullah Siddiqi, for example, 1981 surveyed Islamic economics literature available at that time. He successfully found 700 titles of Islamic economic thought on various topics in his book Economic Thinking—A Survey of Contemporary Literature [6]. This time we believe that the figures of Islamic economic literature have been added exponentially after passing the last two decades. Socialization of Islamic economics in the Islamic world which started about in 1970's was positively corelated with the desire of Muslims to practice Islam as the way of life including in the economic life. But as stated above the attempt to "islamize" conventional economics discipline needs an integration and mastery of conventional economics and Islamic disciplines at once. Unfortunately, we have just generated scholars who have high Islamic spirit but still lacking in having Islamic standard scholarship.

Today the economics studies at the higher learning institution in the Islamic world are still not integrating of studying *Islamic studies* covering some primary courses such as *'Ulum al-Qur'an, 'Ulum al- Hadith, Mantiq, Usul al Fiqh, Kalam, Tasawwuf, Fiqh and the Islamic history.* Socializing Islamic economics at the higher learning institutions should be started with the integration of Islamic studies with conventional economics. This is because from the Islamic epistemological point of view, those of Islamic studies are in fact compulsory upon all Muslims (fard 'ayn), let alone to the Muslim scholars, whereas studying conventional economics is only optional (fard kifayah). But what is happening today, the Muslim society, as a result of following Western education, begin their academic journey with the optional one (fard kifayah). They have high qualifications of economics studies but their personal obligatory knowledge (fard ayn) is not as the same qualification as the former. The question is, how can Islamization of economics possibly be carried out via the scholars who do not equip themselves with the authoritive disciplines of Islamic studies? What the contrary happened is that; these scholars begin questioning and blaming the genuine Islamic principles which are in contradiction with the the the principles of conventional economics. This is the result of mastery of fard kifayah knowledge among the Muslims being more dominant than that of the fard ayn. The knowledge of Fardu kifayah instead of guarding and preserving the Muslim society, now start questioning the very foundation of Islamic principles which are held by the majority of Muslims. This is what has been done by the so-called liberal Muslim thought.

When scholars of conventional economics understand Islamic thought correctly, they will be better off than just being conventional economics scholars. "Khiyarukum fil-jahiliyah khiyarukum fil-Islam, idza faquhu" (those of you who are the best in your pre-Islamic time will also be the best in your Islamic era if you have understood) as stated by the prophet (p.b.u.h) in the hadith narrated by Imam al- Bukhari. Therefore, an exemplary scholar of conventional economics would also become an excellent Islamic economics scholar if he understood Islamic disciplines properly.

The awareness of islamizing conventional economics started with the scholars who have fard 'ayn knowledge and the fard kifayah. Figures like Muhammad Nejatullah Siddiqi, Muhammad Baqir al-Sadr, and Umer Chapra are among those who have a good mastery of Islamic disciplines. Siddiqi, for example, had become a professor and held the head of the Islamic Studies Department at Aligarh University [7]. Baqir al-Sadr in Iraq's Shi'ite community was considered mujtahid mutlaq and marja' [7]. So does Umer Chapra, in his new book, presented a multidisciplinary Islamic economics concept which at once showed his good mastery in Islamic Studies. In fact, since 1986 the same issue had been confirmed in the proceedings of a symposium related to Problem of Research in Islamic Economics which was organized by The Islamic Research and Training Institute

(IRTI), Islamic Development Bank (IDB). In that proceedings, Prof. Dr. Nevzat Yalcintas had stated that:

It is natural for Islamic economics to be related to other areas of Islamic knowledge, because it derives from the same sources as they do and deals with an aspect of human behaviour whose other aspects are tackled by other branches of Islamics. Yet Islamic economics has closer ties with some Islamic disciplines especially ethics, usul, (axioms) fiqh, theology (Aqidah), and history.

As a consequence, he put forward certain conditions for those who want to embark in Islamic economics and doing research related to it subsequently to have some qualifications as the followings: "A researcher working in Islamic economics must have, I believe, the following academic qualifications in order to be able to contribute in this new field:

(i)   Sound, deep and up-to-date knowledge of economics;
(ii) Solid background of Shari'ah
(iii) Proficiency in Arabic to be able to use primary sources

I think, these are the basic requirements for any researcher working in this new domain. Some might find it difficult and unnecessary, especially for the third qualification. But those who are serious about research will appreciate it. We have also to bear in mind that no important step in Islamic studies can be realized without sufficient knowledge of Arabic. As we have seen in this paper, the ties of Islamic economics with other branches of Islamics are direct and very strong."

After seeing the relationship between Islamic economics with the other Islamic disciplines, let us now go to the methodology of Islamizing the conventional economics itself. I propose Islamization of economics will take simultaneous three approaches towards the conventional economics:

i.   Negation approach
ii.   Integration approach
iii. Value Addition approach

1.1 Negation Approach

Negation approach, like the factor of negating gods except Allah (laa ilaaha illaa Allah), is a part of the process of Islamization. For this reason, in the context of islamization of economics, not all the paradigms of conventional economics are acceptable in Islamic economics. Some conventional economics paradigms, even their fundamental parts must be negated and cannot be compromised with te Islamic teachings. This is what is called by al-Attas as 'Dewesternization of Knowledge'. [1] in the economics context said:

The paradigms of both disciplines are radically different. Then Islamic paradigm is not secularist, value-neutral, materialist and social-Darwinist. It is rather based on a number of concepts which strike at the root of these doctrines.

Obviously the elements of secularism, liberalism, materialism and social darwinism must be eliminated from the worldview of Islam economics. Before the book of The Future of Economics published, in his work Islam and the Economic Challenge, Chapra has already stated the importance of "filter" mechanism which is necessary in the process of Islamization of economics. For instance, in the paradigm of conventional economics regarding the notion of 'scarcity' which is saying that the economic problem begin with the scarcity of resources to fulfill the unlimited wants, this notion of 'scarcity' should be first filtered by "the moral filter" of Islam before being allowed to enter the discourse of Islamic economics. He says;

Islam makes it incumbent upon all Muslims to pass their potential claims on resources through the filter of Islamic values so that many are eliminated before they can be expressed in the market place. In this way claims on resources that do not contribute to positively to or which divert from the realisation of human well-being are eliminated at source before exposure to the second filter of market price.

Eventhough Chapra talks about the filter mechanism on a special reference, but the general filter mechanism can be applied in the process of filtering conventional economics which is not parallel with the Islamic worldview. In this case the filtering is carried out by way of negation and elimination.

Parallel with Chapra, another Islamic economics thinker, Baqir al-Sadr, was also presenting the same case. He is even more "radical" by saying that Islamic economics is "Islamic economics school of thought" (al-mazhab al-iqtisadi li al-Islam) which is totally different with the ones of capitalism or socialism as well as communism. Al Sadr said [8]:

When we say "Islamic economy" this does not mean political economy as this discipline just recently appeared. In addition to it, Islam (which appeared much earlier) is the religion of da'wah and the way of life, and it is not its task to do that kind of academic research... Subsequently what we mean by Islamic economy is Islamic economic school which actualizes Islamic values and practices in managing the economic life. With what this school possesses and with all are being demonstrated in its main thought, (Islamic economics) combines Islamic thoughts in ethics, intellectualism, economy, and history then relating them with political economic issues (such as in capitalism case) or with the human history (in the case of marxism).

Furthermore al-Sadr made a bold claim that Islamic economics is not a science and has not yet become 'scientific' so long Islam is not being practiced in the life of society so that the complete data and facts can be abstracted to form the positive Islamic economics theory. It is clear from this case that al-Sadr has given the stressing on the "inductive" method of science itself. However, al-Sadr also acknowledged the other method to imagine the presence of Islamic economy without being conditioned by having the existence of perfect Islamic society first. This is the 'deductive method' by using the principles of Islamic teachings which can be used formulate the theory of Islamic economics. Because of his notion to science which is more "inductive" in nature, this notion which is also shared by Muhammad Nejatullah Siddiqi, then according to the latter the status of Islamic economics is still classified as "ideational and not empirical" economics [5] (Siddiqi, 1989). Another Muslim economist, Muhammad Akram Khan, also called the nature of Islamic economics as a mere "statement of the Shariah position on economic issues" [7]. (Khan, 1989). Nevertheless, in my humble opinion both these inductive and deductive approaches actually can be applied simultaneously in formulating the theory of Islamic economics. Among the philosophers of science for example, like Karl Popper

(1902 -1994) who used to be in the London School of Economics (LSE), did not consider that inductive method as the only methodology in science. Even more general than that, science is a discipline of knowledge which possesses the scientific research programmes (SRP), according to Imre Lakatos (1922–1974), who was one of the Philosophers of science and used to give lectures in London School of Economics. Based on those theories of science, Islamic economics can also be called a science provided the SRP is there.

Irrespective of the above condition, the approach of negation of some conventional economics paradigm theoretically and practically would be an important part in the process of dewesternization of economics. The fact is seen in the views of Islamic economics scholars who stated that Islamic economics possesses certain sides which are different from the conventional economics. Probably the clear example which can be cited as the case of "negation" in the conventional economics is usury case. By consensus the discourse of riba (usury; interest) will not be accepted, and should be discarded from, Islamic economics.

1.2   Integration Approach

Beside negating what is contrary to it, Islam also admits the good things from other system. "Wisdom is the lost belongs to the believer, wherever he finds it then he has right to take it". As has been stated the beginning of this paper there many of conventional economics elements which can be applied in Islamic economics. In this case the task of Islamic economics is to take and make it as an integral part of it. Once again we can see the approach of Dr. Umer Chapra in his book when it is being reviewed by another other prominent figure in Islamic economics, Prof. Khurshid Ahmad, in the preface of that book.

As a professional economist Dr. Chapra is aware of the usefulness as well as the limitations of economics as it has developed in the Western capitalist context. Conscious of the intrinsic value of economic analysis and the contributions it can make towards the amelioration of the human situation on the globe, he identifies the weaknesses that have marred the discipline from playing its rightful role. His approach is not negative, it is positive and creative. He identifies where things have gone wrong and suggests what is needed to set them right. He is not an iconoclast. He is an innovator and a reformer who wants to build on what exists, yet build in a manner that rectifies what has gone wrong.

Integration is also one of the elements of Islamization. Conventional economics which is not contrary to the Islamic teachings must be accepted and integrated into the Islamic economics. Therefore conventional economics must again be appreciated properly by Islamic economics scholars. In other words, those who intend to islamize the conventional economics must also be preferably graduated from economics faculty so that knowing what are corrects and acceptable in the economics need to be preserved and appreciated. To negate totally a knowledge in which he has no authority about it, even under the name of Islam, is only showing his ignorance and foolishness causing the loss to Islam itself. Al-Ghazali, nine centuries ago when discussing the part of philosophy that was possible to be integrated with Islam, had warned us about a kind people "who are friends of Islam but foolish" (sadiq li al-Islam jahil). This group, with such attitude, according to al-Ghazali, had contributed and shared in making "the philosophy to be loved even more and Islam to be hated even more" (fazdada li al-falsafah hubban wa li al-Islam bughdhan), as the consequence of their attack on philosophy indiscriminately without sufficient knowledge. A similar case can happen to conventional economics. If this discipline is not given a fair appraisal, or even totally refused erroneously without enough knowledge, eventhough with an Islamic spirit, will possibly bring the same effect; Islamic economics will be disliked even more and the conventional economics will instead be loved more. Consequently, the process of socializing Islamic economics will be hindered and slowed down by that kind of attitude.

Integration approach is one of the islamization methodology throughout the generations. The Prophet (peace be upon him) was sent solely to make a perfection on the morality. He preserved whatever good moral and good deed of the pre-Islamic time. Generosity (karam) in the pre-Islamic era was preserved and even being upgraded in Islam. In the case of economic activities, the mudarabah and salam which being practiced in pre-Islamic era are perpetuated in Islam, and even their rules were refined in Islamic Jurisprudence later. Likewise the Prophet (peace be upon him) did not disturb the usage of Roman gold money (Dinar) which was showing the pictures and the symbols of their kings on its sides. Moreover, such a kind of money was also used to pay zakat and buying-selling in Islamic societies in the time of Caliph Abu Bakr.

In the history of Islamic civilization, not all sciences originated from Greek civilization were debunked straight away. Some of them in fact were translated into Arabic. Medical books belonged to Galen (Jalinus), the astronomy of Ptolemy, and some of peripatetic philosophies which did not go against Islam were welcomed into the Islamic civilization. As long as such sciences are "wisdoms" then they have been considered as parts of Muslim's possession. Therefore, the contemporary conventional economics will also be subject to the Islamic "integration" methodology. The fact that discipline of economics was produced in the Western civilization does not make Muslim scholars to behave unjustly in acknowledging their contribution. If it is without this integration methodology, why should we burden ourselves to create a so-called Islamic economics, notwithstanding the fact that the term "economics" itself was even the by-product of in Western civilization. So the undeniable proof that the integration is an important methodology, we keep using the terminology of "Islamic economics" without being able to free ourselves from term of "economics" at all.

1.3 Value Addition Approach

Islamic economics can also contribute something new, better, and more beneficial to the economic life of humanity. At this level the role Islamization of economics is to include specific Islamic values that do not exist in conventional economics. The concept of zakat, for example, only exists in Islamic economics and nothing in conventional economics. Indeed we know the concept of tax, but the concept of zakat is different from tax. The tax exists because of the existence of government. So if there is no government, then there is no tax. But in Islamic economics, zakat will still exist, whether there is government or not. In addition, the function of zakat is more oriented toward the distribution aspect, and not the collection one. The point is, we can pay zakat directly to those who are entitled to receive it, without necessarily going through its intermediary. While tax needs to be paid to the government first, as an intermediary, then distributed to the people. So tax needs the collection first then distribution, while zakat does not. Obviously in this matter zakat is a value added to the fiscal system, because the tax objective can also be achieved via zakat, even faster.

Another example is the "mudarabah" system, or with another name "qiradh", which is a unique characteristic of partnesrship in Islamic economics that does not exist in other system. Historically "mudarabah" had influenced the world partnership method of the Medieval Europe with the name "Commenda." A France historian, Andre-E Sayous in his book Le Commerce des Europeens a Tunis depuis le XII siecle jusqu'a la fin de XVIe (Paris: 1929) states:

Muslims in the 10th-11th centuries had trading methods who were more perfect than, and were incomparable with, people of Europe. Since the era of Muhammad, even without a doubt, since pre-Islam, a type of contract that contains a refund and participation in the profits generated, has been one form which was almost the same shape as the commenda appeared shortly after that in Christian countries, Western Mediterranean… Europe Christians cannot surpass them [9].

Another economic historian, Abraham L. Udovitch, even states that the commenda method that developed later in Europe has characteristics that are totally the same as "qiradh" or "mudharabah" in Islamic economics which are more advanced than that of the Europe in the 9th, 10th, and 11th centuries AD. In the last paragraph of his article which had shocked the Western historians, Udovitch said:

The qirad, it can be unequivocally stated, is the earliest example of a commercial arrangement identical to the latter commenda, and containing all its essential features. Whether the qirad was taken over wholesale by Italian sea merchants and transformed into the commenda or evolved independently to meet a need created by commercial expansion is something which cannot be stated with certainty. However, even in the darkest period of the Dark Ages trade between the Catholic West and the Muslim World did not come to a complete standstill. The political and economic contracts between Islam and the West during the eight, ninth, and tenth centuries offered Western merchants numerous and convenient opportunities to learn and adopt commercial techniques and practices from their more advanced Eastern colleagues [10].

Based on his research also, a Muslim economic historian, Murat Cizakca, states explicitly that the commenda came from the Islamic world. In his book published by E.J. Brill, Prof. Cizakca said:

… it should be up to those who argue that commenda is originated from non-Islamic sources to furnish the proof. Until they are able to do so, this author, at least, feels safe with the argument that the commenda is originated in the world of Islam.

There are many more Islamic economic concepts that can have value added to conventional economics, both intellectually and practically. This is where the Muslim economists would play their role in researching and studying the history of Islamic economic institutions which can be shown vis-a-vis the conventional economic institutions. There are many legacies of Islamic literature which still need to be re-studied, especially those directly related to the scope of the economy. Literature about hisbah, kharaj, amwal, kasb, nuqud, tijarah, etc., are among the sources of direct references concerning the history of Islamic economic thought and institutions [11].

It cannot be denied either that the ideas and practices of contemporary Islamic economics have contributed to the conventional economics value added. Ideas and practices about Islamic banking, Islamic insurance, Islamic Capital Market, etc., are examples of new ideas comparable to conventional economic institutions. There are certainly many more tasks that the Islamic economics must take up to improve the economic conditions of the world in the future. Islamic economics is expected to be "the future economics", borrowing the term of Chapra, which has "a far more difficult task than conventional economics" [1].

Ibn Khaldun stated that the emergence of new disciplines or sciences are directly related to the civilization ('umran) which produces it. Islamic civilization used to produce its own sciences, as did the Western civilization. When Islamic civilization re-emerges, then a synthesis of Islamic sciences will be born. As a matter of fact the Islamic civilization is not dead, because so long there is the Religion of Islam and the Muslims themselves, the Islamic civilization will always be there.

Sometimes ago I have stated that:

... the 'tamaddun' of Islam has its unique characteristic allowing it to survive eternally and not to be part of the past history. This is because there is a close relationship between the Islamic civilization and the din itself. This relationship is very significant at the etymological level, which according to Prof. al-Attas, the word of tamaddun is closely related to the word din. Starting from this concept it can be said that Islamic 'tamaddun' is the manifestation of the aspect of the din in life. The degree of this manifestation can be broad and large and dominating the entire human life like what happened in Islamic history. However, its degree of manifestation can also be confined to certain aspects of life as it happens today. But even when there is only a small aspect of this manifestation, Islamic 'tamaddun' is still surviving. This means that as long as there is religion of Islam and Muslims, then Islamic civilization keeps on existing [12].

Today in the field of Islamic economics especially the Islamic banking and finance is moving forward with some breakthroughs in its products and services noticeable by the conventional banking and finance. The fruits of Islamic civilization and its 'tamaddun' is now growing again with the emergence of such disciplines. At this stage, Islamic economics is a universal economics that can be enjoyed by all humanities, irrespective of their religions; Muslims or non-Muslims. With this value addition approach Islamic economics emerges as the economics for all as the rahmatan lil 'alamin.

Negation, integration and value addition approaches in the process of socialization of Islamic economics must go together hand in hand simultaneously. The Islamic economics, therefore, must show its own wisdom. It rejects the bad, accepts the good, and adds more good at once. At the level of the negation approach, its stand must be firm and uncompromising. Because this is the level where distinction (furqan) between Islamic economics and non-Islamic economics should be highlighted. At the level of integration approach too, the attitude of Islamic economics is to embrace and welcome all the beneficial ones from the conventional economics. While at the level of value addition, the attitude of the Islamic economics does not force others to follow its economics, as reflected in the attitude of la ikraha fid din (no compulsion in religion).

Islamic economics should also welcome criticisms and comments from various parts of scholarships for the sake of making the discipline more matured. Despite the growth of literature promoting the Islamic economics, there are also some literature criticizing the ideas and implementation of Islamic economics, in particular Islamic banking, both from among the Muslims themselves and non-Muslim scholars [13, 14]. Whether the criticisms are valid or not, Islamic economics must also be able to conduct a dialogue and address the criticism accordingly. We must also realize that this Islamic economics movement are noticeable by non-Muslim scholars too around the world. If indeed we can add value to the existing economics, automatically those who are honest and sincere will recognize and acknowledge its contributions. Criticism usually arises due to non-genuine process of "Islamization" which is cosmetical in nature and only polishing the "outer" part of it, whereas the "inner" one is not touched at all. It is not surprising that a non-Muslim observer, for example, makes negative comment between the implementation of Islamic banking in some countries:

In Pakistan, the government imposed the 'Islamization' of the economy in 1985. This process was carried out without serious attention to Islamic legal doctrine, leaving the interest-based banking system fundamentally unchanged, but covering it with an Islamic varnish. Thus much of the scholarly literature relating to the Pakistani system either discusses theories which are totally irrelevant to actual Islamic banking practice, or lists the verious ruses used to hide interest-based banking practices in Islamic terminology. This hypocrisy has led the few Western bankers who know of Islamic banking to see it as a mere semantic sacralization of normal banking, and to discount its originality and importance. While these conclusions founded with respect to the Pakistani system, they are much less so in relation to Arab Islamic banking, which is developing a system based on the framework provided by medieval Islamic law [15].

From the Muslim side, the same concern was voiced out by Dr. Umer Chapra:

Islamization was introduced in Pakistan by President Ziaul Haq in July 1979. He certainly deserves credit for taking the initiative. Since this was done in response to popular demand, there was a whole-hearted public support for the same. However, even though the Council of Islamic Ideology had clearly warned that "the elimination of interest is but a part of the overall value system of Islam and this measure alone cannot be expected to transform the entire economic system in accordance with the Islamic vision", no serious effort was made to implement the recommendations of the Council or to introduce greater integrity into the financial system [1].

Anything associated with Islam and given the 'Islamic' pre-fixed as in the case of 'Islamic economics' will have no exception to be cross-examined from various aspects related to Islam itself. Therefore an Islamic economics is not just a shariah economics. It is an economics symbolizing Islamic civilization and its 'tamaddun' in a broad sense. In this case the link between Islamic economics and Islamic studies clearly are not only with fiqh (Islamic jurisprudence), but with other Islamic disciplines within the domain of Islamic civilization discourse.

2   The World-View of Islam

The negation, integration and value addition methodology that we stated above are no other than the techniques and methods of Islamizing conventional economics in partic-ular, and other conventional disciplines in general. However, there is something more fundamental than the stated methodology which needs due attention in the process of Islamization, so that the targeted objectives are attainable and not distracted by the contra-productive processes. For sometimes the branches of the Islamization methodology may look like helping the whole process of Islamization, however, the same method can hinder the essential process instead. For example, the methodology "masjid dirar" in the time of the Prophet (peace be upon him) which physically looked like establishing a mosque as the most sacred Islamic institutions to support the Islamization process. However, since it was established as a counter-program, it was actually hindering the Islamization. The Prophet (peace be upon him.) should have carried out the "integration" methodology on a mosque being established, but what he did was executing the "negation" methodology by burning and destroying the mosque itself. This implies that there is something more fundamental and essential in determining which needs to be rejected, integrated, or added value in the Islamization process. The essential and fundamental thing that what we mean here is no other than the Worldview of Islam itself. This process of Islamization of worldview that will guide and direct the negation, integration, and value addition methodology in the process of Islamization of knowledge and disciplines need to be given a priority.

As we stated briefly at the beginning of this paper, Islamic worldview is Islamic view of life that does not change by time and space. It constitutes usul of Islam, qat'i of Islam, muhkam of Islam, ma'lum bi al-darurah of Islam, thawabit of Islam, ijma' of Islam, and the core of Islam itself which are projected in its fundamental aspects such as in understanding (ma'rifah) of the attributes of God, the nature of revelation, nature of the universe, nature of man, nature of knowledge, nature of religion, nature happiness, nature of values and morals, the nature of happiness [2]. Today all those understandings have been secularized by Western philosophy and civilization, so the Muslims who are duly influenced have misunderstood their own religion. For example, many Muslims are increasingly influenced by Western ways of thinking and claiming that all religions are the same. Some of them even declare themselves as atheist-Muslims. If this kind of understanding is not settled first, what is the meaning of building Islamic economics and its economy, when Islam is considered the same as other religions or when God is not considered to exist? Take for example in the case of Indonesia, when the liberal group of Muslims calling themselves as 'Islam Liberal' or Islib who dare enough to say that Islamic shari'ah does not exist, where can we expect an Islamic economics would come from them? Again when some of them wanted to edit the Qur'an and to produce the so-called Critical Edition of the Qur'an, for sure not just an Islamic economics that will never emerge, even Islam itself will collapse with this type of thinking. Obviously the issues that this group are promoting are directly related to the problem of Islamic worldview. In other words, their thinking as such are actually beyond the matrix of the Islamic worldview. So if this problem is not settled first, let alone if it is accepted by general Muslims, then there will be no meaning of Islamization at all. We can imagine if such opinions are accepted by some Islamic economics scholars, can we expect the genuine Islamic economic concept coming from them?

The problem is that the alien understandings of the Islamic worldview are now being propagated in Islamic universities themselves. Nowadays we find university lecturers who teach 'Ulum al-Qur'an, but having a doubt with the authenticity of the Qur'an. The professors who teach Islamic thought teaching to the students that all religions are the same. Can we expect a proper Islamic economics thought is coming from these intellectuals or from the students who follow them? As a natural fact we will deal with this kind of people first before going forward with others, such as non-Muslims who reject the existence of Islamic economics in the first place. So it is clear that re-Islamising the worldview is a prerequisite for the process towards Islamization of the economics and the economy itself. In other words, behind the problem of economics and the economy that we want to solve, there is more fundamental problem that we need to handle as well, that is the worldview problem. Therefore, the problem of Islamic economics can be likened to an iceberg that appears on the surface of the Islamic worldview problem. In other words, the problem of Islamic economics is only a tip on the iceberg of that of the Islamic worldview.

3 The Role of Islamic Epistemology

As we said above, one of the elements of the Islamic worldview is the recognition of the nature of "knowledge" itself. In this context I want to take the attention of the readers that Islam affirms the possibility of human being to receive knowledge. It is out of intention that statement has been given an italic since there is a particular worldview stating that knowledge is not possible. The worldview which states that human being cannot receive knowledge is not new. The history has noticed it since the time of Greek civilization ever, which is about 5th century BC. This view is referred to as the epistemology of the Sophists [17]. The words sophistry and sophisticated in English come from the words of this sophist or sophism [18]. At the time when this view was absorbed into Islamic civilization, the Muslim scholars call this view as Sufasta'iyyah (sophism). Since there is a danger that the worldview sufasta'iyyah was posing towards this Islamic creed (aqeedah), then the scholars of kalam (theologians) classified this view as a view that is contrary to Islamic faith. The clearest statement was made by a 6th Century Hijrah theologian 'Umar Najmuddin al-Nasafi (d. 537/1142) in his Aqidah book which is well-known throughout the Islamic world entitled al-'Aqa'id al-Nasafiyyah [2].

This book has been given many commentaries, but among the most famous commentary was by Sa'duddin al-Taftazani (d. 791/1387). In his remarks, al-Taftazani mentioned three groups of Sufasta'iyyah: (1) al-'Inadiyyah, (2) al-'Indiyyah, and (3) al-La'adriyyah [19]. I only want to take just an example from this case, namely the second group, al-'iIndiyyah, which states that the truth is subjective in nature. To them the truth and certainty depend on the person, the place and the time. Accordingly, people will have different view and understanding of the truth and certainty due to the differences of place and time. The truth in the past possibly wrong by now and the false of the past maybe true now. To them there is no common absolute truth, namely there is no eternal truth in the past, the present, or in the future. In short, no universal truth to them; the truth is relative and subjective. If this kind of view is accepted by Muslims, do not expect Islamic economics will exist in their mind. Instead, Islam itself will disappear with this worldview. So the epistemology of Islam is integrated in aqidah books with the aim to keep the knowledge from being destroyed and corrupted by the opposing worldview and epistemology.

We can take another example of "deconstruction" concept which is propagated nowadays by the philosophy of post-modernism. To this view, any established disciplines or concepts must be dismantled and deconstructed, so that they are open for criticisms from various angles, especially for the historical cases. We can imagine when the Qur'an needs to be "deconstructed" as proposed by Muhammad Arkoun, a liberal thinker from Algeria. Will there be Islam any longer? How about the existence of Islamic economics, if al-Quran must be deconstructed?

We can take an example from economics which is more toward capitalism, although the opponents such as the socialism and marxism ere also there. If we "deconstruct" this economics, then we will see that this discipline is indeed only benefiting the capitalists and rich people who dominate both the physical as well as the financial capitals. As for poor people and those who have no capitals, then there is no significant place in economics. It is true that the topic of "poverty" is discussed in development economics, but the way to overcome this problem is only dependent on market via taxation and public finance. Certainly, this economics discusses the variety of theories of development, but at the end again in favor of the rich people. Apparently the economics that we study now is in line with the industrial revolution happened in the Western countries in the 18th century. To industrialize the economy the country must have factory, and to have factory they must get capitals. Finally, the capital is the main factor of production. When the capital is there, so factory (land) and labor can easily be bought by the capitalist entrepreneur. As a result the rich becomes richer and the poor becomes poorer, though the poverty is only a "relative poverty" and not 'absolute' in nature.

4 Conclusion

Where does the position of Islamic economics lay in in the contexts of conventional economic paradigm? In my humble opinion, it first lies in thought and the worldview of Muslims and their scholars. The scholars who see this world with Islamic worldview will perceive the existence of imbalances and discrepancies in the life of world economy. One of the causes of this discrepancy is the science of economics being taught so far. Prof. Dr. Mubyarto once said that the teaching of economics in Indonesia is a big fault because, "economics teachers and lecturers are only "aping" what the American scholars have taught,".... whereas "the economics which is really reflecting the Indonesia's economy remains underdeveloped since all what is taught are only importing and not necessarily suitable to the condition of Indonesia" [20]. The same argument can be used for the Islamic economics. He suggested that there must be "efforts of Indonesianization of the discipline for the sake of the welfare and happiness of the Indonesian people." This is also our desire on the part of Muslim scholars to struggle on the great efforts in the process of Islamization of knowledge for the sake of the welfare and happiness of all human race in this world and in the hereafter.

References

1. Chapra, M.U. (1992). *Islam and the Economic Challenge.* Leicester: The Islamic Foundation.
2. Al-Attas, S.M.N. (1988) The Oldest Known Malay manuscript: A 16th Century Malay Translation of the Aqa'id of al-Nasafi. Kuala Lumpur: Department of Publication University of Malaya.

3. Laktos, I. (1984). *The Methodology of Scientific Research Programmes*, ed. John Worral and Gregory Currie. Cambridge: Cambridge University Press.
4. Sadeq, A. H. M. (1989). *Factor Pricing and Income Distribution from an Islamic Perspective.* Journal of Islamic Economics. Petaling Jaya: International Islamic University, January, 45-64.
5. Khan, M. F. (1995). *Essays in Islamic Economics.* Leicester: The Islamic Foundation.
6. Siddiqi, M.N. (1981). *Muslim Economic Thinking.* leicester: The Islamic Foundation.
7. Haneef, M.A. (1995) *Contemporary Islamic Economic Thought.* Petaling Jaya: Iqrak.
8. Al-Sadr, S.M.B. (1991). *Iqtisaduna. Beirut:* Dar al-Ta'aruf li al-Matbu'at.
9. Khan, M.A. (1989) "Islamic Economics: The State of the Art," dalam Readings in the Concept and Methodology of Islamic Economics, eds. Aidit Ghazali dan Syed Omar. Petaling Jaya: Pelanduk Publications.
10. Cizakca, M. (1996). A Comparative Evolution of Business Partnership The Islamic World and Europe, with Specific Reference to the Ottoman Archives. Leiden: E.J. Brill.
11. Udovitch, A.L. (1962) "At the Origins of the Western Commenda: Islam, Israel, Byzantium?" Speculum, 37, 207.
12. Orman, S. (1997 and 1998).*Sources of the History of Islamic Economic Thought.* al-Shajarah Journal of the International Institute of islamic Thought and Civilization (ISTAC), vol. 2 no. 1 dan vol. 3 no. 2.
13. Suharto, U. (1989). Persoalan-Persoalan Mengenai Sumber-Sumber Rujukan Kajian Tamadun Islam. Al-Hikmah – Forum ISTAC, bil. 1, Tahun 4, Januari-Maret, hal. 24.
14. Jomo K.S. (1993). Islamic Economic Alternatives – Critical Perspectives and New Direction, ed. Jomo K.S. Kuala Lumpur: Ikraq.
15. Haque, Z. (1995). Riba – The Moral Economy of Usury, Interest and Profit. Kuala Lumpur: Ikraq.
16. Ray, N. D. (1995). Arab Islamic banking and the renewal of Islamic law. London and Boston: Graham & Trotman.
17. Hatta, M. (1982) *Alam Fikiran Yunani. Kuala Lumpur:* Dewan Bahasa dan Pustaka.
18. Ayto, J. (1990). *Arcade Dictionary of Word Origins.* New York: Arcade Publishing.
19. Elder E.E. (1950), *A Commentary on the Creed of Islam.* New York: Columbia University Press.
20. *Pengajaran Ilmu Ekonomi di Indonesia Keliru Besar (2003)* "Ekonomi Syariah Magazine", Jakarta: Ekaba-Usakti, vol. 2, No. 1. 24.

Marketing Efficiency of Organic Rice in East Lampung Regency
(Case Study in Multi Baliwo Farmers Group, Purwokencono Village, Sekampung Udik District)

Sri Handayani$^{(\boxtimes)}$, Dwi Eva Nirmagustina, and Ni Siluh Putu Nuryani

Politeknik Negeri Lampung, Bandar Lampung, Indonesia
`sri.handayani84@polinela.ac.id`

Abstract. Organic rice has a large market potential in the community, this is based on the increasing demand for organic food products. However, the basic problem experienced by organic rice farmers is limited market information for organic rice products and marketing channels. The purpose of this study was to identify marketing channels for organic rice products and to analyze the marketing efficiency of organic rice in East Lampung Regency. The location of the research is located in Purwokencono Village, Sekampung Udik District, East Lampung Regency which has been cultivating organic rice since 2010 and has obtained organic certification Inofice. The data analysis method used marketing margin and farmer's share for organic rice marketing. Total respondents were 16 farmers, 1 farmer groups namely Multi Baliwo, 2 collecting traders namely Yabima and community group, and 1 retailer. Research results show that marketing channels formed by marketing organic rice in East Lampung Regency are 3 (three) channels, namely channel I (farmers – farmer group – yabima – retail - consumer), channel II (farmers – farmer group – yabima – consumer), and chanel III (farmers – community group - consumer). The results of organic rice marketing efficiency can be shown that marketing channel II is categorized as efficient because it has the lowest marketing efficiency value of 22.52%.

Keywords: marketing channels · organic rice · marketing efficiency

1 Introduction

Sustainable development is a central issue in the development of community welfare. The United Nations, starting in 2015, has even established a development program titled the welfare of the world community with the Sustainable Development Goals (SDGs) program [1]. One of the efforts emphasized in this program is the existence of sustainable and environmentally friendly agriculture, namely organic farming. One of the strategic commodities in supporting the development of the economic sector and the fulfillment of national food needs is rice. The need for rice as a staple food commodity continues to increase. Research result [2] this is in line with the increase in population and the increase in consumption per capita, so that optimizing rice productivity is one of the

© The Author(s) 2023
R. Martini et al. (Eds.): FIRST 2022, ASSEHR 733, pp. 196–208, 2023.
https://doi.org/10.2991/978-2-38476-026-8_22

efforts to increase national grain production. Awareness of the importance of health and environmental sustainability encourages people to return to organic farming systems because the products are free of chemical fertilizers and pesticide residues. Besides being environmentally friendly, the cost for organic farming is lower because the fertilizers and pesticides used come from nature around the farmers [3].

Lampung Province as one of the rice producers that contributes to the national rice production surplus always experiences an increase in production every year. Rice production in Lampung Province reached 2.65 million tons of dry milled grain, increased by 486.20 thousand tons or 22.47 percent compared to 2019 which was 2.16 million tons of dry milled grain [4]. The rice harvested area in 2020 is 545.15 thousand hectares, an increase of 81.05 thousand hectares or 17.46 percent compared to 2019 which was 464.10 thousand hectares. The development of organic rice on a large scale is very potential and can be implemented through agricultural extensification programs and market development [5].

East Lampung Regency is one of the organic rice production areas that has implemented an organic farming system for rice plants since 2010. One of the farmer groups that cultivates organic rice is the Multi Baliwo Farmer Group. This farmer group consists of 34 farmers and the number of farmers who have implemented organic farming systems is 16 farmers. Multi baliwo farmer groups have received INOFICE organic certificates from 2018 to 2021. Organic rice production performance is going well so far, the certified organic rice plant area is 10.7 hectares and capable of producing a production of 28 tons of organic dry milled grain. Organic rice milling is carried out independently by farmer groups and is able to produce 16,600 kg of organic rice.

The bargaining position of agricultural products is quite weak because agricultural products are seasonal and do not last long. Organic rice plants cultivated by farmers are seasonal which causes limited income during the harvest season that occurs. Furthermore, limited market information and marketing channels cause organic rice to be marketed locally at a selling price that is still low and almost the same as the price of conventional rice. If farmers do not immediately sell their organic rice products, it will have an impact on damage to organic rice products. The impact on the acceptance of organic rice farmers is less than optimal. The selling price of organic rice at the farmer level when managed by a farmer group is Rp. 13,000/kg, while for non-organic rice Rp. 8,000/kg. The price margin should be an opportunity for farmers to increase their farm income. Marketing activities can run efficiently if farmers get the most benefit from organic rice value chain activities and have clear marketing channels. Based on the background of the research above, the objectives of this study are:

1. Describe the marketing channels for organic rice from the farmer level to the final consumer of the Multi Baliwo Farmer Group, Sekampung Udik District, East Lampung Regency.
2. Analyzing marketing efficiency in each organic rice marketing channel in the Multi Baliwo Farmer Group, Sekampung Udik District, East Lampung Regency.

2 Proposed Method

The research method used in this study is descriptive and mathematical analysis. The descriptive method is a method used to describe or analyze a research result but is not used to make broader conclusions [6]. The research was conducted in East Lampung Regency as one of the centers for organic rice farming, then the Multi Baliwo Farmers group, Purwokencono Village, Sekampung Udik Subdistrict, was selected using the case study method, considering that this group has the largest planting area of organic rice in East Lampung Regency and has been certified organic INOFICE. Further more, that it is expected to represent the upstream and downstream areas of organic farming.

2.1 Sampling Method

Data collection methods were carried out through observation, surveys, in-depth interviews and focus group discussions, with the respondents consisting of 16 organic rice farmers using proportional random sampling technique. Determination of marketing agencies using the snowball method (snowball sampling). The snowball method is a sample selection technique by first determining one key information (key person), then selecting the next sample depending on the first informant, and so on until the information obtained is sufficient [7]. Total respondents were 16 producer farmers, 1 farmer groups, 2 collecting traders, and 1 retailer.

2.2 Data Analysis Method

Analysis of the marketing channel of organic rice products in Multi Baliwo farmer groups was carried out using descriptive analysis based on the results of tracing the organic rice starting from farmers, farmer groups, traders, retailers and consumers. Marketing channel is a set of organizations involved in the process of distributing organic rice products ready for consumption or use by consumers.

Marketing Margin. Marketing margin is the difference between farmers' prices and consumer prices. The marketing margin also includes all costs incurred by marketing channel, starting from the farmer to the marketing agencies involved. The organic rice marketing margin is calculated based on the reduction of the selling price and the purchase price at each institution involved in marketing organic rice or the sum of the marketing costs incurred and the profits earned by the marketing agency [8]. Marketing margin can be formulated as follows [9]:

$$M = Pr - Pf$$

$$M = C + \pi$$

$$Pr - Pf = C + \pi$$

Marketing institution profits:

$$\Pi = Pr - Pf - C$$

Total marketing margin:

$$MT = \Sigma M$$

Information:
M = Marketing Margin
Pr = Price at consumer level (Rp/kg)
Pf = Price at producer level (Rp/kg)
C = Cost institution
Π = Marketing institution profits i
MT = Total Margin

Farmer's Share. Farmer share can be calculated based on the percentage of the total price received by farmers divided by the price formed by consumers. Farmer share calculations are obtained from comparisons between farmer prices and consumer prices measured in percent units (%). The farmer's share formulation is as follows [10]:

$$Fs = \frac{P_f}{P_r} \times 100\%$$

Description:
Fs = *Farmer's share*
Pf = Farmer price (Rp/kg)
Pr = Customer price (Rp/kg)

Marketing efficiency is the ratio between marketing costs compared to the price of the product, so that marketing is said to be efficient and effective if it can provide incentives to actors who can encourage them to make appropriate and efficient decisions [11].

3   Result and Discussion

3.1   Respondent

Age. Working age is the age level of a person who is expected to be able to work and generate his own income. Age is one of the factors that determine the activities of farmers in managing their farming. In general, the higher the age, the work ability will increase to a certain extent. The age of respondent farmers in Purwokencono Village varied from 22 to 80 years. The average age of respondent farmers in Purwokencono Village is 46.75 years, meaning that the age of respondent farmers in Purwokencono Village is of productive age. In Table 1, it can be seen the details of the age level of the respondent farmers in Purwokencono Village, Sekampung Udik District, East Lampung Regency. Based on Table 1, it is known that the largest age group for sample farmers is the age group of more than 50 years, as many as 8 people (50%). Based on this age classification table, it shows that the average age of farmers is more than productive, closer to the elderly. The application of technology may not be easily absorbed by farmers, so it requires an intensive mentoring process.

Table 1. Classification of respondents by age group

Age (year)	Respondent	
	Farmer	Persentage (%)
< 40	4	25
40 – 50	4	25
> 50	8	50
Amount	16	100

Table 2. Classification of respondents based on education level

Education level	Respondent	
	Farmer	Persentase (%)
SD	6	37,5
SMP	3	18,75
SMA	7	43,75
amount	16	100

Education. The level of education is one of the factors that play a very important role in business activities, because it can affect the ability of farmers to manage their business. Formal education plays a very important role in determining the pattern of technology adoption decisions in the businesses it manages. The education classification of respondents can be seen in Table 2.

Table 2 shows the education level of organic rice respondents. The level of formal education of respondents is very diverse, ranging from elementary to high school level. The highest level of education is at the high school level, this shows that most of the respondents received a relatively high education, namely as many as 7 respondents or 43.75 percent. However, some of them have low education, namely only graduated from elementary school as many as 6 farmers (37.5 percent).

Experience. The length of experience of respondents of organic rice farmers in East Lampung Regency in rice farming is one indicator that can affect the success of rice farming carried out as a whole. On average, respondents at the research sites had 8 years of farming experience. The classification of respondents' business experience can be seen in Table 3.

Table 3 shows that the experience of respondents in farming is still quite new. As many as 50 percent have 10–20 years of business experience and another 50 percent are less than 10 years old, this shows that many new farmers are starting to cultivate rice. Generally, respondents who have been farming for a long time are supported by financial needs because farmers are the main occupations of all respondents. Organic rice

Table 3. Classification of respondents based on business experience

Business experience (year)	Respondent	
	Farmer	Persentase (%)
< 10	8	50
10–20	8	50
> 20	0	0
amount	16	100

farming has only been cultivated for 8 years and generally knows organic rice farming from agricultural extension workers.

3.2 Marketing Channel

Marketing is a process of planning and executing the realization, pricing, promotion, and distribution of goods, services and ideas to create exchange by self-milling. Meanwhile, for non-organic rice, farmers sell in the form of grain, so that the rice mill acts as one of the marketing institutions involved in the non-organic rice trade system. The selling price of organic rice products is generally higher than non-organic rice.

A marketing channel is a set of interdependent organizations that are involved in the process of making a product or service ready for use or consumption [12]. The marketing system for organic rice products tends to be different from non-organic marketing in general. The pattern of organic rice business at the farm level is usually selling in the form of rice, while in non-organic rice most farmers sell in the form of unhulled rice. The efficiency of organic rice marketing reflects the distribution of profits and the profits obtained by each organic rice marketer. In this study the performance of the organic rice market was analyzed through marketing channel analysis, farmer share, marketing margin ratio and profit margin.

Marketing channel for organic rice in East Lampung Regency consist of:

1. Marketing chanel 1: Farmer, Farmer Group, Yabima, Retail, Customer
2. Marketing chanel 2: Farmer, Farmer Group, Yabima, Customer
3. Marketing chanel 3: Farmer, Community group, Customer

In general, the marketing channels in the Multibaliwo Farmer Group, Purwokencono Village, Sekampung Udik District, East Lampung Regency can be seen in Fig. 1.

Organic rice production by farmers in Multi Baliwo farmer group is 17,271 kg with a planting area of 5,125 hectares. The average productivity produced is 3.4 tons/hectare. The total sales of organic rice for all farmer respondents is 11,568 kg (67%), they use as much as 324 kg of seeds (2%), and the remaining 4,946 kg is consumed by farmers (29%).

The first marketing channel, farmers sell organic rice to farmer group (Multi Baliwo). The selling price of organic rice is IDR 12,000. Farmer groups do organic rice milling

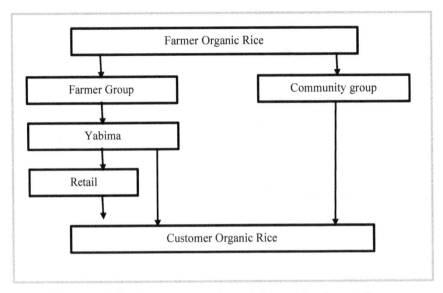

Fig. 1. Marketing channels of organic rice in Multi Baliwo Farmer Group.

and product packaging in sacks. Farmer group sell organic rice products with their own packaging and sold at a price of IDR 13,000 to Yabima. Yabima carries out organic rice sorting activities, packaging using a vacuum sealer machine, and transportation from the Farmers Group in East Lampung Regency to Yabima in Metro City. Yabima sells packaged organic rice products to retail at a price of Rp. 16.000. Retail sell organic rice IDR 20,000 to customer.

The second marketing channel, farmers sell their product to farmer groups (Multi Baliwo) with farmer selling prices of IDR 12,000. Farmer groups do organic rice milling and product packaging in sacks. Farmer group sell organic rice products with their own packaging and sold at a price of IDR 13,000 to Yabima. Furthermore, Yabima sell products at a price of IDR 18,000 to consumers. In addition to channels 1 and 2, farmers also sell their crops on the third channel, which is selling products to community group due to economic pressure. The selling price of rice is low price is IDR 10,000. The community group sell product is IDR 15,000 to consumer.

One of the indicators used to determine the efficiency of a marketing system is the marketing margin [13]. Marketing margin is the difference between the price at the producer level (Pf) and the price at the consumer level (Pr). Marketing margins have an important role in determining the size of producer income, because it directly affects the formation of organic rice prices at the producer level.

Marketing Margins in Marketing Channels I. The first marketing channel consists of farmers, farmer groups, yabima, retail, and consumer. Farmers sell their organic rice product directly to collectors at an average price of IDR 12,000 per kilograms. Farmers pay marketing costs including harvest costs, drying, transportation, and the farmers net profit of IDR 3,941 per kilograms. Based on this, the farmer share in the first marketing channel is 60% (Table 4).

Table 4. Analysis of marketing margins of organic rice at marketing channel I

No	Market institution	Price (IDR)	Share (%)
1	Farmer		60
	Production cost	7,454	
	Harvest cost	330	
	Transportation	50	
	Drying	225	
	Selling Price	12,000	
	Profit	3,941	
2	Farmer Group (Multi Baliwo)		65
	Purchase price	12,000	
	- Packing (sack)	200	
	- Milling	450	
	Total cost	12,650	
	Selling Price	13,000	
	Profit	350	
	Marketing margin	1.000	
3	PP (Yabima)		80
	Purchase price	13.000	
	- Packing	1.000	
	- Sorting	500	
	- depreciation	500	
	Selling price	16.000	
	Profit	1.000	
	Marketing margin	3.000	
4	Retail (Polinelamart)		100
	Purchase price	16.000	
	Marketing cost	1.500	
	Selling price	20.000	
	Profit	2.500	
	Marketing margin	4.000	
5	Consumer purchase price	20.000	
	Total Profit	7.791	
	Total marketing cost	4.755	
	Total marketing margin	8.000	
	FS	60%	

Based on Table 4, it can be seen that the share received by farmers in marketing channel I is 60 percent of the selling price at the consumer level. Then the share received by the farmer groups is 65 percent of the selling price of the farmer groups to consumers. While the share received by Yabima is 80 percent and at the retailer/retail level is 100 percent because in this marketing channel retailers sell organic rice directly to consumers.

Marketing Margins in Marketing Channels II. The second marketing channel consists of farmers, farmer groups, yabima, and consumer. Farmer sell their organic rice to farmer group and collectors at an average price of IDR 12,000 per kilogram. Farmers pay marketing costs including harvest costs, drying, transportation, and the farmers get a net profit of IDR 3,941 per kilograms. Based on this, the farmer share in the second marketing channel is 66.67%. (Table 5).

In marketing channel II, it can be seen that the share received by farmers is 66.67 percent of the selling price to consumers. Meanwhile, the share received by traders is 72.22 percent of the selling price of farmer groups in this channel. Furthermore, Yabima sells products directly to consumers.

Marketing Margins in Marketing Channels III. The third marketing channel consists of farmers, community groups, and consumer. Farmer sell their organic rice to community group at an average price of IDR 10,000 per kilogram. This price is cheaper compared to other marketing channels because the farmers do not deliver the products, but the buyers come to the farmers to buy their products. Farmers pay marketing costs is drying and harvest cost. Community group buys organic rice at a low price because it will resell organic rice using community selling price of IDR 15,000. Based on this, the farmer share in the third marketing channel is 66.67% (Table 6).

Table 6 shows that the marketing margin obtained by cpmmunity is IDR 4,000 per kg and farmer profit of IDR 2,991. Farmers' profits in channel III are smaller than channel II, that is IDR 3,941.

Marketing Efficiency. Marketing efficiency (Ep) can be calculated by the formula [11] which is the comparison between marketing costs and product prices. The decision rules on marketing efficiency according to [14] are as follows:

- Ep 0 - 33% = Efficient
- Ep 34 - 67% = Less Efficient
- Ep 68 - 100% = Not Efficient

Based on Table 7, it can be explain marketing channel II gives the lowest share marketing efficiency, which is 22,55%, because farmers selling prices are higher and the role of farmer groups in accommodating farmers' harvests and milling. Yabima buys organic rice from farmer groups and packs rice products using a vacuum sealer will be gives added value of organic rice. The Yabima also plays a role in finding customer in the Bandar Lampung or Metro region. Collaboration with Yabima is the key to successful efficiency on maketing channel II.

Table 5. Analysis of marketing margins of organic rice at marketing channel II

No	Market institution	Price (IDR)	Share (%)
1	Farmer		66.67
	Production cost	7,454	
	Harvest cost	330	
	Transportation	50	
	Drying	225	
	Selling Price	12,000	
	Profit	3,941	
2	Farmer Group (Multi Baliwo)		72.22
	Purchase price	12,000	
	- Packing (sack)	200	
	- Milling	450	
	Total cost	12,650	
	Selling Price	13,000	
	Profit	350	
	Marketing margin	1,000	
3	PP (Yabima)		100
	Purchase price	13,000	
	- Packing	1,000	
	- Sorting	500	
	- depreciation	500	
	- labor	800	
	Selling price	18,000	
	Profit	2,200	
	Marketing margin	5,000	
4	Consumer purchase price	18,000	
	Total profit	6,491	
	total marketing costs	4,055	
	Total marketing margin	6,000	
	FS		66.67

Table 6. Analysis of marketing margins of organic rice at marketing channel III

No	Market institution	Price (IDR)	Share (%)
1	Farmer		66,67
	Production cost	7.454	
	Harvest cost	330	
	Drying	225	
	Selling Price	10.000	
	Profit	2.991	
2	Community group		100
	Purchase price	10.000	
	- Packing (sack)	500	
	- Milling	550	
	- Labor	1.700	
	- Transportation	435	
	Total cost	13.185	
	Selling Price	15.000	
	Profit	1.815	
	Marketing margin	5.000	
3	Consumer purchase price	15.000	
	Total profit	4.806	
	total marketing costs	3.740	
	Total marketing margin	5.000	
	FS	66,67%	

Table 7. Marketing Channel Efficient

Marketing chanel	Total cost (Rp)	Price (Rp)	Efisiensi (%)
Chanel I	4.755	20.000	23,77
Chanel II	4.055	18.000	22,52
Chanel III	3.740	15.000	24,93

4 Conclusion

The conclusions obtained from the research results that.

a. The marketing channel for organic rice products identified results obtained that there are 3 (three) channels, namely tha first maketing channel (farmers – farmer group – yabima – retail - consumer), second marketing channel (farmers – farmer group – yabima – consumer), and third marketing chanel (farmers – community group - consumer).

b. The results of organic rice marketing efficiency can be shown that marketing channel II is categorized as efficient because it has the lowest marketing efficiency value of 22.52%.

References

1. Devi Devi, S. R. M., & Hartono, G. Faktor-faktor yang mempengaruhi keputusan konsumen dalam membeli sayuran organik. Agric, 27(1), 60-67. (2015)
2. Pramono. J, Basuki. S dan Widarto. Upaya Peningkatan Produktivitas Padi Sawah Melalui Pendekatan Pengelolaan Tanaman dan Sumberdaya Terpadu. Agrosains 7(1): 1–6. (2005).
3. Handayani, Sri, and Muhammad Irfan Affandi. "Supply Chain Management Performance Of Organic Rice In Pringsewu Regency." Journal of International Conference Proceedings (JICP). Vol. 2. No. 1. (2019).
4. Badan Pusat Statistik. 2015. Planting, Data Rice Production and Productivity. http://bps.go.id.Accessed on September 4, (2015).
5. Handayani, Sri, Irmayani Noer, and Rini Desfaryani. "Development Strategy of Organic Rice in Lampung Selatan Regency." IOP Conference Series: Earth and Environmental Science. Vol. 1012. No. 1. IOP Publishing, (2022).
6. Sugiyono. Understanding Qualitative Research. CV. Alfabeta. Bandung. (2005).
7. H. Irianto, and T. Mardikanto. Methods Agribusiness Research and Evaluation. Agribusiness Department / Study Program, Faculty of Agriculture, UNS. (2011).
8. S. Handayani, & M.I. Affandi. Supply Chain Management Performance Of Organic Rice In Pringsewu Regency. In Journal of International Conference Proceedings (Vol. 2, No. 1). (2019)
9. Kohls, R.L. Dan J.N. Uhl. Marketing Of Agricultural Products. Ninth Edition. Macmillan Company. New York. (2002).
10. B. Swastha and I. Sukotjo. Pengantar Bisnis Modern. Edisi Keenam. Liberty. Yogyakarta. (2002).
11. Soekartawi. Analisis Usahatani. UI–Press. Jakarta. (2016).
12. Kotler, P. dan K.L. Keller. Manajemen Pemasaran Edisi Ketiga Belas Jilid I. Erlangga. Jakarta. (2009).
13. A.I. Hasyim. Agricultural Trade Administration (Diktat Kuliah). Faculty of Agriculture, University of Lampung. Bandar Lampung. (2003).
14. Yuniarti, D., Rahayu, E. S., & Harisudin, M. Saluran Pemasaran Beras Organik Di Kabupaten Boyolali. Agrisocionomics: Jurnal Sosial Ekonomi Pertanian, 1(2). (2018).

CPSIA information can be obtained
at www.ICGtesting.com
Printed in the USA
LVHW030714050423
743535LV00004B/110